FPCC
OCT 21 1994

On Fashion

Edited by

SHARI BENSTOCK
and SUZANNE FERRISS

RUTGERS UNIVERSITY PRESS

New Brunswick, New Jersey

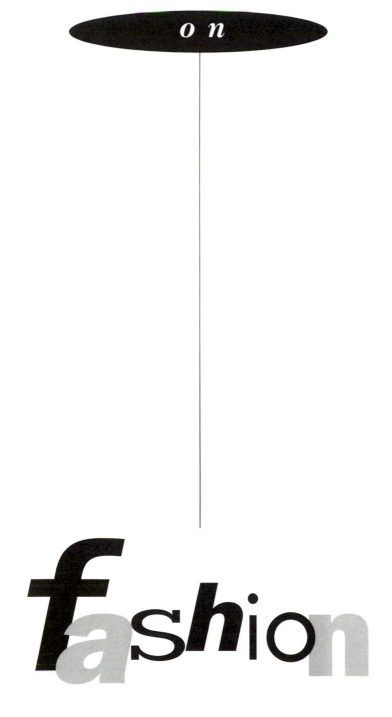

Library of Congress Cataloging-in-Publication Data

On fashion / edited by Shari Benstock and Suzanne Ferriss.
     p.   cm.
    Includes bibliographical references and index.
    ISBN 0-8135-2032-0 (cloth)—ISBN 0-8135-2033-9 (pbk.)
    1. Fashion—Social aspects. 2. Fashion—Psychological aspects.
I. Benstock, Shari, 1944–   . II. Ferriss, Suzanne, 1962–   .
GT525.06 1994
391—dc20   93-13886
                                                         CIP

British Cataloging-in-Publication information available

    Sonia Rykiel, "From *Celebration"* first appeared in *Celebration* (Paris: Editions des Femmes, 1988).
    Kaja Silverman, "Fragments of a Fashionable Discourse," from *Studies in Entertainment,* ed. Tania Modleski (Bloomington: Indiana University Press, 1986), reprinted by permission of the author.
    Iris Marion Young, "Women Recovering Our Clothes," from *Throwing Like a Girl and Other Essays in Feminist Philosophy and Social Theory* (Bloomington: Indiana University Press, 1990), reprinted by permission of Indiana University Press.
    Diana Fuss, "Fashion and the Homospectatorial Look," from *Critical Inquiry* 18 (Summer 1992), reprinted by permission of the University of Chicago Press.

For Berni and Steven

Contents

B ODY POLITICS

Acknowledgments

The idea for this collection emerged at the University of Miami after we screened *Mildred Pierce* while investigating feminist film theory with the English department's Critical Theory Discussion Group. We briefly considered co-authoring an essay on Joan Crawford's shoes, but soon abandoned that idea in favor of a larger project exploring fashion and its representations. Avid fashion collectors, consumers, and critics, we have spent many happy hours compiling these essays.

We would like to thank our editor, Leslie Mitchner, for her encouragement and support from the very beginning of this project. With her acute critical skills and her fine fashion sense, she has been instrumental in shaping its direction and scope. (She also promised to buy us shoes when we finished.)

Our well-dressed partners provided support in their own inimitable fashion. We dedicate this book to them, even though we did not take seriously their suggestion to call it *D. H. Lingerie*.

**Shari Benstock
Suzanne Ferriss**

ntroduction

> She wore diamonds on the soles
> of her shoes.
> **—Paul Simon**

Shoes. Dream shoes. Shoes to power the imagination. We sat spellbound before *Mildred Pierce*.[1] Our eyes followed her feet as she metamorphosed from abandoned housewife and single parent selling pies out of her kitchen to successful restaurateur, to alleged murderess, to martyr to her daughter's precocious sexuality, to her final apotheosis as the woman who speaks the truth (see figure 1). Through all these transformations her shoes were the one constant, and they made no concession to economic privation, practicality, or comfort. Inevitably black, they featured three-inch talons, a slightly raised platform, and a delicate strap encircling the ankle. Her shoes were a sign—but of what, we asked ourselves.

The intriguing significance of those shoes, ill suited to Mildred Pierce's daily life but essential to Joan Crawford's place in the Hollywood star system, signaled a larger preoccupation with both the so-called fashion system evidenced in movies, magazines, and shop windows and the role of fashion in modern culture.[2] What held true for *Mildred Pierce* still holds true: nothing stands outside fashion's dictates. Urban chic and urban violence, terrorism and tribalism, rage and rapture all have their mode—"attitude dressing." The monopolies and mythologies of the old fashion system have been shattered. No one aesthetic holds sway over our imaginations or controls market forces; even designers of haute couture have had to acknowlege individuality, innovation, and personal choice. On the streets, style wars map the cracks and fissures of fragmented and beleaguered societies: "looks," which have replaced "the Look," are the signs of our times, from hip hop to grunge, techno to eco. We are drawn to ask: what are the economic and libidinal investments, the power struggles and

1

Figure 1. Joan Crawford (right), with Zachary Scott and Ann Blyth, in Mildred Pierce.

ideological fractures of these new fashions? And what fragments of the old hegemony (Joan Crawford in her star shoes) are reflected in the aggressive postmodernism of the late twentieth century?

The essays in this collection trace certain threads in this complex fabric. Grouped into three major categories—consumerist, visual, political—they share an interest in the *discourses* of fashion, how we talk and write about clothes and style, how our identities are woven into and through these discussions. A variety of critical discourses shape current debates about fashion and its representations. These include feminist criticism, film theory, post-structuralist theories—especially psychoanalysis and deconstruction—as well as analyses of consumer culture and popular culture. Within and across these discourses the "F-word" generates new and often contradictory meanings: fabrication, fad, fake, false-consciousness, fancy, fairy world, fantasy, feel, feminine, fetish, figure, finery, freak, frivolous, frumpery, frustration. . . .[3] The voices of this volume speak in their own styles—individual, idiosyncratic, by turns strident, soothing, urgent, and celebratory. As editors we have made no attempt to homogenize styles or tone down differences in critical approaches, political attitudes, or disciplinary viewpoints. Nor do we hope to have been fully representative or to have "said it all." The gaps and resistances, open spaces and silences, are places for the reader to enter.

If fashion is always ahead of the time, its seasons in advance of the real season, it is always in some sense dated—and so are these discussions. The questions we ask are at once "nouveau" and "retro," as our contributors take in the sweep of twentieth-century fashion, from Victorian shirtwaists to contemporary street style. For example, what does it mean to be "in fashion"? Should we consider fashion a business, concerned with consumerism and consumption, or an art form? To what degree is fashion expressive, repressive, revolutionary? Is clothing an aesthetic object separate from the body it encases or does it protect and enhance the human form? A central concern is not only the clothes that cover our bodies but the bodies we recover under our clothes. How does fashion shape the body to its changing ideals? Do fashion's representations—its photos and magazines—submit the female form to the scrutiny of the male gaze? Do fashions enforce gender distinctions? As a product of consumer culture, does fashion necessarily enslave or constrict us? Or can it empower those without means? What accounts for the hegemony of Western modes of dress in other parts of the world while Western designers rely on the perceived exoticism of native dress to rejuvenate their collections? Are the stylish those who purchase the preconstructed designs of haute couture or those who fabricate their own individual designs from the castoffs found in thrift shops?

We raise anew the question of how fashion makes its appeal. How it calls first to the "eye" (the gaze, the look, the to-be-seen) and plays into the psychic field of desire for exhibitionism and voyeurism. To look is to desire, to want to touch and caress, to slip a hand into a seam or fold. Whatever the price or pain, we want Joan Crawford's shoes. But is it the shoes we want, or the fantasy of a fashionable existence—the secret dream of Mildred Pierce? The shoes hint at her sexuality, the otherness of her desires—the desire for empowered elegance. They are a clue, the telltale detail that betrays the contradictions of her world. The disjunction between the social and economic realities of life and the impossible perfection of her dress is not to be ignored. We know nothing about how she inhabited her clothes. Did her shoes pinch as she stood at the kitchen table rolling out the pie dough? (Would she have let on if they did?) *Mildred Pierce* draws us back again to issues of desire and empowerment, of women inhabiting their clothes. Fashion and fantasy: fashion and identity: identity and sexuality.

The pleasures of viewing are different from the joys of wearing. Costumed, one experiences an intimacy with one's own skin, the inside—unseen—of oneself, as Hélène Cixous says about Sonia Rykiel's clothes: "With my hands, with my eyes in my hands, with my eyes groping like hands, I see—touch the body hidden in the body." Synesthesia of sensations, forbidden pleasures of the self, immodesty veiled—and unveiled.

But violence lurks just around the corner of these hidden pleasure grounds, the eye taking aim, sighting the subject. In *Still of the Night,* the camera glimpses Meryl Streep's pale skin through the back slit of her blue satin gown, the seam opening and closing as she walks. The camera tracks her; she is oblivious to her attacker taking aim through the door crack. Dressed to kill, she is prey to the Look.[4]

When we speak in this book of the body clothed, we are in virtually every case talking about women's bodies, fashion having served traditionally as the cultural sign of the feminine. We take up the hinged question of how the cultural feminine uses fashion to shape women's bodies and women's desires to its profitable designs and, further, how fashion has—over time—redefined notions of the cultural feminine in gendered reversals to include men—or at least the comfort of men's dressing and the dreams of men's power. Feminism of the early 1970s opened a debate around these issues, focusing on the "beauty myth"—a debate that continues within the pages of this volume. For whom does the fashionable woman dress—herself or others?—and in what measure are her dress choices her own, and to what degree are they shaped by advertising and business? Feminists of a generation ago, echoing their suffragist precursors, taught women that interest in dress and beauty was the result of a socially produced false consciousness that placed women in league with patriarchal and capitalist power structures.[5] High fashion signaled (hetero)sexual and social oppression, and even "real clothes"—what we wore every day—cinched waists, smoothed out curves and bumps, and constrained our movements. What relief to unhook brassieres, unzip girdles, and step out of the cage of Jackie Kennedy box suits. Letting our hair down, we proclaimed Our bodies, Ourselves. If our shoes pinched, we went barefoot.

Fashion entered the academy by way of "French theory," whose stylish, wickedly witty, playful intellectualism made our heads spin. That academic feminism could no longer avoid the fashion question (or the issues raised by French *critique féminine*) was made visually evident in the Summer 1982 issue of *Diacritics* (see figure 2).[6] A headless, handless, high-heeled figure in a pantsuit posed, knee on chair, à la Marlene Dietrich. "Cherchez la femme," the black-on-white title announced. Inside, the dialogue that would dominate the 1980s staged itself as a debate about signifiers and signatures, the relation of women's writings to women's lived experiences. The metaphor was shoes: sensible, low-heeled for American feminists, shapely and seductive for French theorists. The back cover figured *la femme* as paper-doll cutouts, her body and the chair that supported it an empty white space in which were suspended the essential (yet ephemeral) "accessories" of her wardrobe—hat, gloves, jewelry, belt, and open-toed shoes (see figure 3). The scent of French perfume floated imperceptibly in the air. The disturbing disappearance of the woman's body, the suspension of fashion's signifiers, appeared to underscore Jean Baudrillard's claim that fashion is a simulacrum, that "the signs of fashion are free-floating and not grounded in the referential."[7]

Yet we still perceive fashion as embedded in material culture and invest it with referential power—hence the seminal role dress plays in the "mystery" of *The Crying Game* and its phenomenal success.[8] The film's surprise hinges on taking Dil's trumped-up dress and long hair as evidence of femininity. Like the protagonist, the audience (or, at least, the heterosexual viewer) readily accepts fashion as a sign of sexual identity. Later twists in the film highlight the slippage inherent in this equation: the gun-toting IRA member, Miranda Richardson, disguises her "masculine" aggression under the cover of a dyed Louise Brooks bob and the crisp outline of a stylish suit, while Dil escapes her detection (at least for a while) by passing for "male" with newly shorn hair and wearing a polo sweater, white pants, and sneakers. Into fashion's fabric, the film neatly interweaves sexual politics and the revolutionary terror of the IRA.

Indeed, fashion often serves political designs. We can chart the struggle for sexual and political liberation, for example, as a change in style: 1970s bell-bottomed pantsuits signaled freedom from feminine dress codes. As women entered the professions in ever greater numbers in the late 1970s, they were Dressed-for-Success in business suits accented by men's ties. By the early 1980s, the women warriors of Wall Street and Washington had donned jackets with power shoulders, and wore short skirts and stiletto heels. Those suits of armor are passé now, their sharp corners and acute angles rounded to follow the lines of the body rather than draw the lines of battle. Gone are styles glorifying bondage and S/M, the steel-plated bustiers of Thierry Mugler and Jean-Paul Gaultier and the torturous straps of Gianni Versace and Azzedine Alaïa. We return to a more innocent time, to the flowered prints of Edwardian garden parties, to London's Chelsea in the 1970s. But with a difference, we are told: sensuality has been joined to sensibility.[9]

Figure 2. Front cover of Diacritics *12, no. 2 (Summer 1982). Reprinted by permission of the Johns Hopkins University Press.*

Figure 3. Back cover of Diacritics *12, no. 2 (Summer 1982). Reprinted by permission of the Johns Hopkins University Press.*

Fashion is no longer afraid to be feminine. As several essays in this volume point out, this advance is also a return, a folding back on and overlayering of cultural history. The new looks remind us not only of the 1930s but of the 1960s, periods of social and cultural unrest when tensions between the sexes escalated, when the world was yet again poised for war, when enormous gulfs divided rich and poor, white and black, men and women. Behind the scenes of contemporary fashionable discourses—with their rhetoric of elegance and exoticism, and emphasis on the sumptuous and sensual—are social issues of real moment, of bodies in pain, of the homeless who wrap themselves in the "layered look" in order to survive, who make of their clothes a "home."[10]

Contemporary fashion may be in pieces, no longer cast in a dominant mode of one look, one hem length, but its desiring gaze searches the world for "looks" to appropriate. St. Laurent exploits African dress, defined as *mode exotique*. Giorgio Armani, the jackets-and-pants man, announces a new evening line from the seraglio–beaded bodices, exposed midriffs, harem trousers, ankle bracelets. Jean-Paul Gaultier admits, "I love the idea of taking the traditional dress from each country and mixing it up." Today's fashions promote a "kaleidoscope of cultures" gathered together in a "global village."[11] But the traditional associations and cultural meanings of national cultures are erased or confused by this mix-up of modern technology and never-out-of-fashion piecework and cut-rate labor that redesigns "native" as an exoticized Other. One imagines this scene: a first-world designer lands in a private plane in Peru, Bali, or West Africa, eyes the designs of native goods displayed in local markets and bargains for a few representative samples. This is a reconnaissance mission, the sketches quick and covert. The samples are then sent to textile factories in Korea and Hungary where low-waged weavers and seamstresses produce clothes sold in Milan, Paris, and New York. Who gains and who loses by this stylish buccaneering? At home in Guatemala or Bolivia, traditional Indian dress marks its wearer for silencing, persecution, genocide. The same design, woven in cashmere or leather, is the last word in style in London, Miami, or L.A.[12]

In contrast to doomed native peoples, the proponents of antifashion are vocal and aggressive in their resistance to the oppression of fashion and bourgeois conventions. Flaunting ripped jeans and slouched flannel shirts, this mode does violence to the very fabric of fashion. Yet it cannot escape fashion's dictates, only despoil them—and it is only a matter of time before high fashion exploits antifashion, whose effects—both psychological and economic—are costly. Reversing the principles of sumptuous display and the pleasures of voyeurism, antifashion challenges us to look—a look that hurts and is thrown back at us in mockery and defiance, but we cannot overlook the self-laceration at the heart of this "attitude," this refusal to be left out. Antifashion's challenge to look assumes alternate form as a parody of haute couture: hip hop's exaggerated gold chains and watches or glamorized sportswear, including baseball caps and football jackets. Whether torn in shreds or folded against itself, fashion *is* the cultural fabric. And in its purposeful affront to sensibilities and norms of aesthetics and ethics, antifashion reminds us that dress is always in some way self-conscious, and always about power. It may be a mistake, then, to assume that native peoples do not dress self-consciously or that their costumes can only be read as signs of their political and economic oppression and victimization. Are they any more dressed for death, "dressed for kill," than khaki-clad revolutionaries—the Provos and Senderos, with their terrorist chic?

Fashion is a material culture, clothing bodies that come in different sizes, shapes, and sexes, bodies open to desire and pleasure and vulnerable to pain and death, bodies regulated by the forces of capitalism and commodification. What relations of power and persuasion are at work in articulating fashion through the body—human bodies? We begin here.

Design Dictates

The essays in this section emphasize that fashion stakes out the body as its territory. Analysts of fashion have repeatedly turned to Michel Foucault's study, *Discipline and Punish,* for assistance in charting this terrain. In his work, Foucault demonstrates that the body is subject to various forces, social, economic, political and sexual among them, and he promotes the rights and pleasures of the body against their oppression.[13] The usefulness of such an approach for studies of fashion is abundantly clear, as Kim Sawchuck explains: "When we are interested in fashion, we are concerned with relations of power and their articulation at the level of the body."[14] Instilled with a false need to consume an ephemeral product, the fashionable body is held captive to its own desires for adornment and subjected to economic and market forces. As Elizabeth Wilson has noted, fashion's link to commodification can be traced to its origins in modernity; it is coincident with the rise of industrial capitalism and the market economy.[15] Fashion can exert a repressive power over the consumer, even the youngest, as Ingeborg O'Sickey demonstrates.

In "*Barbie Magazine* and the Aesthetic Commodification of Girls' Bodies," O'Sickey insists that in our love-hate relationship with the Barbie doll we have overlooked its textual offshoot. The doll embodies an illusory and partial definition of woman (as blonde, white, affluent, and inordinantly thin) that the companion *Barbie Magazine* further delineates and enforces as a "normative" ideal of femininity and consumer behavior, beginning a training that adult fashion magazines will continue. Extending Foucault's insights about disciplinary power, O'Sickey identifies the tactics employed by the beauty industry to subject the female form to its control as they appear in the pages of a magazine directed toward the youngest of consumers. The Mattel Corporation not only promotes its own products but also holds out the promise of an ideal beauty that readers can attain by investing in the right diet, exercise, clothing, and makeup. Encouraging identification with Barbie, the magazine further prescribes girls' play, enforcing sexist, racist, and classist stereotypes. And since no girl will ever be able to be Barbie, "*Barbie Magazine* taps into and fosters the same kind of self-dissatisfaction that sells products to adult women."[16]

Like O'Sickey, Karla Jay considers fashion as a commodity that promotes a normative ideal of femininity. She further argues, however, that it enforces heterosexuality as the norm of sexual identity. In "No Bumps, No Excrescences: Amelia Earhart's Failed Flight into Fashions," Jay examines Earhart's pioneering efforts to market practical, comfortable, fashionable sportswear for women. Earhart's failure, Jay argues, was due not only to lack of interest by the major fashion magazines and the economic depression of the 1930s but to the disjunction between the image of Earhart the aviator and the self-consciously feminine Earhart the fashion promoter. Instead, sportswear only gained acceptance when donned by movie stars, particularly Katharine Hepburn and Marlene Dietrich. In films featuring female aviators, such as *Christopher Strong* and *Dishonoured*, the screen idols appropriated Earhart's image but glamorized and sanitized her work clothes. Their seductive femininity succeeded in popularizing sportswear when Earhart's commitment to practicality and comfort placed her at odds with fashion's elite. In Jay's words, she fell prey to a "genderized schizophrenia."

More than thirty years later, the much-hyped period of sexual, social, and political revolution, the 1960s, flouted such simplistic gender distinctions in its marketing of fashion. Drawing on her own experience as a teenager captivated by Twiggy and the Mods, Linda Benn DeLibero lends credence to O'Sickey's claims about the process of identification encouraged by consumer culture, particularly in its youngest consumers. DeLibero notes that she and her adolescent companions "were exceptionally susceptible to the spurious involvement consumption offered," viewing their purchase of mod fashion as a way of buying into the politics of liberation of the sixties (the Vietnam War, the civil rights movement, and the dawn of feminism). Yet she notes that the Twiggy phenomenon merely substituted innovation in fashion and style for political and social change. Uneducated, working-class, and vaguely androgynous, Twiggy served as a fairly innocuous image of gender and class "violations." She sold a diluted version of Mod politics, grafting it onto American consumer culture. DeLibero thus glimpses in the early 1990s an uncanny echo of the Twiggy phenomenon in the much touted "return of the gamine."[17] Once again, American designers have capitalized on the marketing potential of "subversive" style, selling what had been the low-cost antifashion of grunge rockers (Doc Marten boots and flannel shirts from the Salvation Army) as haute couture.

Leslie Rabine notes that fashion magazines embody the contradictions suggested by DeLibero. In "A Woman's Two Bodies: Fashion Magazines, Consumerism, and Feminism," Rabine argues that magazines such as *Vogue* and *Glamour* construct two separate and distinct bodies: one is subjected to culturally imposed images of the feminine form, while the other pleasurably exploits fashion's link to theater and fantasy as a means of self-production, self-expression, and even liberation, including political liberation. Contemporary fashion magazines schizophrenically represent both forms: "While these magazines are well-known as instruments for consumer capitalism, non-readers are often surprised to learn that they have increasingly served as a forum for North American feminism (as well as civil rights and ecology movements) during the past twenty years." Fashion's symbolic representations thus exhibit the logic of postmodernism, for they both expose and uphold forces of dominance.

Shifting emphasis from the selling of style, Hélène Cixous returns our attention to the fundamental relation of fashion and the body. In "Sonia Rykiel in Translation," the French theorist reflects on the significance of the French fashion designer's clothes, particularly her own personal attachment to a black jacket created by Rykiel. To Cixous, Rykiel's designs establish a continuity between "world, body, hand, garment" and communicate across barriers of time and memory as "dresses like dreams full of history." Cixous claims that the model for Rykiel's fashions is "the body's internal sensation of itself, the secret of the body," and that "there is no rupture with the body hidden in the body."

In her own voice, Sonia Rykiel concurs that it is "as if body and dress were mirrored images of each other, each the consecration of each other." Her epigrammatic and fragmentary comments in *Celebration* establish a complex network of images: textile, texture, text, tissue, web, word. Fabric, fashion, figure, figuration, fabrication, fabulation. In her first published text, *Et je la voudrais nue*, Rykiel meditated on the related meanings

of "creation," linking vestimentary composition, writing, and preg-
nancy.[18] Here she explores the intersections of fashion design and literary
creation, emphasizing the textual constructedness of fashion: "He who
utters the word fashion knows not what he says. Lean closer to hear the
rustle of fabric, the words of the artist, his passion for dress."

SIGHT LINES

Fashion's artists are not only its designers; they are also those who capture
fashion on film. This section of the book looks at how the camera and
cinematic apparatus support (and sometimes subvert) dominant psycho-
sexual and social attitudes, especially notions of the feminine and of the
female body (clothed or unclothed) as something-to-be-looked-at. Our
contributors ask the following questions: Do "still" images of fashion
photography frame subjects in ways similar to cinema narratives? Do
magazine images of fashion models situate the reader (usually a woman)
in the same ways that screen images frame audience responses? How are
the acts of filming, photography, looking, and reading gendered? In what
ways can the photographer, filmmaker, and actor-model invert or undercut the cultural assumptions that inform their work? This discussion focuses on how we are taught to look at pictures and movies (and what
"looks" these media throw back at us) and on the techniques fashion photographers and cinema directors use to structure our responses to the fashioned body that invites our gaze. This debate implicitly challenges a
founding premise of feminist criticism and film theory, that the camera
eye = masculine gaze.[19] Also in question is John Berger's framing of the
cultural axiom: "Men look at women. Women watch themselves being
looked at."[20]

For Diane Arbus, who used the camera to "stare down" her subjects,
the photographic moment captures a certain kind of tension between imaginative desire (the urge to create) and the pain of frustrated or failed hopes.
In "Off the (W)rack: Fashion and Pain in the Work of Diane Arbus,"
Carol Shloss examines the dialectic established between Arbus's early fashion photography, which represented the American dream of Beauty
through "snapshot realism," and the later, darker work, which rejected
the social norms of the beautiful and focused on freaks and outcasts, capturing the body in pain. Arbus's later photos testify to the failure of fashion
to fulfill its false promise of enacting a change in character or fortune
("woman + garment = security, esteem"). These photographs also expose Arbus's own early role in upholding fashion's false fabrications.

Man Ray certainly did not "stare down" his subject. Instead, he manipulated the photographic image and its props in such a way as to direct our attention to the many ways the camera's subject is fashioned (i.e., constructed). How, asks Mary Ann Caws, is the observer "seduced into collaboration with the photographer's sight?" In "An Erotics of Representation: Fashioning the Icon with Man Ray," she considers the surrealist photographer as both a French fashion and a fashion*er*. She argues that Man Ray's representations of fashionable dress construct an image of his own self fashioned as Other. Her essay explores the tension between viewer and viewed as the camera eye imposes its surrealist vision— Man Ray's signature—on the photographic subject.

Maureen Turim examines an earlier kind of filmic seduction that paved the way for "feminine modernity." "Seduction and Elegance: The New Woman of Fashion in Silent Cinema" reads silent cinema as a record of women's rejection of the confining and discreet Victorian shirtwaist in favor of high-fashion extravagance, a shift that announced a "self-conscious sexual desirability." The "Gibson Girl" served in life, art, and film narratives as a transitional figure between the virginal Victorian victim and the activist "new woman" who sought romance, employment, class ascendancy, and fine clothes. D. W. Griffith's films established the Gibson Girl as an ideal type, fashionable yet modest, and positioned her within a conflict of values between fashion and social space, or power. Cecil B. DeMille's epics then recast and recostumed the Gibson Girl, employing orientalism, primitivism, and exoticism to reveal the new woman's seductive power as an inversion of social and sexual codes—reminding audiences that dress and decoration are "essential elements of self-presentation."

Pop culture diva Madonna perhaps best personifies for late-twentieth-century media culture the inherent possibilities for manipulating self-presentation. Douglas Kellner surveys her career in "Madonna, Fashion, and Identity" and argues that she deploys fashion and sexuality to construct an identity as rule-breaker and transgressor. He identifies three stages of her controversial and contradictory self-fashioning and concludes that the Madonna phenomenon is paradigmatically postmodern: first, because identity is constructed through image, fashion, looks, pose and attitude; second, because Madonna belongs to commodity culture, her self-fashionings (and the lucrative Madonna-imitations they spawn) "reinforce the norms of the consumer society, which offers the possiblities of a new commodity self through consumption."

In "Fragments of a Fashionable Discourse," Kaja Silverman maps the history of vestimentary self-fashioning from a psychoanalytic viewpoint. She observes that in making the body culturally visible, clothing and ornamentation map the shape of the ego and reveal the complex visual exchange of the psyche—seeing (voyeurism) and to-be-seen (exhibitionism). Reviewing the history of Western fashion, she reminds us that dress was once a signifier of class status rather than sexual difference. While male dress has become fixed and stable, frozen into a "phallic rigidity," female dress has changed frequently, shifting emphasis from one erotic zone to another. During the same period that dress became a form of contestation in contemporary life, a way of challenging power structures and cultural norms, North American feminism reacted against the female narcissism and exhibitionism associated with fashion. Contemporary "new women" either adopted muted imitations of male dress (the business suit) or parodied the masculine vestimentary codes (the tuxedo look, sequined ties). Silverman offers an escape route from this mirroring binarism by turning back on history in "retro dress." Vintage clothing reconceives the past and at the same time puts forward a masquerade that allows an ironic distancing between the subject and her clothes. It also allows us a way to recycle fashion's "waste."[21]

Iris Marion Young reimagines the psychic and physical space of fashion's gaze by liberating the Look from the sole provenance of the organ of sight. "Women Recovering Our Clothes" articulates pleasures that exist outside the "orbit of self-reference" that the gaze establishes. The first pleasure, touch, recalls Sonia Rykiel's notions of sensual dressing, a sensory recovering that allows woman to experience the private and unseen pleasures of her body clothed: "Sensing as touching is within, experiencing what touches it as ambiguous, continuous, but nevertheless differentiated." The sense of touch counters the painful sense of being stripped naked by the (masculine) gaze. The second pleasure, bonding, joins the individual woman to her sisters, clothes serving as "threads in the bonds of sisterhood." The final pleasure, fantasy, challenges and unsettles both the reigning orders of the gaze and the tyranny of exploitive consumerist mass culture by playing with (and thus recognizing) that the fashion myth is "the fantasy of multiple and changing identities."

Diana Fuss distinguishes the "photographic contract" from the "cinematic contract" in terms of how each structures desire (through fantasy) to create the heterosexual female subject. In "Fashion and the Homospectatorial Look," she argues that although fashion photography presumes a heterosexual viewer, it offers eroticized images of the female body that encourage women to look, see, and view as lesbians. She explores the "self-fashioning" of the female subject by revealing how fashion photography plays upon the homosexual identifications of the pre-oedipal mother-child dyad in creating the "norm" of heterosexual object choice. Fashion photography situates the viewer so as to awaken the daughter's unconscious homosexual desire for the mother and holds out to her the fantasy of repossessing the lost object—the face, smile, gaze, touch, even smell of the maternal.

BODY POLITICS

Fashion serves as site for exploring not only sexual identity but also political expression, as the essays in this closing section forcefully demonstrate. In "Terrorist Chic: Style and Domination in Contemporary Ireland," Cheryl Herr analyzes fashion from the point of view of dispossessed but politically engaged women in Northern Ireland. She argues that "the disappointing legal status of women in the Republic and the crossfire situation that many in the North encounter resonate in the discourse about what people in Ireland wear and why they wear it." In particular, Herr analyzes the paramilitary wear of the IRA and the marching bands that promote its cause. This "resistance style" marks its members out for British surveillance but simultaneously serves as a sign of their collective identity. Their clothing "pointedly follows its own history in implied resistance or even indifference to that of haute couture."

But if fashion can indeed serve revolutions waged abroad by the Provos and Sandanistas and on the popular culture front by grunge rockers and rappers, it can also be a means of oppression and exploitation. Barbara Brodman argues in "Paris or Perish: The Plight of the Latin American Indian in a Westernized World" that the process of Western colonialism is evident in the increasing adoption of Western clothing in Central America, where native people suffer social disintegration, persecution, and even death for retaining tribal patterns of dress. Further, Brodman observes that the fashion world liberally "borrows" from native designs, usurping the creative potential of others and reaping a tidy profit in the process. The hegemony of Western style works in two ways: we instill a desire for Western clothing in others while coopting native designs and textiles for our high fashion. Designers romanticize the Other, and by purchasing such creations we participate in this exploitive cooptation. We overlook the material struggle of native peoples and we do violence by erasing the traditional associations of dress in the daily life of those for whom it is a national costume.

The same pattern of cooptation occurs when designers turn to the streets for their "Radical Chic." Christian Lacroix (of pouf fame) exclaims in the pages of *Vogue*, "We are all nomads. . . . Modern technology and communication have created a kaleidoscope of cultures. And the result is a kind of nouveau folklore. I'm not talking about ethnic embroidery, I'm talking about new fabrics such as leather decorated with modern elements like metal. It doesn't come from the archives, it comes from the street."[22] Yet, as with "ethnic embroidery," such cannibalism of style effaces the political significance of street style. Dick Hebdige, Angela McRobbie, and others consider "style wars," subcultures, and the antifashion aesthetic as a means of political or economic emancipation.[23]

Thus, in "Tribalism in Effect," Andrew Ross examines contemporary street style, particularly among young black males in the inner city of Los Angeles in terms of its political suggestiveness. He argues that hip hop fashion may in fact reverse the pattern of the fashion world "ransacking street style." Instead, "the logic of the marketplace has become an object of sartorial terrorism," as rappers produce their own versions of high-fashion luxe. He points to the role of their fashions in the rebellions taking place in urban centers like Los Angeles. Ross suggests that consumer culture does not always enforce the status quo, but instead may serve as the battlefield in the struggle of disenfranchised groups for access to power. But, as he notes, we can discern no common political purpose behind such designs. Instead, fashion serves not to unite but to distinguish individual communities or "tribes" seeking to define young black masculinity. Style tribalism in L.A. subverts the call for "multiculturalism" and echoes the trend toward ethnocentrism in Eastern Europe and sub-Saharan Africa.

Power fashion. Terrorist chic. How far we've come from Joan Crawford's high heels.

NOTES

1. *Mildred Pierce* (1945), dir. Michael Curtiz, with Joan Crawford, Zachary Scott, and Ann Blyth.

2. Roland Barthes, *The Fashion System,* trans. Matthew Ward and Richard Howard (New York: Hill and Wang, 1983). In this early semiotic analysis of the rhetoric of fashion, Barthes demonstrated that, like language, fashion is "a system of signifiers, a classificatory activity, much more semiological than sociological" (280).

3. In intellectual circles, fashion is no longer the "F-word." See Valerie Steele, "The F-word," *Lingua Franca* (April 1991): 17–20. Recent publication of a number of full-length works exploring the topic testify to its newfound "seriousness." See, for example, Fred Davis, *Fashion, Culture and Identity* (Chicago: University of Chicago Press, 1992), and Marjorie Garber, *Vested Interests: Cross-Dressing and Cultural Anxiety* (New York: Routledge, 1992).

4. *Still of the Night* (1982), dir. Robert Benton, with Roy Scheider and Meryl Streep.

5. Andrea Dworkin documented the oppressive effects of foot binding, for

example. See Andrea Dworkin, *Pornography: Men Possessing Women* (New York: Perigee Books, 1979), 123–127. More recently, Naomi Wolf has followed Betty Friedan's early example to argue that the "beauty myth" is a patriarchal conspiracy to keep women in their place. See Naomi Wolf, *The Beauty Myth: How Images of Beauty Are Used Against Women* (New York: William Morrow, 1991).

6. "Cherchez La Femme: Feminist Critique/Feminist Text," *Diacritics* (Summer 1982).

7. Douglas Kellner, *Jean Baudrillard: From Marxism to Postmodernism and Beyond* (Stanford: Stanford University Press, 1989), 97. Baudrillard argues that fashion dominates and refigures that which it is supposed to represent. Perhaps for this reason, Fredric Jameson chose Andy Warhol's *Diamond Dust Shoes* for the cover of *Postmodernism: Or, The Cultural Logic of Late Capitalism* (Durham, N.C.: Duke University Press, 1991). Note that both Jameson and Baudrillard have moved away from more thoroughgoing Marxist analyses of market forces towards analyses of the semiotic systems governing consumer culture. On the link between fashion and the postmodern, see especially Julia Emberley, "The Fashion Apparatus and the Deconstruction of Postmodern Subjectivity" and Gail Faurschou, "Fashion and the Cultural Logic of Postmodernity," in *Body Invaders: Panic Sex in America,* ed. Arthur and Marilouise Kroker (New York: St. Martin's Press, 1987), 47–60 and 78–93, respectively.

8. *The Crying Game* (1992), dir. Neil Jordan, with Stephen Rae, Miranda Richardson, and Jaye Davidson.

9. "Wanted: A Few Good Clothes," *Mirabella,* March 1993, decries the recent trends toward transparent layers and slit shirts and skirts. These designs "reflect a prevailing mindset that considers fashion fun and games, runway entertainment." The real world of women's lives, however, demands clothes "strong enough to be taken seriously, different enough to be interesting" (57). In the same issue, "Of Women's Bondage" (116–118) fantasizes a Murphy Brown-as-dominatrix, whose "bullying" tendencies are displayed by leather harnesses and whips, chains and garters. The point seems to be that to appear truly powerful women must still be seen as threatening, intimidating.

10. "Bazaar," *Harper's Bazaar,* February 1993, 111.

11. "Radical Chic," *Vogue,* July 1992, 102–113.

12. See "Ethnic Ware" in *Mirabella,* March 1993, 114–115.

13. Michel Foucault, *Discipline and Punish: The Birth of the Prison,* trans. Alan Sheridan (New York: Vintage, 1979).

14. Kim Sawchuk, "A Tale of Inscription/Fashion Statements," in *Body Invaders: Panic Sex in America,* ed. Arthur and Marilouise Kroker (New York: St. Martin's Press, 1987), 62.

15. Elizabeth Wilson, *Adorned in Dreams: Fashion and Modernity* (London: Virago, 1985).

16. Karen Avenoso reports that the new talking Barbie doll was "recently deprogrammed so she wouldn't say, 'Math class is tough,' after the American Association of University Women argued that the doll could discourage future female rocket scientists." See "Feminism's New Foot Soldiers," *Vogue,* March 1993, 118.

17. See *Vogue,* January 1993.

18. Sonia Rykiel, *Et je la voudrais nue* (Paris: Grasset, 1979).

19. See Laura Mulvey, "Visual Pleasure and Narrative Cinema," *Screen* 16 (Au-

tumn 1975): 6–18; Mary Ann Doane, *The Desire to Desire: The Woman's Film of the 1940s* (Bloomington: Indiana University Press, 1987); E. Ann Kaplan, *Women and Film: Both Sides of the Camera* (New York: Methuen, 1983); Annette Kuhn, *The Power of the Image: Essays in Representation and Sexuality* (London: Routledge & Kegan Paul, 1985); Jacqueline Rose, *Sexuality in the Field of Vision* (New York: Verso, 1986); Teresa de Lauretis, *Alice Doesn't: Feminism, Semiotics, Cinema* (Bloomington: Indiana University Press, 1984), and *Technologies of Gender: Essays on Theory, Film, and Fiction* (Bloomington: Indiana University Press, 1987). For a comprehensive overview of feminist positions, see Jane Gaines, Introduction to *Fabrications: Costume and the Female Body,* ed. Jane Gaines and Charlotte Herzog (New York: Routledge, 1990), 1–27.

20. John Berger, *Ways of Seeing* (London: Penguin, 1972), 47. Also see Jacques Lacan, *The Four Fundamental Concepts,* ed. Jacques-Alain Miller, trans. Alan Sheridan (New York: Norton, 1978), and "Introduction of the Big Other," *The Seminars of Jacques Lacan, Book II: The Ego in Freud's Theory and in the Technique of Psychoanalysis,* ed. Jacques-Alain Miller, trans. John Forrester (New York: Norton, 1988); Shari Benstock, *Textualizing the Feminine: On the Limits of Genre* (Norman: University of Oklahoma Press, 1991), chs. 1 and 2. Three troublesome issues that feminist film theorists might further investigate are these: (1) why do we assume that the gaze is a function of the organ of sight? (2) why do we (mis)read Lacan's psychic theory of the gaze as a theory of masculinity? (3) why does society assign the right to look (voyeurism) to men and the necessity to be seen (exhibitionism) to women?

21. Naomi Wolf, author of *The Beauty Myth,* comments that third-wave feminists feel free to reject the toned-down or downright unfashionable dress of their feminist precursors. "You can wear lipstick or high heels or combat boots and be a feminist, sleep with whomever you want, follow your bliss. The image is about tolerance and pleasure." See "Feminism's Newest Foot Soldiers," 116.

22. "Radical Chic," *Vogue,* Summer 1992, 102–113.

23. See Dick Hebdige, *Subculture: The Meaning of Style* (London: Methuen, 1979); Angela McRobbie, ed., *Zoot Suits and Second-Hand Dresses: An Anthology of Fashion and Music* (Boston: Unwin Hyman, 1988).

design

dictates

Ingeborg Majer O'Sickey

*b*arbie *Magazine* and the Aesthetic Commodification of Girls' Bodies

From Barbiemania to Barbienoia

Barbie is indisputably the most successful doll ever marketed. One sign of its success is that it has "broken out of Toyland and moved into Artville," as Alice Kahn puts it in her article "A Onetime Bimbo Becomes a Muse."[1] Barbie populates the avenues of Artville in a variety of guises: Marge Piercy wrote a poem about her, performance artist Jeffrey Essmann impersonated her, Andy Warhol painted her, designers like Oscar de la Renta and Bob Mackie fashioned gowns for her, Kenneth and Vidal Sassoon coiffed her, New York's Modern Museum of Art, London's Victoria and Albert Museum, Washington's Smithsonian Institution, and the Oakland Museum exhibited her.

Perhaps the most impressive testimony to the doll's power came in 1986 when Mattel financed a $1.5 million exhibition titled "The Barbie Retrospective and New Theater of Fashion." The multimedia show, which was organized by BillyBoy, "a self-confessed Barbie maniac," toured Europe with a production that would rival that of any mega rock star: top couturiers from both sides of the Atlantic designed sixty original outfits, and artists created life-size Barbie habitats and holograms in celebration of Barbie's consumer euphoria. After its European tour the show climaxed in a New York extravaganza during which Warhol unveiled his painting of Barbie and 1,300 guests danced until dawn to "Barbie and the Rockers."[2]

Clearly, Barbie had moved beyond her original doll-dom and gone on to become an icon on America's Main Street.[3] From the moment she made her grand entrance at the New York Toy Fair in 1959, Barbie Doll became the consummate material toy-girl, a role model for many members of the Baby Boomer generation. As a late-twentieth-century icon Barbie's success is measurable in hard currency: conceived as the most acquisitive doll in history, Barbie, the brainchild of Mattel Toy Company founders Ruth and Elliot Handler, earned over $700 million in 1990 alone. *In toto,* Barbie and her entourage of family, friends, and pets have inspired a labor-intensive industry that has produced 600 million plastic dolls and more than one billion outfits, including 1.2 million pair of shoes and 35,000 handbags.[4]

BarbieMania inspires collectors to travel from all corners of the world to Barbie conventions. Over 500 Barbie-collecting aficionados attended a three-day-long "Barbie Forever Young Convention" in Garden Grove, California. They came to buy, sell, and trade Barbie items, from plastic bags containing Skipper shoes for $1.00 to a $1,000 Barbie Airplane. BarbieMania has motivated one woman to set up the Barbie Hall of Fame in Palo Alto, California; it boasts more than 16,000 dolls in a permanent exhibit. Barbiephiliacs have been regaled with a number of Barbie biographies during the last decade, from Susan and Paris Manos's *The World of Barbie Dolls: An Illustrated Value Guide* (1983) to BillyBoy's *Barbie: Her Life and Times* (1987).

The fashion industry has capitalized on BarbieMania as well. Mattel's designers copy Parisian haute couture for Barbie, who "possesses a specially-designed outfit for every occasion that could possibly enter a little girl's dreams."[5] Cultural mimic and culturally mimicked, Barbie has inspired, as *Elle* documents in a photo-fashion spread titled "What a Doll!," a number of top designers to "toy with the look of America's favorite doll, in sixties suits made modern."[6]

BarbieMania, America's love affair with the 11½-inch plastic doll, has its antithesis, BarbieNoia. Articles by feminist critics trace the back-and-forth shuttle from doll to woman and woman to doll, exposing the influence the doll has had on America's feminine beauty ideal. In "Living Dolls" Anne Taylor Fleming comments on the Barbie doll-woman-consumer nexus when she asks, "Are we crazy, or is everyone starting to look like Barbie?" and illustrates the Barbie-wanna-be's wave by juxtaposing images of six "Plastic Versions" of Barbie from 1961 to 1985 to six "In the Flesh" versions; the photographs of Dianne Brill, Faith Ford, Jane Fonda, Marla Maples, Dolly Parton, and Deborah Norville in uncannily lifelike Barbie-looks, speak for themselves.[7] A number of artists, inverting Warhol's glorifying, straight painting of Barbie, have generated a "Barbie

Noire" wave. Peter Galassi, curator of "Pleasures and Terrors of Domestic Comfort" at the Museum of Modern Art, notes that Barbie's aesthetic significance lies in her ordinariness, in the fact that Barbie is "a kind of ubiquitous consumer item found in the home. . . . Barbie isn't just a doll. She suggests a type of behavior—something a lot of artists, especially women, have wanted to question."[8] Commenting on her exhibit "Berkeley, Calif., 1987," artist Sage Sohier says, "I've taken a lot of pictures with Barbies . . . symbolic of society's ideal of the perfect woman—but I've also photographed kids on the beach decapitating them, then floating their heads in the water."[9] Taking a different perspective, "Barbie Noire" artist Ken Botto's photographs, exhibited at the Oakland Museum, make explicit what he perceives to be the doll's darker side for males. According to Botto, replicas of Barbie's looks portrayed in fashion magazines strike fear in men, "like they're going to eat you alive. I saw her as a reflection on what we think of femininity. It's not flattering.[10] To make his point about Barbie as a "dominatrix," he photographed a comatose Ken on the ground, with Barbie towering over him.

> Life is a beauty contest.
> **—Thierry Mugler,** designer,
> *Elle*, March 1991

BARBIE MAGAZINE

America's love-hate relationship with Barbie, what I have called Barbie-Mania and BarbieNoia, has been commented upon extensively. What we have not paid attention to before is the doll's textual offshoot, *Barbie Magazine*. In 1965 more than 100,000 readers subscribed to the bimonthly magazine for girls aged four to twelve. The current textual wing of the Barbie doll, *Barbie Magazine,* was started in winter 1984 and is, as of this writing (January 1993), in its thirty-first issue. At first glance, the magazine seems merely another money-making dimension of the Barbie doll. Undeniably, the magazine makes no secret of its function as a showcase to sell more in-house Mattel products. But it is not that simple. *Barbie Magazine*'s primary function is the production and reproduction of images of certain kinds of femininity in order to train girls to become perfect consumers of beautifying commodities. All women's fashion and beauty magazines are ultimately manuals for particular kinds of training in femininity; *Barbie Magazine* is the preparatory text, the basic-training manual, for the girls' later reading of teen magazines like *Seventeen* and *Mademoiselle*. These, in turn, prime teens for adult fashion magazines like *Glamour, Elle*, and *Vogue*.

The role of *Barbie Magazine* within the larger context of adult women's fashion and beauty magazines cannot be overemphasized. Whereas these magazines are a part of the vast American apparatus of industries that sell feminizing products, *Barbie Magazine* works for these industries by laying the textual groundwork for what the plastic doll personifies: the girls are not only instructed in consumerism, but taught to accept their passage from childhood to adolescence in terms of commodities.[11] *Barbie Magazine* builds upon ideas the doll manifests, and it initiates its readers into practices that adult women's magazines will continue. Essential to the magazine's lessons on femininity is the premise that being feminine is to be in constant need of "aesthetic innovation"; to teach girls that women, like cars, must be restyled every year.[12] In the following pages I will discuss the tactics in three basic sections that *Barbie Magazine* recycles in each issue to convince its readers that they are in perpetual need of renovation: the editorial section (which includes beauty guides, an advice column, and fashion spreads); advertising (ranging from beauty products and clothes to Barbie-related paraphernalia); and the "Barbie photodrama."

> I made my living from looking young. It was really a good thing that I stopped in time. I aged quickly. You do that in America.
> —**Greta Garbo,** quoted in
> *Allure,* February 1992

A MANUAL FOR DISCIPLINING THE BODY

The regularly featured editorial beauty guides in *Barbie Magazine* code the child models' bodies as a *territory* upon which a systematized and rigorous basic training toward a normalized femininity is dictated. It is useful to look at the magazine's techniques of feminizing its readers in terms of Michel Foucault's analysis of "disciplinary power" in *Discipline and Punish*. By "disciplinary power" Foucault means "a policy of coercions that act upon the body, a calculated manipulation of its elements, its gestures, its behavior" through a "machinery of power that explores it, breaks it down and rearranges it."[13] For our purposes, we can think of "the policy of coercions that act upon the body" as the tactics various beautifying industries employ. Foucault's "docile body" is a male body that stands for both male and female (student, soldier, patient, worker, prisoner).[14] If we want to apply Foucault's insights about disciplining practices to the way femininity is inscribed on girls textually in *Barbie Magazine,* we have to broaden his categories. To the places Foucault mentions (schools, factories, prisons, barracks, hospitals, and so on), we have to add those sites where the *female* body is made docile: fashion magazines, beauty salons, spas, so-called fat farms, body sculpting clinics where cosmetic surgery is used to redesign the female body, body-reducing businesses (such as Weight Watchers),[15] body-shaping businesses (such as health clubs), pageant grooming schools (such as Success Marketing, Inc., for children), and modeling/self-improvement schools (such as Barbizon). Since Foucault locates the disciplining practices in Western societies in a "political economy" of the body, it is possible for us to discuss the way the body is used materially as a commodity. He says, "The body is . . . directly involved in a political field; power relations have an immediate hold upon it; they invest it, mark it, train it, torture it, force it to carry out tasks, to perform ceremonies, to emit signs."[16]

Barbie Magazine's strategies for exerting disciplinary power upon the girls' bodies recalls Foucault's account of a "micro-physics of power" (a power that derives its force from fragmenting and carving up the body in temporal, spatial, and gestural ways). The most sustained examples of a Foucauldian "micro-physics of power" in the magazine can be seen in editorials that maneuver the girls' bodies into temporal schemes (times of day, seasons), into feminizing spaces (beauty salons, bathrooms, dance studios), and gestural regimes (certain ways of moving, standing and sitting, smiling). The girl models' bodies are frequently presented in time slots determined by when beauty treatments of specific body parts are deemed appropriate (for example, creams to be applied in the morning, nails to be buffed in the evening). For this purpose, parts of the body are photographed in segments. Lips are painted following specific rules for color and shape, creams are applied in certain places according to a time schedule, and so on. Face, arms, hands, hair, and so on are territorialized and made to conform to notions of ideal femininity by treatment with exercise, cosmetics, and embellishment with accessories.[17]

In one notable example, the "Fall Beauty Fling" feature poses the girls in front of mirrors as they demonstrate ways to repair their skin and hair after a summer in the sun; the program shown operates on a Foucauldian micro-physics of power, designed to teach girls how to regain "smooth skin" on their hands, feet, elbows, knees, and shoulders, body parts that, according to the magazine's beauty editors, have been abused during the summer months. Other after-summer advice includes how to do a manicure, how to choose the right kind of perfume, how to condition hair, how to get rid of chapped lips, and how to have a "sunny smile" with a "sparkling-clean mouth."[18] Similarly, the feature entitled "Punky Brewster's Beauty Guide" treats the girl's body like a territory, segmented by rules that govern the regimentation of each part. The model, nine-year-old actress Soleil Moon Frye, demonstrates to her peers how to take care of their hair, their skin, their hands, their nails; how to apply makeup; what to eat; and so on. The 1992 winter issue of *Barbie Magazine* featured a "before and after" hair make-over in a beauty salon, showing girls how to turn frizzy hair into smooth hair, and straight hair into "angled" hair.

In a slightly different manner, editorial fashion layouts segment the children's time into slots of specific activities. Specialized "theme" clothing, such as clothes for school, sports events, parties, and holidays, suggest that the accoutrements are more important than the activities. In one such layout, titled "Jungle Fever," the models are photographed in "safari attire" against a background of junglelike vegetation. The implicit suggestion is that they need new outfits in order to have an "adventurous" play time. The theme approach to fashion camouflages this suggestion, however, in that it pretends to educate the children about cultures other than their own. But as is evident from the copy that accompanies the photographs of the little girls "in" the jungle, this "other" world is completely stripped of otherness and denuded of difference: "If you are heading south to explore the Amazon, or whether you're just taking a few fashion cues out of Africa, the jungle look is hot stuff this spring! So let *Barbie Magazine*'s models guide you on a style safari."[19] The text's allusion to the film *Out of Africa* and its pop descriptions of Africa homogenize this other world into a commodity for the children's consumption.

Another conspicuous example of presenting children's clothes in terms of theme clothing is the fashion layout "Flamenco Fashion" (figure 1). Here the models (ranging in age from six to ten) are posed in what is popularly conceived to be Spanish ethnic clothing. The copy makes believe that the feature will teach children something about Spanish culture: "If you have a passion for fashion, you'll fall for these fabulous fall styles. They have a romantic tale to tell and they tell it in an exotic Spanish accent! Flamenco fashion is a fiery look that will remind you of fearless toreadors, singing troubadours, and lovely ladies with red roses."[20]

As is clear from the trivialized and highly romanticized descriptions of other cultures, however, the world presented in these fashion editorials is a world that is finally not outside at all. It is imploded into the compass

Figure 1. "Flamenco Fashions," Barbie Magazine, *Fall 1988, 18–19.*

of the department-store-like world created by the Barbie doll and the magazine and then consumed by the magazine's child-reader. The self-contained consumers' world that we find in the magazine's editorials fosters a fantasy of power in the readers that ultimately backfires. The fashion spreads encourage the little girls to strive to achieve a role, but since roles based upon merchandise require no investment of the self on the part of the little girl, they are empty and, therefore, ultimately deeply frustrating.

A similar fantasy of power is promoted in advertisements in *Barbie Magazine.* An especially striking example is a full-page ad for the girls' streetwear line called "Unique" (figure 2). The child model is posed sitting on a railing with sailboats in the background. She is dressed in a feminized sailor outfit, with a seductively unbuttoned white shirt; the upturned collar and loosened tie create a look of throwaway chic. The slogan "She's unique!" is printed in a slanted position toward the focal point of the photo (the girl's head), in the top left corner of the photograph. The girl is set in affluent surroundings, whose status is condensed (and collapsed) into a code, the Yachting Club. Set against this background, the image of the little girl in "unique" clothing suggests to its readers that the identity of a female person is to be on display as affluent, white, blonde, blue-eyed, and slim. That she is said to be unique at the same time as she is used to seduce many others to become like her seems at first a contradiction. The claim

She's Unique!

Now Showing Spring 1986
Toddlers - 4 to 6x - 7 to 14
112 W 34th Street, Rm 1412
New York, NY 10001
(212) 714-9476

UNIQUE!
STREETWEAR FOR GIRLS

Figure 2. "Unique,"
Barbie Magazine, *Winter*
1986, 3.

is justified, however, since her image can command her spectators' gaze without returning it. Her image "receives" its viewers' envious looks only as a recognition of its own supposed self-sufficiency. The model's self-absorbed look reflects the Freudian view of the female as passive and ultimately narcissistic.

This view of women has been reproduced in countless representations of women from paintings to advertisement. Only the most self-confident among the young viewers of the photographed girl can avoid feeling somehow lacking, somehow insufficient by comparison with the self-regarding girl in the photograph. The only way the girls can escape the anxiety of insufficiency is by identifying with the photographed girl in order to compete with her. The two emotional axes activated by the advertisement, then, are identification and competition. These axes make it impossible for the girls to accept or appreciate their own difference and thus block feelings of self-worth. In that the advertisement constructs in its targeted viewers a self that is chronically insufficient, it stifles the possibility for meaningful, noncompetitive interaction with others. That this model is said to be "unique" *like* the name of the line of clothes she is advertising is another example of an explicit collapse of girl into product.[21]

The degree to which the idea that women are the product and the product is the woman has become introjected in mainstream American thought becomes especially clear in *Barbie 30th Anniversary Magazine* (Winter 1990), in which Barbie's career from 1959 to 1989 is documented (figure 3). A central feature in this special issue, a five-page spread entitled "Here's to You! A Celebrity Tribute to Barbie," promotes the illusion that the 11½-inch plastic doll is a human celebrity. Even though the comments celebrating Barbie's thirtieth birthday are made by prominent people of varying ages and professions, their testimonials are remarkably similar. What is significant is that their remarks about the doll's conspicuous consumption, resistance to water-weight gain, cellulite-free body, and the fact that it doesn't have to go on diets and won't get crow's feet or need a "tummy tuck" are made in an anxious humor that reflects the four major

Figure 3. "1959. In the sleepy Fifties, we wanted to conform. Unwinding from the rat race meant a backyard get-together with the hubby, housewife, and 2.4 kids from the split-level next door," Barbie 30th Anniversary Magazine, *Winter 1990, 9.*

cultural anxieties in the United States: affluence, age, weight, and feminine beauty.

The celebrities cited in *Barbie 30th Anniversary Magazine* relate these anxieties misogynistically by contrasting Barbie's appearance to their own. Danielle Steel's remarks are representative of the edge to some of the observations:

> Most of us face 30 with trauma, trepidation, and terror. I approached my 30th birthday as though it were an impending earthquake. . . . Only later did I realize that women are at their most beautiful at 30. So it is with Barbie, who has turned 30 with luxuriant hair, a tiny waist, firm arms, slim thighs and a huge wardrobe.[22]

Whereas we hear an unmistakable tone of anxiety and competition in the women's testimonials, the men's reveal the confidence of those who consider themselves to be authorities on female beauty. Designer Bill Blass puts it epigrammatically: "Happy Anniversary—you've never looked better!" Beauty Queen crowner Bert Parks gushes: "Having crowned 25 Miss Americas, I am somewhat of an authority on beauty, and Barbie, you are among the prettiest. You are the personification of eternal youth, and you have inspired many generations of young girls."[23] Oscar de la Renta remarks, "Barbie is the ideal customer. She looks like a perfect size 6, and she keeps her figure. She's the all-American girl,"[24] unwittingly revealing the correlation between Barbie, the commodity, and women, the consumer.

Of course, Mattel's public relation move to make Barbie one of the celebrities for girls to emulate reflects a fact already "understood" by its consumers. Judging from the letters to the magazine, the girls who play with Barbie play-act as if she were a unique, grown-up star, and often in scenarios in which they "become" dolls, or, perhaps more to the point, "miniature women." One reader writes, "Dear Barbie, what I like best about your magazine are the hairstyles. I wear them all the time and I get ideas for Barbie's hairstyles, too." Another girl writes: "Dear BARBIE Magazine, one day I was thinking about what to wear. Then I opened BARBIE Magazine and found a *great* idea!"[25] *Barbie Magazine*'s boast that "all little girls could see themselves in Barbie's eyes" is taken more than literally by its readers. Indeed, the way the magazine fulfills its dual function of promoting Mattel products and encouraging acceptance of a particular feminine beauty ideal in its readers makes clear that play with a Barbie doll is pre-scripted in a way that circumscribes the girls' play in the narrowest sense.

THE "BARBIE DRAMA"

The most conspicuous example of pre-scripted play comes by way of the "Barbie Drama," a photographed melodrama that appears in the magazine at regular intervals. Letters to the editor reveal that these dramas are very popular with the magazine's readers. The girls use the script, their dolls, the clothes, and equipment necessary to reenact the drama's simple plots. In the photo soap opera titled "The Show Must Go On" (Winter 1986), for example, Barbie stars in a fashion show that is staged for the benefit of a children's charity. I chose this particular photo soap opera to discuss because it most clearly reveals the magazine's official view of femininity. In this drama the dolls, or "miniature women," are depicted in a classic situation, the fashion show. They enact a scenario in which they display commodities (clothes and accessories) at the same time that they become or embody a commodity on stage; each is the object for the spectators' gaze. Spectacle by virtue of the spectator, the miniature women's life is presented in terms of a show in which the female self is role-modeled and constituted by the way others see her. They are outfitted, coiffed, gestured, and smiled into existence to appear in what Laura Mulvey calls women's "traditional exhibitionist role" in which they are "simultaneously looked at and displayed, with their appearance coded for strong visual and erotic impact so that they can be said to connote *to-be-looked-at-ness.*"[26]

This understanding of women's social position as objects to be looked at is elaborated upon in John Berger's explanation about women as spectacle *and* spectators of themselves: "*Men act* and *women appear* [emphasis added]. Men look at women. Women watch themselves being looked at. This determines not only most relations between men and women but also the relation of women to themselves. The surveyor of woman in herself is male: the surveyed female."[27] Indeed, it is striking that traditional gender-specific representations that reproduce the customary heterosexual division of labor, which feminist critics have identified in high-brow dramas, can be found in the low-brow "Barbie Drama" as well. Maintaining the "men act and women appear" formula, Mattel promotes Barbie and her female friends as *dolls,* and Ken and his male friends as *action figures.* More-

Figure 4. "The Show Must Go On," Barbie Magazine, Winter 1986, 25.

over, in the last frame of the "Barbie Drama," the "action figure," Ken, validates the entire drama by coming forward as the representative of the "Foundation" to give Barbie an envelope with a check for the children's benefit (figure 4).

Not all "miniature women" are equally unequal in this drama, however. Whereas social power is explicitly shown as belonging to the male "action figure," the imbalance enacted in the drama is not merely an embodiment of general female social powerlessness. Manifest is the dominant view of how women of all races and economic classes should appear: with long slender legs and body, wasp-thin waists, large eyes and delicate features, basically straight but curled hair, elaborate living spaces, flashy cars, and state-of-the-art leisure equipment. Erased are all racial traits and attributes that deviate from white European ones, and erased also are all class distinctions other than those that mark the affluent upper class (figure 5). By presenting an impossible-to-reach beauty ideal and generally unattainable economic wealth, the drama lets *all* readers know what they are lacking

Figure 5. "The Show Must Go On," Barbie Magazine, Winter 1986, 23.

and where and why they are lacking, and lets its nonwhite and/or non-affluent readers know that they are even more lacking than most.

Even though *Barbie Magazine*'s message that "whiteness is rightness" reproduces the racialist and classist attitudes of the dominant media in the United States, Mattel's public relations department converted the need for coming out with new Barbies into an opportunity for giving the company itself a progressive image. The fact that it took twenty-one years to produce a black or Hispanic Barbie did not stop Mattel from exploiting the black consciousness movement. It unabashedly entitled the announcement of its production of "ethnic" Barbies "Her-itage" and claimed, "Now all little girls could see themselves in Barbie's eyes."[28]

In the Barbie photodrama "The Show Must Go On," a homogenizing process has stamped out racial differences. The miniature women of color exhibit the same beauty ideal as the white Barbies. This makes it difficult for the girls to imitate adult role models in an imaginative way, that is to say, in a way that reaches toward a "fantasy" or "reality" beyond the play that the doll itself creates, because it is this doll itself, a particular miniature woman, they are imitating.

Although toys and children's magazines are only a part of the vast feminizing technology in American culture, they are especially noteworthy because they are the site where the free reign of imagination, fantasy, and play is said to be encouraged. The Barbie doll, as presented in the magazine, however, is not only not the site of free play but is a site where narrowness of vision is dictated textually. Thus, it is in some ways useful to think about the Barbie drama in terms of filmic spectacle and spectation, since, like spectators of films, the readers of *Barbie Magazine* are looking at images of a normative ideal of femininity as they are using the textual and visual frames for acting out the roles prescribed in a rearticulation of female bodies *as* spectacle.

This rearticulation, while implicitly sexual on the one hand, is curiously asexual on the other. The doll's persona (Barbie is a "good" girl) and its body (without nipples, navel, or pubic hair) present an image sanitized of the "messier" aspects of physicality. Despite Eartha Kitt's edict that "good girls go to heaven, bad girls go to Bergdorf's [a high-price, high-fashion New York specialty store]," Barbie, the Good Girl, does go to her equivalent of Bergdorf's. Although generally analytically critical of Barbie-Mania, Marilyn Ferris Motz argues that by playing with Barbie a little girl "can imitate adult female behavior, dress and speech and can participate vicariously in dating and other social activities, thus allaying some of her anxieties by practicing the way she will act in various situations." Motz also claims that by playing with a Barbie doll a girl "can establish the limits of acceptable behavior for a young woman and explore the possibilities and consequences of exceeding those limits."[29] These arguments are difficult to support since the practice of being a woman in our society is *predicated* on anxiety. As in the Doris Day song, this practice is shot through with *Angst:* "Will I be pretty?" (Will I be pretty like Barbie doll? Will I be slim like Barbie?) "Will I be rich?" (Will I have all the things I need to have the kind of life Barbie has?). This *Angst* is, as I have argued, created in bourgeois commodity culture with Barbie and *Barbie Magazine* among its most prominent players. As to establishing limits (in sexual terms) and learning the consequences of these limits, this is impossible with Barbie: trying out the limits of sexual behavior by play-acting can obviously only take place when sexual function is made visible.[30] Furthermore, as Anne Taylor Fleming suggests, there may well be a sinister side to Barbie's asexuality: "A naked Barbie doll is somehow bizarre, the original dashboard princess, all T&A and nonstop legs. . . . So that's what Barbie is: She's a fantasy object for men for little girls, if that makes sense."[31]

I agree with Fleming that, rather than alleviating anxiety as Ferris Motz suggests, the doll's body image has a disempowering effect on girls, a disempowerment that can be seen in the way "adult women are aping her appearance, being surgically trussed up and staying anorectically thin."[32] Indeed, the child models who populate the magazine's pages range from slender to anorectically thin, and although slimming diets have not yet found their way into the magazine, the American mania for the right body architecture is promoted through *Barbie Magazine* as well. In 1984, at about the time that Jane Fonda began marketing her aerobics videos, a "Great Shape Barbie" was merchandised in the United States. As *Barbie Magazine* boasted, "Whatever new ways Americans devise to stay in shape, Barbie is there!" More recently, a casting call for roles in a video called "Dance! Workout With Barbie" brought 350 girls to a Los Angeles studio for auditions. The 9 girls chosen (ranging in age from seven to eleven) rehearsed for eight months in a Foucauldian regime of "teleological exercise" and "tactical control" before the final video was produced.[33] In what I take to be an ingenuous comment, a writer for *Barbie 30th Anniversary Magazine* makes an important point for critics who see the negative effect of Barbie's body: "Her striped 1959 'birthday suit' revealed a figure that every little female baby boomer hoped would some day be hers."[34]

There can be no doubt that Barbie's body, which translates into real-life measurements of 5′9″, 36-18-33, shapes the young girls' body ideal and continues to influence women in adulthood. Barbie, of course, does not do this by itself. But as Susan Bordo argues in "Anorexia Nervosa: Psychopathology as the Crystallization of Culture," self-disciplining practices that result in eating disorders are not only medical cases, but culturally induced in that they are clearly linked to the "consolidation of patriarchal domination," a domination, I might add, that plays itself out in consumer capitalism in Western industrially developed nations.[35]

Insofar as Barbie dolls have professional titles from astronaut to physician, Barbie's image has been seen progressive in its alternative to the *Kinder-Kirche-Küche* scenarios of the 1950s.[36] The other side of this "progressive" image, however, is that by fostering an impression that an asexual and anorectically thin body is the ideal feminine body, the doll represents a denial of the sexual functions of the female body, including reproduction. As Bordo writes, "Adolescent anorexics express characteristic fears about growing up to be mature, sexually developed, potentially reproductive women." In a commentary on the influence of representations of women in the media, Bordo tells the story of a little girl she saw in Central Park, "perhaps ten years old . . . gazing raptly at her father, bursting with pride: 'Daddy guess what? I lost two pounds!' "[37] The little girl's anxieties reflect Americans' obsession with pounds, which has taken a dizzying upward spiral in the last thirty years: 31 percent wanted to lose weight in 1951; by 1991 the figure had jumped to 52 percent. Naomi Wolf's research shows an estimated 8 million anorexics in the United States and reveals that 90 percent of the 8 million Americans with severe eating disorders are women. She reports that 20 percent of American college women "binge and purge regularly."[38]

We have seen the fantasy to look like Barbie enacted by film stars such as Cher, who has undergone radical surgery to "resculpt" her body to fit the ideal upheld by Barbie. The back-and-forth shuttle of influence is clear: while many models and actresses strain to attain Barbie-like figures, there is no doubt that young girls look to actresses and models for role models. For years Barbizon's ad campaign to attract young women to take its modeling courses has capitalized on this fact: "Be a model. Or look like one!" As Susan Bordo writes, "What used to be acknowledged as extremes required of fashion models is now the dominant image that beckons to high school and college women."[39]

As is evident, the editorials and advertisements in *Barbie Magazine* organize and package messages on how to be (sexually) attractive, as an aesthetic. The grown-up little-girl models in *Barbie Magazine* bear a striking resemblance to their childlike adult counterparts in fashion magazines for adults. As in adult fashion magazines, the girls' faces and bodies are used as the canvas for beauty products and clothes. In this way *Barbie Magazine* taps into and fosters the same kind of self-dissatisfaction that sells products to adult women. The collapse of a doll (product) into a woman is entirely consistent with the commonly held view of woman as the "perfect consumer of commodities as well as images," since her role as a consumer is, as Mary Ann Doane puts it, "indissociable from her positioning *as* a commodity and results in the blurring of the subject/object dichotomy."[40] It is important to keep in mind that the collapse of product into woman and woman into product must always (however else we talk about femininity as a social construct) also be understood as a construct marked with *investment,* measurable in capital in that the material basis for women's self-alienation is anxiety about not measuring up to the standards of feminine beauty generated in commodity culture and consumer capitalism. In this sense, it is crucial to recall, as Doane does, that woman "is the object of exchange rather than its subject," a fact that points to the "asubjectivity of the commodity. The woman's objectification, her susceptibility to processes of fetishization, display, profit and loss, the production of surplus value, all situate her in a relation of resemblance to the commodity form."[41] Thus, for marketing purposes the girls and women themselves are, like the doll, shown to be in need of continual "aesthetic innovation." Female bodies and parts of women's bodies are represented and addressed *as* commodities in more or less direct ways in magazines from *Barbie Magazine* to *Seventeen* to *Elle* and *Vogue*. Slick ads for creams promising rejuvenation and products for slenderizing are brazenly aggressive in their strategies. In *Barbie Magazine,* the basic training manual, girls are given lessons in what "well-groomed" women know. Clearly, the injunction to be "perfectly feminine" alienates girls from themselves and each other in that they begin to see themselves as inadequate—that is, fat and ugly. Studying the photographs of the models in *Barbie Magazine,* one can see that the girls look "naturally made up" (from the youngest model, aged about four, to the oldest, who looks about twelve), by virtue of having undergone a strict regimen of disciplinary practices. In the piece on repairing summer damage, in the lessons Soleil Moon Frye imparts, and in the dictates of how to be dressed properly for every occasion and time, the magazine sets the foundation for the lessons that those girls who do not want to be seen as "unnatural" will follow into womanhood: that being perfectly feminine is deferred until the next beauty product, the next dress, the latest diet.

NOTES

I am especially grateful to Linda Alcoff, Dympna Callaghan, and Robyn Wiegman of the "Feminist Study Group" at Syracuse University for their insightful and critical readings of earlier versions of this essay. I also thank those friends, students, and colleagues who have sent me Barbie-related news and suggested resources to me.

1. Alice Kahn, "A Onetime Bimbo Becomes a Muse," *New York Times,* September 29, 1991, 1.

2. Ibid., 1.

3. Barbie even made it into the evening news in December 1989, after the historic opening of the Berlin Wall. CNN reported the story of an East German girl of seven, who, when asked what she would like to have now that the border to the West was open, answered unhesitatingly, "a Barbie doll." The girl's linking of political freedom and consumerism was rewarded by Mattel. They flew her to their New York headquarters for a tour and feted her.

4. *Barbie 30th Anniversary Magazine,* Winter 1990, 27–31.

5. *Barbie 30th Anniversary Magazine,* Winter 1990, 30.

6. *Elle,* February 1991, 176–181.

7. Anne Taylor Fleming, *Allure,* March 1991, 128, 130. It has long been recognized by critics of the doll that it has negatively molded girls' body images. The doll's influence on girls' intellectual capabilities has also recently come under at-

tack. Mattel's latest creation, "Teen Talk Barbie," with its statement, "Math class is tough," has prompted the National Council of Teachers of Mathematics to object to the "negative impact" Barbie's wail will have on girls (*The Washington Post,* January 10, 1992).

8. Quoted in Kahn, "Bimbo," 25.

9. Quoted in ibid.

10. Quoted in ibid.

11. Susan Willis devotes a chapter in her recent book, *A Primer for Daily Life,* to Barbie's influence. In "Gender as Commodity," she makes a point similar to mine: "My hypothesis is that both toys [Barbie and He-Man] play on the child's conscious and unconscious notions about adolescence. They focus the child's conception of the transformations associated with adolescence in a singular fashion, and they suggest that change is somehow bound up in commodity consumption" (*A Primer for Daily Life* [London: Routledge, 1988], 27).

12. The phenomenon of "aesthetic innovation" is described by W. F. Haug, *Critique of Commodity Aesthetics* (Minneapolis: University of Minnesota Press, 1986). Most manufacturing industries, like Mattel, face the problem of marketing products that may not wear out fast enough. "Aesthetic innovation" is promoted in a way that makes consumers accept the "new" product as *necessary.* A survey of women's fashions (both clothing and cosmetics) of the last thirty years shows that "aesthetic innovation" has become the main marketing strategy of appearance-related industries.

13. Michel Foucault, *Discipline and Punish: The Birth of the Prison,* trans. Alan Sheridan (New York: Vintage Books, 1979), 138. Foucault identifies four disciplinary procedures which provide the conditions for imposing the regimens upon the body; these are "cellular" control, which refers to public spaces that are made into grids, compartmentalized, and carved into units where "each individual has a place and each place has its individual"; "rhythmic" control, which refers to time tables for the management of activities; "teleological exercise," which is based on a schedule with the goal of getting better and better; and "tactical" control, which refers to the way signals (whistles, hand-clapping, bells, and so on) are used to call individuals to perform (143).

14. As Sandra Lee Bartky notes, the story of the regimentation and subjugation of women's bodies ("bodies [made] more docile than the bodies of men") cannot be simply collapsed into the account of disciplinary practices rendered upon male bodies. She looks at three categories of disciplinary practices that are "peculiarly feminine": dieting, nonverbal expressions such as movement, gestures, and posture, and decorative disciplines such as dress, makeup, and other ornamentation. See "Foucault, Femininity, and the Modernization of Patriarchal Power," in *Feminism and Foucault,* ed. Irene Diamond and Lee Quinby (Boston: Northeastern University Press, 1988), 61–86.

15. Isolating only one of these industries predicated on a technology of the body, the body-reducing business, clearly reveals the link between beauty ideals and consumer capitalism: Weight Watchers sales in 1990 were $1.6 billion, and it boasted 750,000 members at 4,000 locations. Nutri/System earned $764 million in 1989 and has 200,000 members at 1,800 locations internationally (*Allure,* February 1992, 78).

16. Foucault, *Discipline and Punish,* 25.

17. Examples of segmenting the female body can be found in adult fashion magazines as well. Some of the more bizarre formulations accompanying the photographs blur the distinction between body parts and fashion accessories: "Hair is a woman's most erotic *accessory*" (*Bazaar,* February 1990, 150), and "today's shifts are shaped in at the waist, *accented by bare arms* and above-the-knee hemlines" (*New York Times,* February 4, 1990, 54; my emphasis).

18. *Barbie Magazine,* Fall 1988, 12.

19. *Barbie Magazine,* Spring 1987, 16.

20. *Barbie Magazine,* Fall 1988, 18.

21. I am indebted to Doug Anderson for development of this line of thought.

22. *Barbie's 30th,* 40.

23. Ibid., 41.

24. Ibid., 31.

25. *Barbie Magazine,* Fall 1992, 4; Fall 1988, 4.

26. Laura Mulvey, "Visual Pleasure and Narrative Cinema," in *Feminism and Film Theory,* ed. Constance Penley (New York: Routledge, 1988), 62.

27. John Berger, *Ways of Seeing* (London: British Broadcasting Corporation, 1972), 46–47.

28. *Barbie 30th,* 50.

29. Marilyn Ferris Motz, "I Want to Be a Barbie Doll When I Grow Up," in *The Popular Culture Reader,* ed. Christopher D. Geist and Jack Nachbar, 3rd ed. (Bowling Green, Ohio: Bowling Green University Press, 1983), 127.

30. Barbie's "just say no" attitude, outlined by Motz, ironically predates the political right's prescription on teenage sexual behavior in the age of AIDS, since practicing abstinence based on ignorance of facts about sexuality is the only sexual behavior that can be rehearsed with Barbie.

31. Fleming, in *Allure,* 132.

32. Ibid., 132–133. Film director Todd Haynes recognized the connection between Barbie's figure and anorexia when he used defaced Barbie dolls in his 1987 documentary film *Superstar: The Karen Carpenter Story.*

33. *Barbie Magazine,* Winter 1992, 52, 27.

34. *Barbie 30th,* 27–28.

35. Susan Bordo, "Anorexia Nervosa: Psychopathology as the Crystallization of Culture," in *Feminism and Foucault,* ed. Irene Diamond and Lee Quinby (Boston: Northeastern University Press, 1988), 87–117.

36. It is surely no accident that "Barbie-inspired" couture made a comeback during a period of high unemployment in the United States during the late 1980s and early 1990s. It mirrors the return to "normalcy" for women following World War II, during the late 1950s and early 1960s (which brought us Christian Dior's baby-doll fashions), when women were forced to return to domestic duties. Similarly, Mattel's plans to market a "Barbie for President" (outfitted with a campaign button and briefcase to go along with a business suit, and an inaugural gown) can be read as mirroring a recovering economy and as a commentary on the Bill and Hillary Clinton phenomenon.

37. Ibid., 102.

38. Quoted in *Allure,* February 1992, 77, 78.

39. Bordo, "Anorexia," 101. Comments by brokers of images of feminine beauty for the media and heads of modeling agencies have become the measure for

feminine ideals and foster an intensely misogynist climate in the United States in the eighties and into the nineties. For example, the head of a top modeling agency in New York, Eileen Ford, is quoted as saying that all women, even nonmodels (i.e., short women), can have great legs, but they must be well proportioned: "To be short from the knee to the ground is a sorry thing. It makes you look underslung . . . calves must be curved—too straight is boring." Dani Korwin, the owner of the "Parts Model Agency," judges that legs must be "long, slender and shapely. . . . The calf shouldn't be too muscular, the thigh shouldn't be too chunky, and ankles must be slim. Ideally, if a girl stands with the legs together, they should touch in three places: the knee, the wide parts of the calf, and the ankle" (*Elle,* June 1991, 174).

40. Mary Ann Doane, *The Desire to Desire: The Woman's Film of the 1940s* (Bloomington: Indiana University Press, 1987), 13.

41. Ibid., 22.

Linda Benn DeLibero

*t*his Year's Girl:

A Personal/Critical History of Twiggy

> As fashion continues to borrow heavily from the 60s, a model with a Twiggy-like physique becomes the logical clothes-horse.
> **—Christian Wright, "Fresh Faces," *Allure*, January 1993**

> For a generation just now generating its own marijuana culture . . . the gamines and their hippie threads provide a link with the past.
> **—John Leland and Elizabeth Leonard, *Newsweek*, February 1, 1993**

A pale-faced model gazes vacantly from the cover of *Vogue,* her cropped hair provocatively tousled, wide eyes framed by a fringe of spiky lashes. At first glance, she bears an uncanny resemblance to the skinny teenager who shook the fashion world in 1967, and for a second I do a double-take in the check-out line. But Twiggy Lawson—as she's now known—is forty-three years old, a semiretired actress whose last brush with fame was a failed sitcom, and this is 1993. The cover girl is Amber Valletta, one of about a dozen Twiggy look-alikes who've been popping up on magazine covers since late 1992; in fact, this is the third time in a month I've had to look twice to determine that I wasn't seeing an apparition from the past. Yet another sixties revival in the fashion world; designers call it "The New Look."

Official histories of the sixties will take you on a tour around the great movements of the decade in terms writ large and apocalyptic ("days of hope . . . years of rage"). But this latest style revival reminds one of another, less official version of that famously tumultuous time: the decade was a shopper's paradise, a consumer explosion for the young and the hip. Today, tie-dyeds and combat boots may indeed be the true and only "link with the past" for the Crystal Pepsi generation. Even for many of us who grew up during those years, it's tempting to remember the sixties as a passing style parade, a collection of attitudes and fashions glimpsed longingly in the pages of *Life* and purchased in bits at the local Carnaby Street—every American city had one. From that perspective, the utopian promise of the decade has been reduced to the things that lasted—a proliferation of recyclable fashions, the politics of simulacra, the youth market, a collection of co-opted subcultural styles: the Hippie Look, the Mod Look, Radical Fringe jackets.

But that would be giving too little credit to the profound effect popular culture can have on people's lives. I lived through the Twiggy phenomenon at an age when it was bound to affect me deeply, at the turn into adolescence. My friends and I were too young to have been in on the "real" events of our time, too old not to have been changed by them. Our awareness of the war, the civil rights movement, the dawning of feminism, was filtered through newscasts and the somber, alien language of adults. We felt powerless to affect that world, even as it imperceptibly shaped us. The fragments of popular culture we consumed were, indeed, our only tangible links to the world "out there": the black armband and "peace" earrings we proudly sported on Moratorium day, the Avedon photo of John Lennon hanging on the bedroom wall. The ads we saw, the magazines we read, communicated to us in the kind of magical language children understand: vivid, immediate, full of promises, full of contradictions. Did the politics come along with the clothes?

As young, white suburban girls, both curious about and frightened by the changes occurring all around us, we were exceptionally susceptible to the spurious involvement that consumption offered, and especially to anything that enticed without too much threat. For a while Swinging London—already pretty much finished in England by 1967—was the most desirable of cultural exotica that passed before us in an exceptional era; besides *Sgt. Pepper,* Twiggy was the most visible commodity Britain produced that year, and we generously complied with the hype, scarfing up skinny little Twiggy pens, Twiggy lunchboxes, Twiggy lashes, an assortment of Twiggy-endorsed cosmetics. Undoubtedly, we were also buying a particular set of ideas about femininity, the malleability of identity, the power of mass marketing. I can't look at the history without wondering what we gained from our investment, or how much it cost us.

> It's the first time that a young girl has had this appeal for the great teenage market.
> **—Thomas Whiteside,**
> ***Twiggy and Justin***

Twiggy: Queen of the Mod, seventeen and enviably famous. Was our fascination only about copying a very cleverly marketed look? For weeks now I've been critically assessing ads for products I once bought, photos I studied with religious intensity, articles that fired my twelve-year-old's conviction that London was the center of the universe, a piece of which could be mine for the price of a Yardley Slicker Stick. The cultural historian in me tries to sort out this material, make sense of the official discourse in ways that will explain our enchantment, our sheer helplessness before it. And yet even as I'm looking, waves of nostalgia overcome me as I remember exactly how potent the charm was of those faces, those clothes. Fashion as a powerful mode of expression, style as a means to another life, the sense of possibility in a purchase—the connection between clothes and the politics of liberation hadn't been so pronounced since the twenties. For a girl on the verge of adolescence, that convergence proved heady. *Vogue* called it "youthquake." Part of me wants to see it—or at least its effects—as something more than the cultivated narcissism and commodity fetishism credited to the original Mod movement. For the young girls I knew, adapting those clothes was a step, possibly a side step that was often painful as well as exhilirating, into a different relation to our bodies, to our ideas about what we could expect from the world, to our sense of place in history.

But the rhetoric surrounding Mod style supported those notions; the figure of Twiggy herself (née the prosaic Lesley Hornby) completed a movement that sought to reverse rigid hierarchies of style, feminine beauty, class, and age. In *Seeing Through Clothes,* Anne Hollander delineates the way in which representations of the human body alter according to changing fashions.[1] Just so, the "Twiggy" body only became visible some time after the clothes it was designed to wear became popular. That skinny, ungainly child of a carpenter, with her sunken chest and swayed back, was the logical endpoint of Swinging London style, when, for a brief moment, all Britain seemed to thumb its nose at the official order.

In 1962, when Mary Quant knocked off Courrèges' haute couture miniskirt for her Bazaar boutique on the King's Road, she was credited with democratizing fashion for the masses. The mini, she claimed, was designed for women "to dance, to move, to be."[2] Implicit in that statement (and in the style itself) was the sense that women of a certain age need not apply. "I grew up," Quant once remarked, "not wanting to grow up. Growing up seemed terrible. . . . To me it was awful; children were free and sane and grown-ups were hideous."[3] Quant became the designer for a generation of reluctant adults and self-styled free spirits, marketing clothes that mocked the elegance of couture and rendered the mature female figure ridiculous. Like most mass-marketed phenomena, this ethos was paradoxically as exclusionary as it seemed inclusive. By the time the Mod movement reached American shores in the person of Twiggy, what had begun as a liberating style solidified into a peculiar sort of tyranny.

The whole world wants to do a story on Twiggy. . . . *Life* did a story seven weeks ago—the little girl from London who's setting the world on fire. And they're going to do another on her—a fashion story. *Look* is going to have a story about Twiggy in a coming issue. I can't begin to handle the phone calls that are coming in about her. There's been nothing out of England like this since the Beatles and the Stones. I guess it's somehow just natural evolution that Twiggy should be

Twiggy's arrival in America in March 1967 was notable enough that even the staid *New Yorker* devoted a long essay to the event. The essay was quickly turned into a book—with the addition of photos, of course. Thomas Whiteside's *Twiggy and Justin* was no puff piece, however, but a remarkably prescient account of hard sell in an entirely new age of the photo op and the mass-marketing of endlessly reproducible images. One photo in the book places Twiggy in Central Park, surrounded by four little girls whose faces have been uncannily blanked out by Twiggy masks (figure 1). In another, a crowd of businessmen at the Automat don the masks, masks so lifelike that it is impossible to tell for a second where the real Twiggy is. These visual jokes are a kind of shorthand equivalent of Whiteside's narrative, which clinically details the manufacture and reproduction for profit of a human commodity.

Most of these machinations were the brainchild of Twiggy's manager/boyfriend, a Cockney named Nigel Davies who, as *Mademoiselle* reported, "blithely slipped into 'Justin de Villeneuve' as a Great Name To Be Famous In."[4] The "blithe" transparency with which Davies concocted his new (and preposterous) moniker provides the clue to a signal difference between Twiggy and previous mass phenomena. Whereas Brian Epstein, for example, had worked assiduously to mask his careful cultivation of a "good boy" image for his moptops, de Villeneuve casually laid bare the manufacturing process with a naive braggadocio that was, itself, a kind of put-on. On the verge of negotiating what one promoter describes as "bigger than anything in the history of the commercial-tie-in field," de Villeneuve indignantly complained to Whiteside about the "jokers" on Madison Avenue: "They must think I'm green. . . . And I've got an office in London that's *twice* as big as that hotel room we were just in."[5] In 1967, when much was being made of England's new class mobility, Davies/de Villeneuve played skillfully on both the resentment and admiration engendered by the Cockney-boy-makes-good narrative. The working-class bounder dressed up in dandy's clothing made the transparency of his charlatanism an inextricable part of the phenomenon.

Figure 1. Multiple Twiggys cavort in Central Park during the model's first trip to America. Photo by Melvin Sokolsky, UPI.

And so it was with Twiggy's entire American excursion. Whiteside reported that "a curious sort of excitement seemed to have been stirred up over" Twiggy's arrival, the source of which was doubtless the very fact of its invented quality.[6] "She is a magic child of the media. Where there are no cameras, she ceases to exist," *Newsweek* exclaimed.[7] It was a condition novel enough to become the story itself. Twiggy appeared at that juncture in the sixties when the media had become increasingly self-conscious about its role as mediator (if not co-optor) of enormous social and cultural change. Fixing on a fairly innocuous image of various mild class and gender "violations," the culture industry turned Twiggy into a myth of the marvelous transformative properties not of politics or social consciousness, but of fashion and style. "Twiggy is the first child star in the history of high fashion, crowned queen of the mod by the same adolescent army of teen-spenders that has already seized and conquered pop music," trumpeted that same story in *Newsweek*.[8] The martial imagery here is disarmingly snide: that "army" of adolescents, rest assured, bears no arsenal of Molotov cocktails, merely a pack of credit cards at the ready: Youthquake.

> Today's look comes from below. The working-class girl with money in her pocket can be as chic as the deb. That's what Twiggy is all about.
> **—Cecil Beaton, quoted in "Twiggy: Click! Click!"**

Reading old articles about and interviews with Twiggy, it becomes immediately apparent that no fashion model had ever signified quite so much. It's probable that neither before nor since has the public known more about the life behind a model's face; neither Suzy Parker, nor Jean Shrimpton, nor even Cindy Crawford has gotten so much ink about her origins. Those origins—working-class, undereducated, untutored—may have meant little in the elite world of *Vogue* photographers like Beaton and Avedon, but the popular American press, representatives of the great American middle, clearly perceived Twiggy as a threat.

The snide tone, bordering at times on outright hostility, characterizes a great deal of the coverage she and de Villeneuve received, much of it aimed at the idea of a pair of upstart, illiterate Cockneys cashing in on Americans' susceptibility to the latest thing. If Twiggy and Justin had expected a "democratic" welcome in the States, interviewers quickly disabused them of that notion. The media aimed its subtle (and not-so-subtle) class barbs at Twiggy's lack of education and Justin's aggressiveness. Reporters mocked the inarticulate interview Twiggy gave upon her arrival at JFK airport ("dunno . . . dunno . . . dunno" she responded to a series of rather inane questions) and relentlessly made fun of her accent.[9] In a scathing front-page editorial, the acid-tongued James W. Brady of *Women's Wear Daily* dubbed Twiggy "the paper girl."[10] Judith Crist, writing for *Ladies' Home Journal,* complained that, with the advent of this "Cockney who cavorts with stuffed animals . . . a near-mindless childishness [has] become the hallmark of our time" (figure 2).[11] Oriana Fallaci, in an extended interview for the *Saturday Evening Post,* gleefully quizzed the high school dropout on history and politics: "Fallaci: '*Twiggy, do you know what happened at Hiroshima?*' Twiggy: 'Where's that?' "[12]

Figure 2. "A mindless childishness . . ." Photo by Howell Conant, Life *Magazine.*

Figure 3. Twiggy and Justin. Photo by Burt Glinn, Look *Magazine.*

The media was equally overt in its hostility toward de Villeneuve. In *Look* his photo was captioned "the man behind the property" (figure 3);[13] the *Daily News* dubbed him "pushy"; and Fallaci described him as "a back street bully . . . handsome in a rather crude way."[14] Clearly, the apparent facility with which young Brits could transcend their origins (a phenomenon aided, ironically, by the media) struck a chord of distinct unease, at least among the mainstream press corps. Thomas Whiteside likened Twiggy to a "sort of modern version of Eliza Doolittle" whose Higgins had been replaced by a skillful p.r. man.[15] Indeed, like Eliza, Twiggy could consort with kings and queens (or at least with Sonny and Cher) without the trouble of learning either proper elocution or the social graces. Status had been frighteningly cut loose from character, origins, breeding, or even hard work, in part because the media itself had made appearance primary. Having created its monster, the press spent much of its time clucking at the alacrity with which the American public took up the latest thing; simultaneously, it milked public resentment toward "the paper girl" for making success look so easy.

Ironically, in fixing its outrage on the Twiggy phenomenon, the American media had singled out perhaps the mildest, most watered-down aspects of a movement that had hardly been a radical subculture in the first place. The Mods, far more than any other sixties youth culture, had, after all, made something of a fetish of the American consumer ethos, the American passion for leisure, the American dream of social mobility. Dick Hebdige has noted that being Mod was "largely a matter of commodity selection. It was through commodity choices that mods marked themselves out as mods, using goods as 'weapons of exclusion' to avoid contamination from the other alien worlds of teenaged taste that orbited round their own (the teds, beats and later the rockers)."[16]

In other words, Mod fashion was a way of distinguishing one's self from the more obvious—indeed "crude," "backstreet," "pushy"—trappings of working-class style with which proles like the rockers adorned themselves. As Stanley Cohen pointed out in his study of the demonization of sixties British subcultures, *Folk Devils and Moral Panics,* the Mods were anathema to lumpen youth (and their elders) precisely because "[t]he glossiness of the [Mod] image, the bright colours and the associated artefacts such as motor scooters, stood for everything resented about the affluent teenager."[17] What the American press conflated into a single mass of upwardly mobile young Justin de Villeneuve veiled the reality of several working-class subcultures vying for a piece of Britain's short-lived economic and cultural boom. In fact, for most rockers and Teds, true class mobility was largely a myth. There is no better indication of this than the fact that in America rockers and Teds remained entirely invisible.

Beyond the clichés of Carnaby Street, Americans (save, perhaps, for some die-hard *Quadrophenia* fans) never really knew very much about the Mods in Britain, knew almost nothing of the darker parts of the movement: the Brighton riots of '64, the penchant for amphetamines, the preening narcissism of the style's more extreme followers. Only the most marketable signifiers of Mod culture crossed the ocean, all those dark parts carefully excised from the spectacle. Diluted too, were the cultural politics behind Mod style. At the core of British Mod rebellion was a blatant fetishizing of the American consumer culture that, according to numerous intellectuals and pundits, had eroded the moral fiber of England. Worshipping leisure and money above all else, scorning the masculine world of hard work and honest labor, the Mods mocked the verities of a class system that had gotten their fathers nowhere. The Mods—and to a lesser extent, the Teds before them—were doubtless among the first subcultures that had based a rebellion on consuming pleasures.

This link to consumerism, the obsession with shopping, was the ultimate affront to male working-class traditions: shopping was a girl's job. As Paul Willis has noted, femininity was the primary characteristic motorbike boys designated as Mod.[18] Their pouffy hair and colorful clothes were "queer." And herein lies perhaps the biggest difference between the British movement and its American counterpart. Underlying this contempt for the feminine was the assumption that Mod was almost exclusively the province of males. Both in the British press and in subsequent scholarship on postwar British subcultures, Mod girls remained invisible. But in America, where style and fashion were the movement's primary imports, Mod culture was girl culture.

All of this was lost on us. Certainly, we girls—and indeed, it was mostly girls who affected Mod style in my school—were entirely unaware of its history or meaning. And yet, for all our ignorance, we unknowingly played out our own version of the Mod/Rocker battle, a bitter subterranean struggle for recognition fraught with similar class tensions, similar clashes over the connection between identity, visibility, and style.

Our school was divided evenly between the sons and daughters of the working class and those whose parents could finally afford, in the postwar boom, to aspire to something a bit better for their children. Except for one Jewish boy and one black girl, we were a homogenous lot on the face of it—mostly Irish and eastern European, with an Italian or two thrown in. Beyond that, the students in our relatively small public junior high were stratified into fifteen separate academic tracks, from Advanced Placement for the exceptional to fifteen for the hopeless. Naturally, those tracks divided rather neatly across economic lines as well, the bottom ranks occupied by children of the marginally employed. These were the greaser boys, who wore a defiantly retro look that borrowed heavily from *The Wild One*. Their female counterparts were "racks" (the derivation of which name I have never been able to trace), bad girls who all looked vaguely like Ronnie Specter—ratted hair, white lipstick, black nylons with seams. In some ways, they might have been Twiggy's American counterparts: They hated school, they were inarticulate, they were uninformed and bored with—or threatened by—the world of culture and current events. But they were throwbacks, wearing their '50s leathers with contemptuous pride and casually beating up anyone prissy enough to care about current fashion. They beat up Mods and Preps for reminding them, with their silly, colorful clothes, that at a time of limitless possibility, they had no future. We were terrified of them.

My girlfriends and I had as little contact with that world as we could manage. It was masculine and violent and, we thought, unconscionably ugly and "out." Why would anyone wear a slicked-back ducktail in 1967? Probably, the greasers reminded us too much of adulthood, its attendant struggles, its sexual mysteries. We tried not to think about them unless we had to: if they'd jumped one of our friends on the way home from school or if we'd stumbled upon a greaser/rack couple necking in the woods. Our fascination with Mod style allowed us safe entry into another kind of exotic world entirely, one that was as childlike and asexual as Twiggy herself. The people who manufactured the American Mod craze understood this well, understood that for many of the prepubescent girls they targeted, the deepest fear a twelve-year-old could harbor was the fear of her own body, what it might turn into, what she might lose. A 1967 ad for Yardley's Londonderry Hair Shampoo ("it shines like when you were little") asks, "Where were you when your hair stopped shining?" Somewhere, apparently, "between your twelfth birthday and Sweet Sixteen." I remember owning a bottle of Londonderry Hair, and I know it would have never occurred to me to equate the loss of shining tresses with the loss of virginity. Yet I knew as sure as anything that I wanted to keep my little-girl shine, just as sure as I wanted to have a body just like Twiggy's.

Dear Twiggy,
     Much like yourself, I am skinny and shapeless and flat. I have a scrapbook on you, my hair is styled like yours and my

I got a tie the Christmas of my thirteenth year. It was a real 1967 tie, bright day-glow stripes of orange and green and red, wide as Carnaby Street, with a pocket handkerchief to match. It was the most beautiful thing I'd ever seen, or rather, it was the hippest article of clothing I'd ever owned, the sort of accessory that would change your reputation, command the respect and attention of the cool kids at school, make your teachers realize for the first time that you were a more interesting girl than they'd given you credit for. Maybe you were even a bit of a troublemaker. Of course, nothing could have been further from the truth. My parents had given me the tie, after all, and the only reason they were disposed to humor my penchant for slightly outrageous clothing was because I was such a good girl and so ungainly that it couldn't possibly have signaled rebellion of any sort—it was just a love of fashion, pure and simple. Of course, nothing about style is really pure and simple. So easily deployed by marketing experts and advertising moguls, cut free of historical underpinnings, a style that once signified something—rebellion, subversion, irony—may still be invested with its original power to provoke, whether the wearer knows it or not.

I wore the tie to school the first day back from Christmas break, with a white oxford button-down and a navy skirt, short but not too short, because my mother wouldn't allow it. Sometime during the day I rounded a corner where some greaser boys were leaning against the lockers and knew immediately that I was in trouble. I don't remember their words, but if I think hard enough about it, the sense of humiliation is enough to make my face burn twenty-five years later. I knew, somehow, that it was a kind of sexual humiliation, which made the moment doubly painful. I took the tie off right there at school, carefully laid it away when I got home, and never wore it again.

Of course, from this critical distance, I can see the crime I'd committed against those lost boys; I had affronted their class and sex. A girl—a girl!—had put on the sign of power they could likely expect never to wear, and she hadn't even had the decency to be modest about it. But I couldn't have divined any of this clearly back then; in some dim way I knew that our choice of styles was about more than just fashion, that it was about social choices and possibilities as well. But those boys were too threatening for me to see past the immediate. My misery was attached to something that seemed far more important at the time. A part of me believed that the source of their scorn was simply that I had looked ridiculous in the clothes I so desperately wanted to look good in—ridiculous because I was not boyishly thin, because I had a perfectly ordinary body that was beginning to take the shape of a woman's.

I wanted a body like Twiggy's. I wanted to wear ties so that they would hang straight down my flat chest; I wanted my short skirts to show off knobby knees and slight calves. For an inordinately long time, I believed—or wanted to believe—that most boys preferred that kind of figure. I think now that it was just that we girls preferred it, because the clothes we saw in magazines looked good on those bodies, and because we dressed for each other. I had no desire to starve myself; I never considered doing anything about my "lack." Yet for years I cursed the fact that just as I was beginning to sprout the breasts we'd all been taught to covet, a dumb, skinny girl from London had rendered them passé. At the same time, it was discomfiting to know that the very things I'd been taught I needed to be in order to "get somewhere"—educated, articulate, well informed—had nothing to do with her spectacular success.

> I s'pose most of my fans are girls. I couldn't possibly be a sex symbol, could I, with a skinny figure like mine.
>
> **—Twiggy, in *Twiggy***

And so it was, then, that consumer culture—and Twiggy in particular—made me at times deeply unhappy, fretful and ashamed over what I couldn't change. But if Twiggy made me miserable, she doubtless made skinny girls deliriously happy. I knew some of them, and for those who knew how to sport the look, Twiggy gained them a lot of currency with the popular crowd. Although it's common to think of the sixties—like the twenties—as a "thin" time, the decade was a transitional period in the history of women's body types. The full-figured ideal of the previous decade still obtained in most quarters, and being skinny was, mostly, something to feel ashamed of. Twiggy has often been blamed for beginning the trend toward anorexia, and doubtless the visibility of her body marked a definitive turning point in the shift toward impossibly thin body standards. But we didn't have the language for anorexia then, there was no name for it in common culture, and the teen magazines we read still contained ads for products like "Wate-On" that asked, "Why feel self-conscious and embarrassed because you are thin, skinny, and underweight?" One ad for Yardley's Twiggy Lashes contained the tag line, "With her eyes and your body, who knows how far you can go?"

Given the view from here, in an age when supermodels display manufactured bodies you can only buy or work overtime to achieve, Twiggy's slightness looks like freedom, a space where girls could be girls—could look at other girls—without the intrusion of a masculine gaze or presence. Much was made of Twiggy's androgyny by the popular press at the time ("Is it a Girl? Is It a Boy? No, It's Twiggy" crowed a 1967 headline in *Look*). But it strikes me that her appeal lay not so much in the ambiguity of her sexual identity as in her complete lack of an adult female sexuality. She was, above all and despite her age, prepubescent. Roland Barthes might have been writing of Twiggy when he noted in *The Fashion System* that "the *boyish look* itself has more a temporal than a sexual value: it is the complementary sign of an ideal age, which assumes increasing importance in Fashion literature: the *junior*." [19]

On the one hand, that diminutive status, that emaciated body, signified helplessness and fragility. *Elle* editor Helene Gordon Lazareff said of Twiggy, "She looks pathetic. You say to yourself, 'Poor dear, I ought to take care of her.' " [20] Certainly Justin de Villeneuve's relationship with her was presented—by both the press and the couple—as entirely paternal, and thoroughly traditional. In the popular press, de Villeneuve played Svengali to Twiggy's gullible naif. "Twiggy isn't just me," she gushed in her autobiography, "it's me and Justin. Honestly, I sometimes think Justin invented me!" [21] The threat of both feminism and the youth movement were negated in a sentence.

On the other hand, Twiggy's body, like the anorexic's body, accrued to itself a certain power by virtue of its sexlessness, a power that had a great deal to do with Twiggy's popularity among young girls in the sixties. Susan Bordo has pointed out that such a body ideal, so seemingly defenseless in the eyes of men, may signify for women a freedom from "the encumbrance of domestic, reproductive femininity." [22] No awkward protuberances, no unsightly bulges to remind an adolescent of the destiny still avidly promoted by television and women's magazines (figure 4).

For girls my age, it was a time of increasingly loud and baffling mixed messages. Talk of the sexual revolution was everywhere. Our minis and poorboy sweaters suggested we were alive to its possibilities, but the value

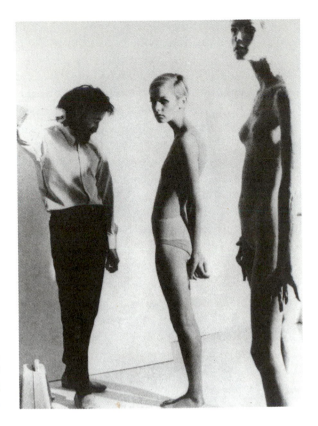

Figure 4. No bumps, no bulges. Photo by Burt Glinn, **Look Magazine.**

system we lived by was as retrograde as the heavy black eyeliner those Ronette girls used to wear, and we didn't want bodies we didn't know what to do with. Sex was either freedom or enslavement. How could one escape it? Go backward, stay young.

De Villeneuve cannily recognized this appeal and carefully honed it. Offered the chance to market a line of sleepwear, he nixed the opportunity: "I don't want filmy Twiggy nightgowns around. It's not good for the image."[23] Ever willing to display his erudition in mass psychology, de Villeneuve once explained to an interviewer: "I don't think boys want Twiggy to be their girl. The kids love her because she's *not* a sex symbol."[24] And that was it exactly. When those boys had ridiculed my tie, I had lost my fashion innocence—I was no longer free to wear what I pleased without calling attention to myself as a sexual being, a girl who should or shouldn't wear certain clothes because her figure might not bear the scrutiny. With Twiggy, for a brief time, girls were free to invest in a spectatorial position that made a virtue of everything deemed undesirable in male eyes. Not only could you transcend your class and be a star, you could transcend the limitations of femininity itself.

Of course, it didn't last; or at least, the celebratory acceptance of a classless, sexless ideal evaporated as quickly as it had appeared. Within months, the androgynous Twiggy had been replaced by the "Young Romantic" on the cover of *Vogue*—adorned in flowing curls and dramatic makeup. Within a year, the anonymous Cockney sprite was masquerading for de Villeneuve's camera as a series of famous Hollywood sirens: Greta Garbo, Rita Hayworth, and, most preposterously, Marilyn Monroe (figure 5). Designer Barbara Hulanicki swathed Twiggy's minuscule frame in the slightly decadent Biba look—all 1930s satins and feathers and black lipstick. In the gloomy years that closed out the decade, Mod fashion itself began to look frivolous and overstylized—ironically, it began to look haute.

What remained was the exaggeratedly thin body type, soon to be sexualized and rendered more unreal by the addition of enormous breasts and

Figure 5. Twiggy as Marilyn. Photo by Justin de Villeneuve.

huge, pouting lips. And the myth of class mobility and freedom promised by Mod culture proved most effective as an example of the incredible marketing potential in "subversive" style. The recent incarnation of sixties fashion, for example, touted as a sign of the new antimaterialism of the nineties, had barely hit the street before it turned up on Paris runways. Similarly, the "new gamines," whose slightly less-than-voluptuous bodies have been hailed as a heartening response to the feminist backlash of the eighties, display figures that can hardly be considered more average or obtainable than Claudia Schiffer's. The pouting lips haven't disappeared; the fashions are routinely provocative and revealing. This new crop of "Twiggy-like" models look disturbingly like sexually precocious children—hardly a liberating image for contemporary adolescents.

I'd like to think that the cultural politics of my own adolescence had something to do with social change, facilitated it in some way or made it visible. A few years after my brief fling with miniskirts and fishnets, I read *The Second Sex,* cut off all my hair, and took to wearing workshirts and baggy jeans. I'm sure I saw this "anti-fashion" as a blow against not only sexism but commodity fetishism as well. The impulse behind it, however, was rooted in the same appeal Mod style had held for me: the desire to transcend my origins, to shake off the boundaries of class and sex and just "be a person." That naive wish, I am sure, was at the root of my emerging political sensibility, as well as my developing aversion to the techniques of mass marketing. But I had myself been deeply enamored of those techniques, had "fallen" for them, and they had given me pleasure as well as pain. Just so, the lithe skinny figure with her arms akimbo, moving—always moving—toward some "luvly" destiny of infinite childlike delights, had been more than just a marketing ploy.

Notes

1. Anne Hollander, *Seeing Through Clothes* (New York: The Viking Press, 1975), xii.

2. Steve Dougherty with Laura Sanderson Healey, "As Hemlines Rise, So Do the Fortunes of Mini Mogul Mary Quant," *People,* September 20, 1990, 37.

3. Deborah Orr, "Minis to the Masses," *New Statesmen & Society,* October 19, 1990, 27.

4. "Justin and Twiggy," *Mademoiselle,* July 1967, 77.

5. Thomas Whiteside, *Twiggy and Justin* (New York: Farrar, Straus, and Giroux, 1968), 127.

6. Ibid., 4.

7. "Twiggy: Click! Click!," *Newsweek,* April 10, 1967, 62.

8. Ibid.

9. Whiteside, *Twiggy and Justin,* 12.

10. Quoted in "Twiggy: Click! Click!," 65.

11. Judith Crist, "What Twiggy's Got," *Ladies' Home Journal,* June 1967, 7.

12. Oriana Fallaci, "My Name Is Twiggy," *Saturday Evening Post,* August 12, 1967, 59.

13. "Is It A Girl? Is It A Boy? No, It's Twiggy," *Look,* April 4, 1967, 90.

14. Fallaci, "My Name Is Twiggy," 59.

15. Whiteside, *Twiggy and Justin,* 142.

16. Dick Hebdige, *Hiding in the Light: On Images and Things* (London and New York: Routledge, 1988), 110.

17. Stanley Cohen, *Folk Devils and Moral Panics: The Creation of the Mods and the Rockers* (New York: St. Martin's Press, 1980), 193.

18. Paul Willis, *Profane Culture* (London, Henley, and Boston: Routledge, 1978), 20.

19. Roland Barthes, *The Fashion System,* trans. Matthew Ward and Richard Howard (New York: Hill and Wang, 1983), 258.

20. Quoted in "Twiggy: Click! Click!," 65.

21. Twiggy, *Twiggy: How I Probably Just Came Along on a White Rabbit at the Right Time, and Met the Smile on the Face of the Tiger* (New York: Hawthorne Books, 1968), 154.

22. Susan Bordo, "Reading the Slender Body," in *Body/Politics: Women and the Discourses of Science,* ed. Mary Jacobus, Evelyn Fox Keller, and Sally Shuttleworth (New York: Routledge, 1990), 86.

23. Whiteside, *Twiggy and Justin,* 137.

24. "Justin Looks At Twiggy," *Mademoiselle,* July 1967, 76.

Leslie W. Rabine

a Woman's Two Bodies:

Fashion Magazines, Consumerism,

and Feminism

Critics of fashion have analyzed clothing as a language, incessantly communicating messages about its wearer.[1] But who speaks this language, to whom is it addressed, what does it mean, and how are its meanings established and transformed? Insofar as fashion communicates primarily cultural messages about the feminine or feminized body as the bearer of social meaning, these questions have no simple answer. They lead instead into the unresolved social and political conflicts of which fashion magazines have become, since the late 1960s, the improbable vehicle. While these magazines are well known as instruments for consumer capitalism, nonreaders are often surprised to learn that they have also increasingly served as a forum for North American feminism (as well as civil rights and ecology movements) during the past twenty years. Between their covers, mainstream fashion has become the figure and arena of the relation between these irreconcilable but interdependent forces.

While critics have traditionally turned a moralizing lens upon fashion, emphasizing its capacity to oppress women, commodify their bodies, and chain their desires to consumerism,[2] others, of whom Elizabeth Wilson is the most noted, object to the view of fashion as a "seamless web of oppression."[3] Yet in asking us to see it as "the most wide-spread medium of women's self expression," she leaves open the questions of how this feminine self is historically constructed, and what is expressed when it expresses itself.[4] An analysis of fashion magazines from 1960 to 1990 suggests that fashion does not merely express this self, but, as a powerful symbolic system, is a major force in producing it. Women of fashion become the "speaking" subjects of a symbolic system which inseparably entangles signs of oppression and liberation within the images of the fashionable feminine body.

In some sense this contradiction has accompanied the history of fashion from the beginning of the twentieth century, as women abandoned heavy, encumbering draperies and torturing foundation garments in favor of simpler, more revealing styles. These have had a double effect, both increasing women's status as objects of male vision and desire and expressing their new independence from the authority of fathers and husbands, their greater physical and economic mobility, their status as self-reflecting subjects, and their release from the restrictions of Victorian womanhood. But through three specific changes in the representation of fashion in the late 1960s and early 1970s, fashion magazines not only allow us to document the emergence of a specifically postmodern conflict, but also perform this emergence in the transformation of their own form.

The look of fashion is the most obvious of these changes. In the early sixties, the pages of *Vogue,* which I am using here as the white, bourgeois authority so influential that its very name is the fashionable synonym of "fashion," displayed the "Jackie Kennedy" style of stiff, boxy trapeze suits and dresses, prim and perky in their elegance. Throughout the decade, these, along with their ubiquitous hats and gloves, gradually gave way to styles more diverse, more body revealing, more specific to a greater range of activities, and more suggestive of daring, exotic costume and masquerade.

The second change could be called anthropological. The world inside the covers of *Vogue* in the early sixties seems to suspend the models' bodies in a vacuum hermetically sealed from the world outside. Neither the fashion photographs nor the copy give any indication of how the readers spend their lives, except for the bathing suit spreads, which show them on vacation. Social and political events and issues are alluded to, if at all, in the vaguest and most indirect terms. Temporal reference points appear almost solely in the form of short clips on the latest in art, literature, theater and music. Recipes for elegant dinners are included in every issue. Since everything about the life of the ideal reader operates on the level of implicit assumption, one must infer that she is married and sequestered, that she does not reflect upon herself, and that her only specific activities are to go to vacation resorts and to give and attend cocktail and dinner parties where she can make charming, informed conversation thanks to the arts-and-letters tidbits in *Vogue.* By the early seventies, social and political issues (the Vietnam war, black liberation, the Equal Rights Amendment, abortion rights) had made their way into the magazine, and by the end of the eighties distinguished journalists and intellectuals were debating every issue. The turning point occurred in the *Vogue* issue of May 1968 (what did *not* occur in May '68?), whose cover broke with convention to announce a "Special Issue: Woman 1968," and which contained an article titled "Who Takes Advantage of American Women?" vigorously attacking woman's "fourth-rate social role," "her socially crippling economic inferiority," and a host of political and cultural injustices. Typical of *Vogue*'s baroquely convoluted position as cutting-edge vanguard of conventional propriety, the article was of course written by a man, Anthony West. Who else in the world of *Vogue* would have the authority to condemn patriarchy and the permission to attack it so aggressively? But he in turn received his authority from his position as son of an outspoken feminist from an older generation, Rebecca West. At the same time that politics entered *Vogue,* the arts-and-letters tidbits expanded to full-length book and film reviews by such intellectuals as Joan Didion and Elizabeth Hardwick. And the notion of culture itself expanded to include not only arts and letters but all manner of cultural phenomena. Consonant with the development of fashion as contradictory symbolic system, the increased inclusion of serious social debate in the magazine paralleled an increasingly sexy style in the fashions. The ebb and flow of this sexiness has to date reached its peak with the ultra-short, ultra-bare, ultra-tight tank-dress style of 1989–1991 that *Vogue* dubbed "body-conscious dressing."

A third change that reinforces this contradiction is a new self-reflexivity on the part of fashion magazines and their implied readers. Instead of relegating everything about the life of the implied reader and her relation to fashion to the level of implicit assumption, the magazines now not only reflect endlessly upon the reader, upon who she is, what she does, what she wants, and what she thinks, but also invite the reader to be more self-reflexive about her relation to fashion, cosmetics, and beauty, and to reflect upon her body in a new, detailed way—as object of her own creativity and control, as instrument of her own social power, and at the same time, as target of men's violence and oppression in a society where gender is still a very lopsided power structure.

Thus a single issue of *Vogue* (February 1990) invites readers to reflect upon themselves in the two following ways. One article offers for our consideration a "new alternative to the black dress" that "Gianfranco Ferre calls the romper—a one-piece jumpsuit with thigh-high shorts" and "a curvy bustier top." Giorgio Armani explains that designers have created it because "The modern woman . . . is 'much more secure about who she is and what roles she plays. Clothes are therefore less traditional and freer.'"[5] The second article offers "the startling statistic that a woman is physically abused at least once every fifteen seconds in the United States," concludes from this that "it is not surprising that domestic violence is the single largest cause of injury to women across the country," and ends by offering a hotline phone number.[6] Left unsaid is that countless women who read *Vogue* to find out how to dress themselves in the newest fantasies are battered women. The "secure," "free" woman and the victim of domestic violence are the same "modern woman."

The conflicting messages that this modern woman's clothing communicates about her situation is illustrated in the two following examples. In the world of *Vogue,* women wear lingerie outside to signify their freedom: "Women today are more confident, so we don't have to be told, 'Now, this is where you wear this. . . .' We are looking at a whole new way of dressing with no categories, no boundaries."[7] Yet in the world outside *Vogue,* say in Fort Lauderdale in 1989, a woman who violated those boundaries found her clothing subject to a univocal masculine reading. When an assailant abducted her from a parking lot, forced her into his car, and raped her at knife point, he was acquitted. The *New York Times* reported, "Members of a jury here say they acquitted a man of rape because the woman's clothing suggested she had 'asked for it.'"[8] Although rape research has consistently denied any connection between the victim's clothing and the rapist's motives, these "twelve reasonable men" projected upon the rapist the authority to decide the single correct reading of the woman's clothing and to determine its true addressee as himself. No ambiguities of message, and especially not the woman's own interpretation of her clothing, were accepted.

These two examples suggest that fashion makes the feminine body into an ensemble of signifiers articulated with two different systems of signifieds. And they further suggest that the two codes are not symmetrical. One accords with the meanings that the dominant culture assigns to the feminine body, while the other is read by the implied readers of fashion magazines as freeing their body from that position. Instead of dismissing this latter reading as an illusion of consumer mythology, we might instead recognize that this other code is real in that it works as a genuine language, that is, as a socially constructed system of signs regulated by a set of shared and accepted conventions. These are readily, if unconsciously, understood by the millions of women attuned to fashion, but not, as a general rule, by men. Fashion therefore harbors a social conflict between these two codes. But since the feminine body remains the central bearer of masculine meanings, this conflict, like those implicit in other forms of popular culture, remains latent. Like any "subversive" language, the sublanguage of fashion is an "outside" of the dominant culture caught within its boundaries. The contradictory symbolic system of fashion works according to a logical figure that modifies two common views of postmodern cultural logic as either the recuperation and containment of resistance within hegemonic culture or as the indeterminate oscillation between two terms. In the logic of fashion, it is not resistance that is contained, but the conflict itself between freedom and dominance. In this conflict, then, the dominant term is doubled, acting as both one pole of the conflict and as the enclosure that contains the conflict. Thus enclosed, the conflict is transformed into an oscillation between the terms that locks the impulse for fundamental change in an historic impasse. Far from illustrating Francis Fukuyama's contention of "The End of History," with its connotations of complacent stasis in a universally homogeneous World Order, the magazines show us the power by which that order blocks the desires and efforts for historical progress of North American social movements.[9]

Within this figure, the three new elements in post-1970 magazines—heightened self-reflexivity, a more blatantly sexy look, and the voice of progressive social movements—work in concert with each other to elicit the reader's desire for identity. These apparently incongruous elements combine to intensify the power of the figure's historical logic by an ability to erase the dichotomy between fantasy and reality at a more obvious level, and to reestablish it more invisibly elsewhere. The fantasies generated by fashion magazines (or videos) do not confine themselves to the page (or screen). They are actually acted out by readers on their own bodies. Imitated from magazines, movies, or videos, and worn in daily life, fashion erases the boundary between the "real" and the "fantastic," between the private escape of fantasy and public intercourse. The pleasure of looking at the photographic images forms one part of a continuum with the pleasure of re-creating the body and the pleasure of masquerade. The continuum turns inside out the commonly accepted opposition between fantasy as internal, unreal, private, and reality as external.

Fashion magazines mediate the continuum between fantasy as mental image and as enactment upon the body through photographs that elicit two different kinds of reader response, each of which plays off the other to foster a particular process of identification. First, the endless repetition of similar images, most of which are inimitable to the point of irreality, invites a look that drifts rapidly through them in a semihallucinatory state. At the same time, other photographs, usually accompanied by articles and captions which assure readers than any woman can achieve the ideal appearance if she learns how to create subtle illusions with clothing, invite a look that scrutinizes and analyzes the photographs in a state of mental concentration so as to permit a future embodiment of the fantasy. The changes in fashion magazines from 1960 to 1980—from showing readers what to wear, say or serve, to showing them how to dress in different styles—carries a deeper change. Aside from increasing the narcissistic seduction of the magazines, it represents a shift from assuming a reader who uncritically imitates an established social role to assuming a reader who produces a self through a proliferation of theatrical roles created through a judicious use of costume and masquerade.

This relation between fantasy and self-production recalls theories of fantasy as a structure that lays the foundation for the "origin of the subject" through "original fantasies" that are also "fantasies of origin."[10] Laplanche and Pontalis are here referring to an infantile "mythical moment of disjunction between the pacification of need . . . and the fulfillment of desire . . . , between the object that satisfies and its sign which describes both the object and its absence."[11] The process of enacting the fantasies of fashion magazines upon the body, the daily act of donning clothing and cosmetics, along with any erotically charged daydream it might include, also entails on the symbolic level a ritualized reenactment of a "mythical moment" itself, covering not the separation between biology and sign but between two signs, that of the unclothed, un-made-up body as sign of unmastered biology and of the clothed body symbolizing a self-produced, coherent subject. The pleasures of fashion include the symbolic replay of this profoundly productive moment when subjectivity emerges. The fantasy of separating from biological indifference into a self that is whole, like the image in the photograph, must end in disappointment, for the resulting woman differs from the hallucination and the photograph in one essential. She does not attain the "frozen" perfection, the completeness of outline that Sylvia Kolbowski calls the "representational plenitude" of fashion photographs.[12] On the contrary, instead of achieving the fetishist's dream of producing a self as whole, she has ended up reproducing a self as alienated, a self-conscious Oedipal subject founded on lack. And she has compounded her dilemma by reproducing her body as the sign of woman, that is, as the sign of lack in a preexisting phallocentric symbolic order. Thus the post-1970 woman of fashion, no longer denied classical masculine subjectivity, but denied the means of transforming the symbolic order that produces it, finds herself in a new form of bisexuality—with a traditionally masculine form of subjectivity and a body marked feminine and subjected as such to gender and sexual oppression.

The changes in fashion and fashion magazines include a transformation of the traditional gender system, but one consonant with their overall figure of contradiction contained and thus turned into oscillation. The subject-object binarism of Western masculine-feminine gender structure is depolarized but at the same time intensified. Fundamental changes in the woman-of-fashion's relation to masculinity and femininity, rather than leading to an equally fundamental change in the gender system's submersion in the subject-object opposition, remain caught within it.

Thus in 1971, three years after *Vogue* published its scathing critique of male chauvinism and began incorporating feminist issues, it published a special issue on the "Sexual Revolution" (April 1971), which contained, among other items, a fashion clip entitled "Scarlet Nails: Male Bait": "Ranked high on every man's list of feminine attractions is, always, hands. Ask one. Men love beautiful hands. . . . And what about these, cream and crimson hands that could have tempted Adam?"[13]

This retrograde call to imitate the most notorious scapegoat of Western patriarchy and to revel in women's objectification by the male look is in fact an innovation unthinkable in the *Vogue* of 1960. This much debated "male gaze," not the gaze of a particular man, but an effect of the male/subject—female/object structuring of the symbolic order, constitutes woman as paradigmatic object.[14] Associated with the eye of the camera in the domain of film, the gaze functions in the domain of fashion as a framing device of the photograph that invests it with desire and provides the erotic charge in which the image is bathed for the female spectator. Whatever the gender of the gaze in feminist photography or film, in the photography of Anglo-American fashion magazines it is, with extraordinary exceptions, emphatically male and constitutes its object as heterosexual feminine. Outside that look, the woman of fashion would not exist. While in the fashion magazines of the early sixties any mention of its potent attraction seems taboo, in the seventies the male gaze is quite frequently and rhapsodically thematized.

Rather than reverse or do away with the gendered subject/object dichotomy, this innovation multiplies it from within and has the woman of fashion play all the roles, although in a historically different way from that analyzed by Mulvey and Doane in forties Hollywood film. The contemporary woman of fashion is expected to become a self-reflecting subject, but reflective about her own status as object, too fundamental to the symbolic order to allow for change. The more she is portrayed as independent, the more she is portrayed as an object of the male look. The woman of fashion is invited to assume custodianship of that look, and to find her own empowerment through managing the power that inevitably reduces her to the second sex. The fashion photograph's function as narcissistic fantasy is expanded, mirroring not only a whole, perfect self, but also the photograph's own process of seducing the woman of fashion as her seduction of the male look.

If fashion erases the boundary between fantasy and reality on the level of achieving a certain look, it reestablishes that boundary with respect to the body's relation to its sociopolitical other. In costuming herself, the woman of fashion also dresses in a fantasy network of social and sexual relations that transforms the masculine power to which she is subject. The encompassing male vision, anthropomorphized in photographs and copy as a real man looking at a woman in detailed situations, is fantasized as paradoxically conferring existence without dominating and controlling. Complementing the fantasy of achieving a certain look, this is a political fantasy that responds to a reader's desire to radically transform the socio-symbolic system that governs her self-other relations. But where that first fantasy blurs the boundary between fantasy and reality, the second one affirms the boundary.

It leaves the woman of fashion with two bodies, both of which are represented in contemporary fashion magazines. One body, represented in fashion photographs and upbeat copy, is the confident, free, sexually powerful image that readers can reproduce through skillful use of clothing and makeup. The other, which could be called the sociopolitical body, is enmeshed in a network of power relations that still subordinate women economically, politically, sexually, physically, and through a symbolic system that requires her objectification. Fashion magazines represent that body through alarming statistics on rape, sexual harassment, spousal abuse, salary inequities, and so on, and through increasingly angry articles (for example, *Glamour,* March 1992: "Why Women Are as Mad as Hell") about the indifferent or malevolent response of white, male institutions.

The magazines play out the dilemma of a politically conscious, self-reflecting, bisexual subjectivity caught in a symbolic order that anchors itself in woman as paradigmatic image or object of representation. Fashion photography, which depends on this reified status of woman, produces an image that denies its premise, and through the derealizing yet super-real effect of photography, projects to feminine viewers the sense of invulnerability and exuberant feminine sexual power that they can dramatize through their bodies. The paradoxical nature of fashion photography thus carries its fantasies beyond a simple illusion not only because they are acted out in the world, but also because the fantasy body constructed by fashion is the visible, physical, seemingly "real" body, while the body subjected to real political relations is the invisible network of relations itself.

From this point of view, the problem for a woman of fashion is not that she could not achieve the look of the fashion model, but the more dire possibility that she could. Fashion magazines enact the dilemma at many different levels. For example, *Glamour,* the most resolutely feminist of the Anglo-American magazines, features a "Fashion Workshop" that instructs the self-reflective reader in the skill of creating the illusion of the ideal body. Non-models are recruited to test clothes and give them "reality ratings." The "Fashion Workshop" of October 1990 invites the reader to analyze a version of the body-conscious adaptable dress to a wider range of body types: "In fact, this dress, shaped by two front seams, flatters more than its ubiquitous, stretchy body-hugging counterparts. That's good to know if you're in the market for bare. The more structured and shaped the dress, the fewer demands it makes on your figure." But the same article shows how the body as enactment of fantasy must confront its evil twin, the body as social relation to the other: "But that skimpiness made Sharon nervous, too. Before she'd walked a block in her test dress, she decided to dash home for a jacket. . . . 'I felt uncomfortable on the street without a coat,' she says. 'Personal safety is too precious.' " [15]

Since *Glamour* has on several occasions since 1970 (for example, in January 1975) published the results of research confirming the absence of causal relation between women's attire and sexual violence, the phrase "personal safety" conveys the unarticulated sense of a historical juncture in which a woman is free make her body into an image of feminine sexual power but not to walk her body down the street. Another example makes even more glaring both the historical moment of clash between the two bodies and the way in which Glamour's commitment to both feminism and fashion creates the clash without seeming to be aware of its presence in the magazine. An article entitled "Take a chance! Nine little beauty dares that turn good looks into great" (September 1990) invites even more imitation than the "Fashion Workshop," since the looks do not depend on body type, and even more intense scrutiny, since they concern subtle details of jewelry, hair style, neckline, makeup, and nail polish. But this article is juxtaposed to a somber, intelligent article by Le Anne Schreiber about the epidemic of campus date rape.[16] The coincidental conjunction of plausible sexual power for women and systemic sexual violence against women turns the conventional structure of the mass-media magazine as random juxtaposition of disparate material into a coherent narrative of struggle between a woman of fashion's two bodies and her two identities.

In fact, the magazines' increasing role as outlets for feminist and (especially in the case of *Essence*) African-American social movements within the confines dictated by commercial consumerism multiplies this sort of coincidence to such a frequency that critical articles and fashion spreads or ads appear as commentaries on each other, with the articles implicitly, and on occasion even explicitly, criticizing the ads, while the ads seem to mock the impotence of the critique. Thus, for example, *Mirabella* scathingly attacks cigarette companies for spending "many millions promoting the image of beautiful, slender women" in the midst of a sea of pages promoting just such an image.[17]

Essence, whose writers and editors negotiate the most intense conflict between the demands of the advertising system and the needs of the readers, consistently carries this process the furthest, though *Glamour* and *Mirabella* have recently begun to follow its lead. From the inception of *Essence* in 1971, even the fashion spreads have acted as political critique of the enforced norm embodied by the slender, light-skinned, thin-lipped models in the ads. Fashion spreads have regularly announced "The Return of the Voluptuous Woman" (May 1975) and have criticized the enforcement of slenderness, even as their photographs of tall, full-bodied women are juxtaposed with advertising images that exemplify the white standard. In the midst of a sea of ads and articles about hair relaxers, one issue features an essay by Audre Lorde entitled "Is Your Hair Still Political?" Lorde begins by describing her fashion decision to grow dreadlocks as a "personal statement," relates the harrowing experience with Virgin Gorda immigration officials that they brought to her, and concludes her analysis by asking: "How long will we allow ourselves to be used as instruments of oppression against each other?"[18] Her question aptly applies to the ads in *Essence* that cynically exploit images of successful, happy black workers or idealized portraits of Martin Luther King. Such ads imitate but are not to be lumped in the same category with fashion features on the politics of African-American style. These articles, as well as social analyses by writers like Angela Davis and June Jordan (May 1990), imply strong criticism of those ads, but within the commercial enclosure of the corporate publication itself.

The fashion magazine has, in this respect, the same structure as the double language of fashion itself, except that in the case of fashion two meanings and their codes oscillate within the enclosure of the dominant code, while in the case of the magazine, two different operations, that of critique and that of recuperation, oscillate in the enclosure of recuperation, with the magazine visibly figuring the economic and ideological enclosure that consumes its own contradictions.

Since fashion is both a symbolic system inseparably linked to the expression of sexuality and an integral part of the global capitalist system, these shifts between different codes, as well as between critique and recuperation, need to be analyzed in terms of the concept of fetishism, so much at issue in contemporary critical debate. As an example of fetishism, fashion casts doubt upon recent views of it as an element "in a deconstruction of phallogocentrism," which works "to the benefit . . . of the feminine."[19] However much fetishism may deconstruct binary oppositions, a closer look at fashion as a notably feminine instance of its operations suggests that deconstruction's very displacement of the phallus leaves its centrality and its effect of masculine primacy intact.

The fetish as a element of deconstruction is characterized by Derrida as a signifier, and thus as a substitute for a special kind of absent referent, "for the thing in itself as center and source of being" of the sign system as a whole.[20] If the sign system produces meaning through a play of difference among signifiers in the absence of a referent, the fetish substitutes for the ever-absent referent that regulates the Symbolic Order itself as its mythic origin and ground. The paradigm of the absent essence of Derrida's *Glas* is the maternal phallus of Freud's essay "Fetishism."[21] By creating substitutes for the absent phallus, the fetishist in Freud's analysis both denies and acknowledges the mother's "lack." By extension, the fetish as signifier creates the illusion of re-presenting its referent, the original "thing-in-itself," while standing in for its absence. Derrida explains that as the model for the "'privileged,' transcendental, fundamental, central signifier, the signifier of signifiers," of the symbolic order, the phallic fetish is a substitute for which there is no original.[22] Since it equally hides and acknowledges the non-existence of this original, the fetish-signifier opens up a "general economy" of "undecidability" of incessant oscillation between meanings.[23]

As a sign system that conforms spectacularly to the preceding description, however, fashion raises questions about the open-endedness and infinite displacement of fetishism's undecidability. The incessant oscillation of fashion fetishism comes not from opening up opposition to infinity, but from a historical process that transforms contradiction into oscillation by enclosing it within an impasse from which neither contemporary Western social movements nor critical theory have found a strategy for release. The debate on fetishism is thus linked to the debates on postmodernism that argue about whether its economic and cultural forms are "paradigmatically different" from or continuous with those of the modernist past.[24] The language of fashion, which is illustrative of postmodernism in general, derives its political significance from both an ambiguity endemic to fashion in capitalist society and a specifically contemporary configuration of that ambiguity.

In feudal society, symbolic systems other than the sign system gave clothing unambiguous referents;[25] clothing designated the wearer's position in fixed hierarchies of class and sex, and, according to Pearl Binder, "constituted a means of enforcing class privilege in a regimented social structure."[26] With the rise of commodity capitalism, workers could dress like the wealthy bourgeois, and so clothing became a masquerade that could *signify* any role in the absence of a referent, instead of *designating* a fixed place in a scale of positions. It ambiguously revealed or concealed the social identity of its wearer.

This ambiguity inherent in fashion, connected in on the one hand to the class structure of capitalist society, is connected on the other to its gender structure. The rise of capitalism brought about, in J. C. Flügel's famous formulation, "the Great Masculine Renunciation."[27] Upper-class men gave up wearing on their own bodies the elaborate masculine fashions of aristocratic society and took up the sober garb of the hard-working, dependable bourgeois. Since a man would contradict the image of his devotion to grave, serious endeavors by displaying his wealth on his own body, he displayed it on that of his wife. Women's clothing thus expressed not their own messages but those of their husbands and fathers. In this function, bourgeois women are analogous to money, which acts as a signifier in what Marx calls "the language of commodities." Its "palpable bodily form," as Marx says, "represents value" but only of another body. Like money, bourgeois women's bodies "can never express the quality of their own value."[28] But as immigrant women formed a feminine working class, and middle-class women also became more active in public life, they adopted fashion for their own self-expression. Where they could not do away with a sartorial sign system through which their bodies were ineluctably condemned to express patriarchy's meanings, they could and did reappropriate this already existing language for their own use, and the conflicting systems of meaning became inextricably overlaid, confused, and difficult to disentangle.

Rooted in this older instability of codes, the semiotics of postmodern fashion have nevertheless a specific relation to fetishism that can be illustrated through an analysis of a fashion photograph from the November 1989 issue of Paris *Vogue*. Included because it illustrates so vividly the political possibilities and impasses of fetishism, this photograph would be inconceivable without the changes in post-1968 fashion magazines and fashion photography discussed earlier in this essay. The photograph enacts a visual joke on fetishism and also illustrates its operations. A model stands both in the middle of the photo and in the middle of an enclosed court whose wall supports the statue of a Church Father holding a sacred book, a book containing the patriarchal law. The model's head has been cropped out of the picture, and her braceleted hand clutches the flashy rhinestone-trimmed shoe of an uplifted foot. All the details in the photo conspire to point attention to this foot or shoe, which Freud has designated as the very archetype of fetish-objects.

As an allegory of the general economy of fetishism, this photo fluctuates

Figure 1. Photo from Paris Vogue *(November 1989). Copyright ©*
F. Scianna/Magnum Photos.

among five simultaneous interpretations: (1) The woman fulfills her role as the traditional object of representation, mastered by the gaze of the patriarch and his law. (2) She disdainfully expresses her indifference to that gaze and its loss of power over her. Her sexy dress no longer refers to the harlotry that he has always forbidden, and she indifferently turns her back on him, making his ruling presence into a joke. Powerless to infringe upon her vitality, he has become the incidental ornament in her picture. (3) But is this her picture? From a more exterior point of view, the woman again appears as an object, this time of the mastering gaze of the photographer, who has set up the oscillation, and made the woman into a mere prop in his visual joke on phallocentrism. (4) The photo replays in symbolic form the very operation of the symbolic order as a whole. This requires the absence of the "thing itself"—the head, traditional symbol of the phallus—and its replacement by a substitute—the foot, traditional symbol of the fetish—under the law of the father. The fetish centers the signifying elements within their enclosure, regulating the undecidable oscillation of meaning between freedom and mastery—but within the framework of mastery. (5) The foot, however, merely plays the role of fetish in the photograph's allegorical content. The "real" fetish, which (literally) stands in for "the signifier destined to designate as a whole the effect of the signified"[29] and therefore centers the play of meaning in the photograph as photograph, is of course the woman. No matter how much this woman can represent her freedom and the changes in the situation of women, this photograph, like innumerable others, and like the culture it expresses, resolves the threat to men's castration posed by the woman's lack of phallus and her indifference to this lack, and resolves as well the maddening undecidability that fetishism triggers, by making woman into the phallus. The photograph still expresses a culture in which man thus gives himself the illusion of possessing the phallus through the illusion that he possesses the woman. The photographer can joke about phallocentrism because he has saved it.

This deconstruction of phallocentrism hardly works to the benefit of the feminine. This photograph, like fashion photography as a genre, suggests that in the symbolic system organized by fetishism, woman is conceived only in terms of having or lacking the phallus, as threatening or warding off man's castration, but cannot be conceived in other terms. If the free-play of oscillation cannot be contained, according to Derrida, "in the space of truth,"[30] it does remain imprisoned within the space of phallocentrism and consumer capitalism that absorbs every signifying act, and from which deconstruction, indispensable though it may be in helping us to understand that space, does not extract us.

That space contains contradiction all the more powerfully in that the "general economy" of symbolic fetishism works in concert with the political economy of commodity fetishism, as "a definite relation between [women] which assumes, in their eyes, the fantastic form of a relation between things."[31] Consumerism conceals the relation between the women who consume clothing and the women (and children) who produce it, often for as little as $1.45 an hour.[32] Commodity fetishism does not simply commodify the subject as consumer, as much cultural criticism suggests. It conceals the transformation of people's labor power into a commodity that capital consumes to produce the whole system of capitalism, and thus conceals the relations between the reader of North American fashion magazines and the immigrant or Third World garment worker. If one task of fashion criticism is to reformulate this obfuscated relation, another is to reformulate the equally if differently fetishized relation between the consumer of fashion and the critic who studies her. Fashion criticism that posits the critic as objective, distant outsider neglects the obvious ways whereby the fashionable institution in which millions of women have practiced a paradoxical feminine symbolic agency reflect the intellectual institution that contains, in both senses of the word, our efforts to conceive feminist theories. Our academic writing, which we use, like clothing, for self-expression and self-disguise, both to reveal and to protect, appropriates theories that posit, implicitly or explicitly, a masculine subject and incorporate Woman as metaphor of their own operation. We liberate them as they imprison us. We write to declare our independence from masculine approval, while necessarily seeking such approval to gain recognition, promotion, and acceptance within the institution. And it is often difficult for us to disentangle our illusions about the effectiveness of our feminist subversions from our reality.

I began this project with the intention of using critical and theoretical resources to understand my very problematical relation to the fashion system, but in the process it gradually revealed an equally, if differently, problematic relation between women and the critical theory of the university. For a feminist critic, the apparent frivolity of fashion and the apparent seriousness of theory, each fraught with its own special variety of real pleasures and anxieties, can change places in disconcerting ways. While fashion and scholarship may begin by presenting themselves as compensations for each other's lack, the critical scrutiny of fashion inexorably leads again and again to its obvious structural analogies with that other institution in which women struggle to engender new meaning.

Women's studies has expanded in the university at the same time that the universities themselves have become more and more the extensions of capitalist enterprises. Our theories have developed in the direction of radical critique and insight as our institutional forms have adopted more and more uncritically the structures of the very institution we critique.

On the other hand, fashion magazine editors and writers, many of them creative, progressive women, have sought to address other women in a "women's world" ultimately controlled by male-dominated publishing and advertising institutions, and use the vast resources from exploitive advertising to provide feminism and minority social movements a forum and a community. An area of future inquiry remains the relation between these two kinds of feminism, popular and academic, both working within structures of domination, and both still seeking a way out.

NOTES

1. See Roland Barthes, *Système de la mode* (Paris: Points, 1967), and Alison Lurie, *The Language of Clothes* (New York: Random House, 1981).

2. See Mary Ann Doane, "The Economy of Desire: The Commodity Form in / of Cinema," *Review of Film & Video* 11 (1989): 23–33; Stuart Ewen, *All Consuming Images: The Politics of Style in Contemporary Culture* (New York: Basic Books, 1988); Stuart and Elizabeth Ewen, *Channels of Desire: Mass Images and the Shaping of American Consciousness* (New York: McGraw-Hill, 1982); Joanne Finkelstein, *The Fashioned Self* (Cambridge, England: Polity Press, 1991); Dean MacCannell and Juliet Flower, "The Beauty System," *The Ideology of Conduct,* ed. Nancy Armstrong and Leonard Tennenhouse (London: Methuen, 1988), 206–239.

3. Elizabeth Wilson, *Adorned in Dreams: Fashion and Modernity* (London: Virago Press, 1985), 53. Also see Caroline Evans and Minna Thornton, *Women and Fashion: A New Look* (London: Quartet Books, 1989), and Jane Gaines and Charlotte Herzog, eds., *Fabrications: Costume and the Female Body* (New York: Routledge, 1990).

4. Wilson, *Adorned in Dreams,* 66.

5. *Vogue,* February 1990, 71.

6. Ibid., 236.

7. Rachel Urquhart, "View," *Vogue,* March 1990, 176.

8. "Defendant Acquitted of Rape: 'She Asked for it,' Juror Says," *New York Times* 7 October 1989. As a result of this case, Florida passed a law barring use of the alleged victim's clothing as evidence in a rape case. See "Rape Victim's Attire Barred as Evidence," *Los Angeles Times,* 2 June 1990.

9. Francis Fukuyama, "The End of History," *The National Interest* (Summer 1989).

10. Jean Laplanche and Jean-Bertrand Pontalis, "Fantasy and the Origins of Sexuality," *Formations of Fantasy,* ed. Victor Burgin, James Donald, and Cora Kaplan (Methuen: London, 1986), 21, 19.

11. Ibid., 24.

12. Sylvia Kolbowski, "Playing with Dolls," *The Critical Image: Essays on Contemporary Photography,* ed. Carol Squiers (Seattle: Day Press, 1990), 151.

13. *Vogue,* April 1971, 121.

14. See *Camera Obscura: A Journal of Feminism and Film Theory* 20–21 (1989); Mary Ann Doane, "Film and the Masquerade: Theorizing the Female Spectator," *Screen* 3–4 (1982): 74–87; E. Ann Kaplan, "Feminism / Oedipus / Postmodernism: The Case of MTV," *Postmodernism and its Discontents,* ed. Kaplan (London: Verso, 1988), 30–44; Laura Mulvey, "Visual Pleasure and Narrative Cinema," *Feminism and Film Theory,* ed. Constance Penley (New York: Routledge, 1988), 57–68; Laura Mulvey, "Afterthoughts on Visual Pleasure and Narrative Cinema, inspired by Duel in the Sun (King Vidor 1946)," *Framework* 15/16/17 (1981): 12–15; Kaja Silverman, "Fragments of a Fashionable Discourse," *Studies in Entertainment,* ed. Tania Modleski (Bloomington: Indiana University Press, 1986), 139–154; and Linda Williams, "When the Woman Looks," *Re-Vision: Essays in Feminist Film Criticism,* ed. Mary Ann Doane, Patricia Mellencamp, and Linda Williams (Los Angeles: University Publications of America, 1984), 83–99.

15. "Fashion Workshop," *Glamour,* October 1990, 206.

16. Le Anne Schreiber, "The *Glamour* Report: Campus Rape," *Glamour,* September 1990, 288–291, 292–293.

17. Sue Woodman, "Target," *Mirabella,* April 1990, 81–84.

18. Audre Lorde, "Is Your Hair Still Political?" *Essence,* September 1990, 40+.

19. Sarah Kofman, *Lectures de Derrida* (Paris: Galilée, 1984), 134.

20. Jacques Derrida, *Glas: Que reste-il du savoir absolu?,* 2 vols. (Paris: Denoël/Gonthier, 1981), 2:292.

21. Sigmund Freud, "Fetishism," *Sexuality and the Psychology of Love* (New York: MacMillan, 1963), 214–219.

22. Derrida, *Glas,* 2:292.

23. Ibid., 2:294.

24. Neil Lazarus, "Doubting the New World Order: Marxism, Realism, and the Claims of Postmodern Social Theory," *Differences* 3 (1992): 109.

25. For a history of the sign system in relation to other signifying systems, see Julia Kristeva, *Desire in Language: A Semiotic Approach to Literature and Art* (New York: Columbia University Press, 1980).

26. Quoted in Ewen, *Channels of Desire,* 122.

27. J. C. Flügel, *The Psychology of Clothes* (London: Hogarth Press, 1930), 110.

28. Karl Marx, *Capital,* trans. Samuel Moore and Edward Aveling, 3 vols. (New York: International Publishers, 1967), 1:51, 56.

29. Jacques Lacan, "La Signification du Phallus," *Ecrits,* 2 vols. (Paris: Seuil, Points, 1971), 2:109.

30. Derrida, *Glas,* 2:292.

31. Marx, *Capital,* 1:72.

32. Sonni Ephron, "How Sweatshop Work Became Family Affair," *Los Angeles Times,* November 27, 1989.

Karla Jay

*n*o Bumps, No Excrescences:

Amelia Earhart's Failed Flight

into Fashions

When Amelia Earhart joined the first group transatlantic flight in 1928, she found fame but left behind everything except her comb, her tooth-brush, and the flight clothes she was wearing.[1] Taking even a small ward-robe seemed to her to be particularly unsuitable since she did not fly the *Friendship,* except for a few short moments when she took the controls near the end of the trip. As she put it, she was merely a "sack of potatoes"; like the coxswain of a rowing crew, she tried to be as light a burden as possible. She wrote in her notes, "Anyway, it [taking no clothing] seemed fairer all around. The men on the 'Friendship' took nothing. Pounds— even ounces—can count desperately on this sort of a show. So why would I load up on non-essential [sic]?"[2] Accompanied by Louis Edward Gordon and Wilmer Stultz, the male crew members, she toured London and Paris in borrowed gowns and dresses, including some provided by Amy Phipps Guest, who had underwritten the costs of the expedition. Afterwards, sev-eral newspapers pointed out that her clothes were "a little large for her in spots," a detail that is confirmed by most of the extant photos of Earhart's triumphant European tour.[3]

Although Earhart was an instant success and the names of her male col-leagues were soon forgotten, the male-dominated press pounced on her lack of glamourous attire. On June 28, 1928, the New York *Sun*'s headline lamented: "Miss Earhart Spurns Fashions." The article went on to explain the horror of this attitude, for anyone who had missed the message: "Clothes she regards as a matteroffact [sic] necessity like food."[4] Even her manager, George Palmer Putnam, wailed about her lack of taste: "Your hats! They are a public menace. You should do something about them when you must wear them at all!"[5] While a man was judged primarily for his achievements, a woman had to be glamorously attired in pursuit of hers. Among the hundreds of telegrams and fan letters she found awaiting her upon her return were several admonitions to comb her hair.

The lesson was not lost on Earhart: by 1935, Fashion Designers of America had named her one of the ten best-dressed women of the year, along with Eleanor Roosevelt and Elsa Maxwell.[6] How and why did Earhart transform herself from the "female Charles Lindbergh" in the crushed leather jacket and jodhpurs to the designer of her own sportswear, raincoats, work clothing, and luggage? Why did most of her attempts to be fashionable make no impact on American consciousness so that her clothing line disappeared from view faster than her plane in 1937?

Earhart's presence on the *Friendship* flight was a lucky accident: Amy Guest intended to make the trip herself, but her relatives refused to permit her to do so. In return for simultaneously obeying her family's demands and continuing to underwrite the flight, she insisted that one American woman go in her place. Earhart was chosen because of her resemblance to Charles Lindbergh and her clean-cut image as a social worker in Boston's Denison House, where she taught English as a Second Language to Syrian immigrants.

After her historic transatlantic flight, Earhart repudiated the idea of cashing in on her new-found fame and declared that she wished to return to Denison House. She wrote in the *New York Times:* "Today I have been receiving offers to go on the stage, appear in the movies and to accept numerous gifts ranging from an automobile to a husband. . . . There will be no stage appearance nor acting in the movies. I am not going to commercialize my flight in the Friendship and I will be happier when the pressure of life in the public eye diminishes."[7]

Although Earhart had earned her share of speed and altitude records, she did not consider an aviation career, especially not the dangerous, but more lucrative, stunt flying. Flying was an expensive pursuit, and enlightened sponsors like Amy Guest were all too rare. Moveover, other pilots were more skillful than she, and several women pilots had broken more records than she had. By the time of her disappearance in 1937, Earhart had already crash-landed several planes. But there were other ways to reach fame than by procuring records that would quickly be eclipsed in any case. As soon as her victorious tour of the United States ended in the autumn of 1928, she published her book, *20 Hrs. 40 Mins.*, about the *Friendship* flight and began a new round of publicity tours.

By then, Earhart had decided against returning to Denison House. Since she had agreed to turn over her royalties to help defray the costs of the *Friendship* expedition, she needed another source of income. As the offers continued to pour in, she began to see the lucrative possibilities of promoting clothing and other items in return for cash or other considerations. Universal Pictures offered her $10,000 for five weeks' work. Riverside Theatre of Medford, Massachusetts, offered her $1,000 for "first personal appearance there for one week."[8]

At first, she accepted gifts in return for promotional considerations:

> For appearing on the NBC broadcast in an auto show at Madison Square Garden, she had been presented with a Blue Chrysler roadster. For her endorsement of a fur-lined, leather "Amelia Earhart Flying Suit," a Fifth Avenue department store gave her one. She had no intention of 'wearing it up and down Fifth Avenue,' as the advertisement claimed, but she had learned from G. P. [Putnam] that there could be considerable gain in such foolishness.[9]

By the end of 1928 Earhart finally decided to endorse products in return for money. Although she didn't smoke, Lucky Strikes cigarettes hired her to appear in their advertisements, in part because she was very trim and cigarettes were being marketed to women as a diet aid. (The company's motto was "For a slender figure—Reach for a Lucky instead of a sweet.") The advertisement claimed, "Lucky Strikes were the cigarettes carried on the 'Friendship' when she crossed the Atlantic" (see figure 1). And yes, someone had indeed brought a pack along. Across the front of one of the advertisements, Earhart sardonically scrawled: "Is this the face of a Lady? What Price Glory!"[10] Unfortunately, the answer to the question she posed was negative, for in the 1920s cigarette smoking for women was still considered "unladylike." As a result, *McCall's* magazine canceled the column she was writing for them (although *Cosmopolitan* soon picked it up), and Earhart donated the one-thousand-dollar proceeds of her cigarette endorsement to Admiral Byrd's Antarctic expedition.

Earhart, it seems, was sending out contradictory signals in ways more complicated than being a nonsmoking promoter of cigarettes. On the one hand, she considered herself a feminist of sorts, although she eschewed the label. She believed that her achievements could be emulated by the average woman, were she given the right opportunity and encouragement. She didn't believe that flying took particular skill or courage. On the other hand, during the 1920s flying was still somewhat of a curiosity, and people

Figure 1. Advertisement for Lucky Strikes, 1928.

were more apt to watch airplanes performing stunts or racing in air derbies than to travel in one. Most of the early female aviators, aware that their very presence in planes was crossing gender barriers, flew in long skirts and feminine hats, even though the unpressurized airplanes were extremely cold. Earhart, on the other hand, liked her

> old flying clothes, comfortably, if not elegantly, battered and worn. High laced shoes, trousers, shirt, and a companionably ancient leather coat, rather long, with plenty of pockets and a snug-buttoning collar. A light leather flying helmet and goggles complete the picture. When it was cold . . . [she] wore—as did the men—a heavy flying suit which covers one completely from head to toe, shoes and all, and in appearance combines the absurdity of a teddy-bear with the shut-in-ness of a diving suit.[11]

Part of the attraction of this outfit was that Earhart was immediately recognized as a pilot and obeyed by ground crews, who might otherwise presume she was someone's secretary along for the ride (see figure 2).

Unfortunately, this was not proper deportment for an American heroine: like endorsing Lucky Strikes, it was "unladylike." Instead of perceiving her as a female Charles Lindbergh, her critics thought her attire suggested that she was Lindbergh in drag. As "Toonerville Folks," a cartoon by Fontaine Fox, put it, "the more pitchers I see the more I'm convinced the feat wuz performed by Lindy, dressed up to look like a gal!"[12] Perceiving Amelia Earhart as a transvestite male was easier for some people than having to consider the implications of a woman soloing across the Atlantic.

By 1929, during her speaking engagements and other public appearances, she had begun to dress fashionably—and femininely—in dresses with frilly or lacy collars. Formal photographs were taken of her in satin or silk dresses. Although she sometimes wore the honorary major's pin presented to her in 1928 by the United States Army Reserve, three strands of pearls also adorned her neck (see figure 3). She cleverly allowed the major's wings to become the primary signifier of her power, while the pearls attested to her femininity and class privilege. Yet she was always uncomfortable in dresses and self-conscious about the appearance of her legs, which "were somewhat shapeless from knee to ankle and her feet were apt to swell."[13] Consequently, she continued to fly and relax in trousers, telling "friends it was to hide her 'thick' legs," although her choice was equally based on comfort and convenience.[14]

She also became quite concerned about her mother's appearance. From 1929 on, Earhart's letters began to be full of admonitions to her mother, Amy Otis Earhart, about what she should wear and say. For example, on December 31, 1930, she wrote:

I sent you two pkgs. yesterday. . . . Please go to a decent tailor and have the brown suit fitted. I think it won't need much. Take Nancy [Balis] with you and get it done right. The blouse will probably be too large for you, but [I'll] try to send another one along anyway. . . .

I want you to go to town with Nancy and buy a lil brown hat to go with suit (a shade or two darker maybe) and a couple of prs. gloves for it if needed. Then while you're at it get a dark blue hat—something like black one you bot yourself last year.

I sent Pidge [her sister, Muriel Earhart Morrissey] some undies and small check.[15]

The casual style of the letter, full of endearing abbreviations, contrasts markedly with the didactic contents. Clearly, Earhart felt that her mother's style—or lack of it—would reflect badly on her. And she was right, for since the press had no boyfriend or husband to ask whether or not Earhart's exploits impinged upon his male privilege, the reporters turned to her mother to discover whether Earhart had parental consent for her unfeminine acts of daring. Mismatched clothing would signify that the entire

Figure 2. Amelia Earhart in her flying suit.

Figure 3. Amelia Earhart, wearing her pearls and honorary major's pin.

family was all too unconventional, or worse, it might suggest that Earhart's achievements were only some exotic form of gender aberration. Ironically, Earhart's concern did not extend to her sister, Muriel Earhart Morrissey. Amelia disapproved of Muriel's marriage and children, but she didn't feel that Muriel's choices would reflect on her own life as dramatically as her mother's would. In her letters, Amy Otis Earhart seemed to acquiesce to her famous daughter's demands, but in actuality she continued to wear and say what she pleased.[16]

Marrying a well-known and handsome man also served to enhance Earhart's public image. After George Palmer Putnam married Earhart on February 7, 1931, he began to devote his full attention to her career and public image, both of which reached a new apex in 1932 as a result of his orchestration. On May 20–21, Earhart was the first woman to fly solo across the Atlantic, a feat performed on the anniversary of Lindbergh's flight, though the connection hardly needed to be underscored. Another round of parades and speeches and another book (*The Fun of It*) followed, but it was soon time to return to fundraising for future ventures.

> Despite his [George Palmer Putnam's] many activities, however, and contrary to popular belief, he was not a wealthy man; most of his private income had been lost when his cousin had taken G. P. Putnam's Sons to the verge of bankruptcy and George never recovered the amount he had left invested in the publishing house. Nor was Amelia a wealthy woman. Between them, . . . they earned a considerable sum, it is true, but their constant entertaining, Amelia's airplanes, the upkeep of [their house at] Rye, the salaries of their retinue, and a high-profile lifestyle used up their income almost as fast as they earned it.[17]

Launching a line of medium-priced women's sportswear was the perfect means of achieving both image and financing. As Roland Barthes has pointed out, fashion "constitute[s] an incontestable element of mass culture, like pulp fiction, comics and movies."[18] Much more so than flying, fashion would take Earhart into every American woman's home (see figure 4). By wearing the Earhart label women could vicariously partake in her adventures without the danger or even the terror of flying—and certainly without family censure. Although the advertisements stressed the practicality of the clothing in terms of the design and the washability of the fabric, what was being marketed was an image. Wearing Earhart's clothing line semiotically indicated that a woman was a star. It brought her closer to one of the two most recognized female public figures in the United States (the other was Eleanor Roosevelt) and gave her a sense of liberation and achievement. This emotional uplift was particularly impor-

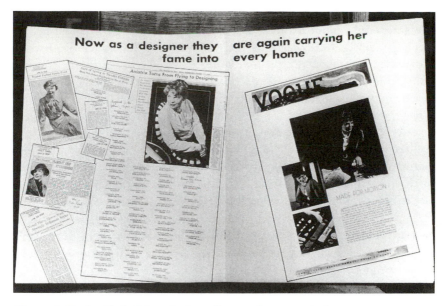

Figure 4. Earhart's fashions being vigorously promoted.

tant during the Depression when women's rights seemed to be spiraling downward, particularly after the heady days of the Roaring Twenties and the first years of suffrage.

Earhart's flying suit was modified so that the commercial version was less androgynous and therefore less threatening than the designer: "Miss Earhart replaces the baggy old windbreaker with a slimly cut suede one, snugly knitted at waist and wrist. Beige, green gold, brown."[19] In short, the look of a flyer with that snug, safe feeling one might get from wearing a sweater (and in fashionable colors, too).

Ironically, the path for transforming flying gear into high fashion was actually paved in films starring two of Earhart's friends, Katharine Hepburn and Marlene Dietrich.[20] In 1933, Katharine Hepburn starred in *Christopher Strong,* directed by Dorothy Arzner. The film revolves around Lady Cynthia Darrington, a woman who, like Earhart, is a record-breaking female aviator. She cares much more about flying than romance until she falls in love with the married and handsome Sir Christopher Strong, played by Colin Clive. (George Putnam was still married when he and Earhart met.) In a Hollywood ending, Darrington crashes her plane rather than tell her lover she is pregnant because Strong would feel obliged to divorce his wife and marry Lady Cynthia out of a sense of "duty" to the unborn child and its unwed mother. In the film, Hepburn dons a glamorized and sanitized version of Earhart's work clothes. The first time we see her enter a plane (most of her feats are twice removed from reality by placing them in the context of newspaper clippings and radio reports rather than flight footage), she is wearing a long, elegant leather trenchcoat with jodhpurs visible underneath. Her hair curls neatly under a fashionable beret, and white gloves indicate that flying isn't a greasy endeavor after all. Strong, dressed in a tuxedo, climbs into the plane after her.

Later, in a round–the–world air race for a prize of $100,000 (an event that seems peculiarly prophetic of Earhart's last flight, down to the accompanying male mechanic/navigator), she wears jodhpurs with a becoming turtleneck instead of Earhart's checked shirt with scarf. Hepburn's leather jacket is lined with a luxurious fur, the collar of which is pulled up to frame her face softly. The flight helmet encases a carefully madeup face, and the goggles remain firmly on top of the head, not over the heavily madeup eyes. Her flight gear is meant to signify an unearthly beauty and an independent will rather than hint at the assumption of male prerogatives. The viewer has already been assured of Darrington's femininity in an early scene in which she appears at a costume ball in a "tight–fitting glittering gold lamé moth costume designed by Walter Plunkett."[21] Although the outfit gives the impression of flight and presages the tragic path of the moth to the flames, the gold antenna make the outfit somewhat whimsical and remove any threat of taking her too seriously.

Marlene Dietrich's appropriation of the Earhart image in the 1931 *Dishonoured* is much slighter than Hepburn's, although the portrayal of the flier who is enlisted as a spy oddly foreshadows the aspersions that would be cast on Earhart after her disappearance near Howland Island, in the same way that Hepburn's film seems prescient about Earhart's tragic end. As an aviator, Dietrich sports a thick, shiny, unwrinkled black leather jumpsuit with some greasy spots of oil around and below the front pocket. A large cowl–like button–down collar adds a feminine touch, although Dietrich stands defiantly, hands placed squarely in the generous pockets. Again, the goggles remain firmly on top of her head. Dietrich also transposes this male masquerade with seductive female outfits. "She could perform a man's espionage tasks without losing the mask of the enigmatic woman of mystery," comments Donald Spoto in his reverent look at Dietrich.[22] Her combination of toughness and femininity is confirmed at the end of the film when, about to face a firing squad, she takes "the blindfold from the nervous young soldier, dr[ies] his tears with it, then adjust[s] her makeup and straightens her stockings before the firing squad dispatches her."[23] For her trip into eternity, Dietrich is dressed in a modest but tightly fitted black dress and a hat with a small black veil.

It was Dietrich's tuxedoed appearance in *The Blue Angel* (1930) and her subsequent partying in Hollywood in trousers that made slacks and then sportswear all the rage for women, much more so than Earhart's feats in the air or in the fashion world. Earhart found Hepburn and Dietrich hard acts to follow when it came to selling clothes, but she tried her own unique angle. For example, in newspaper interviews, Earhart stressed the aerial qualities of her clothing, pressing home the vicarious possibilities for anyone who had missed them. "I have always believed that clothes are terribly important in every woman's life. . . . And I also believe that there is much of beauty in aviation—color and line that is exclusive to the air, which I have attempted to express in sports clothes."[24] "Designing dresses is just another way of making aviation popular with the women of America—for Amelia Earhart at least . . . . 'I never design a frock that I do not see as expressing some of the natural beauty of flying,' she declared."[25]

To underscore the connection to flying, the clothes were streamlined into a semblance of aerodynamic perfection. The promotional catalog informed potential buyers that Earhart "loathes excrescences—anything that bumps up, sticks out, or hangs over."[26] The real gimmick, however, was that airplane fabrics and devices were supposedly used in the manufacture of the garments. In addition to the use of parachute silk in some of the garments, Earhart claimed, "For trimming I nearly always use something characteristic of aviation, a parachute cord for tie or belt, a ball-bearing belt buckle, wing bolts and nuts for buttons."[27]

Close examination of photographs of the clothing, however, reveals ordinary buckles of the type used by firemen, not airmen. Some of the buttons were cleverly shaped like propellers. The buttons that were supposed to represent the wheels of the airplane were really Chinese coins, as even Earhart admitted. The earth tones of her tweed suits and coats, which were almost exclusively in brown, beige, and gray with red and blue highlights, conveyed more a sense of Earhart's unfortunate crash landings than of the wild blue yonder. The neutral colors of the outfits also detracted from claims of bold originality.

Earhart's name was to be the true selling point. During the 1930s, when Paris fashions ruled the Western world and American designer labels like Gloria Vanderbilt and Calvin Klein were still decades away, it was daring, to say the least, to put the name of an American woman—and one with a prior reputation for having a disheveled appearance—on a fashion label. Nevertheless, she convinced several manufacturers, including U.S. Rubber and Stetson Hats, that her name would bring women into department stores. The publicity catalog for U.S. Rubber stressed this point: "Every newspaper, every magazine, has carried her achievements. . . . Now as a designer they are again carrying her fame into every home . . . . You can give your own store this attention-getting feature." The brochure came complete with a list of over eighty newspapers from the *Washington Post* to the Chattanooga (Tennessee) *News* to the New Bern (North Carolina) *Sun-Journal* that had carried news stories or feature articles about Earhart's new sportswear line. For many of the stories, Earhart was interviewed in a hotel room, where she displayed a mannequin onto which she had draped some swatches of cloth. In New York, she would also show reporters her old sewing machine, which she claimed to have kept from her college days at Ogontz, although she never mentioned the machine—or making any clothes on it—in her many letters to her mother. Like most young women of her time, Earhart could make her own dresses, but her sister remembered her as "an unorthodox seamstress. She simply sewed two lengths of the dyed material together, gathered one end on a narrow belt, and turned the other end up so it cleared the floor eleven inches all around."[28] Her high school classmates remembered her somewhat unflatteringly as the "girl in brown who walks alone."

A sense of design and color had never been her strong suit, but it seemed crucial to her image to show that she was not a masculine impersonator: she was an all-around American girl. In fact, she was an archetypal superwoman. Not only was she the first woman to fly across the Atlantic, she thriftily patterned her own clothing at home while sipping buttermilk to keep up her strength. She was a latter-day pioneer woman who could drive the wagons during the day and cook the bacon at night. It is on such images that folk heroines are made.

While she did succeed in becoming a paragon of fashion, it seems unlikely that she ever designed her own clothing. Although several newspapers carried photographs of designs attributed to her, it seems more probable that she suggested colors, fabrics, and ideas, which others rendered into working models. In truth, most of the designs were not that original. Her tricorne hats, which drooped alluringly over one eye, were almost identical to the ones that Stetson was selling under its own label. One three-piece tweed suit with a matching full-length coat with a broad collar and a skirt with a fitted waist and a simple, straight line is attributed to Amelia Earhart on page fifteen of the May 15, 1934, issue of *Vogue;* it is almost identical to another outfit on the very next page of the same issue, attributed to Maggy Rouff of Paris, although the latter advertisement is meant to promote rubber shoes, called Gaytees. And both are strikingly similar to an outfit being marketed by Alfred Dunhill of London in the same issue of *Vogue,* except that in this version, the tweed coat is lined with fur.[29] Rather than being innovative, Earhart's designs reiterated the established fashions of 1934.

The same sorts of exaggerated claims would later be made for Amelia Earhart Luggage, which was manufactured for her in 1935 by the Orenstein Trunk Corporation. Although she claimed (and it was later repeated in biographies of her) that "she helped to design the first line of lightweight, waterproofed, canvas-covered plywood,"[30] the truth is that a year earlier similarly constructed bags of linen or canvas over plywood from Mark Cross and Hartmann Luggage were already being hailed as the suitcases of the future. "They are made in many sizes of a durable airplane silk that—lo and behold!—can be washed. The design is very simple with those new stream-line edges, and the bags weigh practically nothing. . . . The linen luggage that you see about, all called airplane luggage by the way, is light, too. Particularly good, are the Hartmann striped Irish linen suitcases and wardrobe bags."[31]

Through her luggage and clothing Earhart always wanted to stress that flying was for every woman, but the entire fashion system contradicts the idea that a line of clothing will make one woman resemble everyone else. In fact, nothing is more antithetical to fashion than homogeneity. It would not be enough for the propeller buttons and parachute silk to announce that the buyer was an independent, liberated woman ready for any eventuality, it had to raise her to that rare ethereal sphere where only the few had ventured. Eschewing democratization for the sake of sales, Earhart allowed the clothing to be marketed in only one department store in each city—Macy's in New York, Famous-Barr in St. Louis, Strawbridge's in Philadelphia, and Jordan Marsh in Boston.

Hype aside, Earhart's line of sportswear was revolutionary in some aspects of both marketing and design. In addition to being limited to one store per city, the clothing was sold in a discrete Amelia Earhart Shop within each department store. While specialty shops for Ralph Lauren, Calvin Klein, Herve Benard, Anne Klein, Liz Claiborne, and other designers now abound in almost every department store, Earhart's specialty shops were apparently the first marketing effort of this kind. "Most department stores shied away from nationally advertised brands before World War II. They often yielded lower profits than non-branded goods, but managers were primarily concerned that the customer's loyalty be to the firm rather than to a brand which might be purchased any number of places."[32] Department stores had their own exclusive lines of merchandise (as Sears still does today). They declined to carry name brands. They would carry "selected lines—especially in toiletries and major appliances—only when customer demand was irresistible."[33] Department stores sometimes subleased franchises (a hair salon or photography studio), but customers were for the most part unaware that they were not wholly owned by the store. When fashion became more important for women after 1910, "advertisements and catalogs urged women to dress in the mode of the store, stressing the importance of coordinating garments and accessories."[34] Thus, in having her clothing carried in department stores rather than in specialty shops where brand names reigned, Earhart became a fashion signifier. Her name on the shop and a facsimile of her signature on the label (figure 5) were preludes to the designer name appearing on the outside of the clothing—what Alison Lurie calls "conspicuous labeling."[35]

Moreover, Earhart's designs and fabrics rebelled against the systematic repression of women by the then-popular practice of flattening and confining the body and restraining its movements through the use of rubber girdles and brassieres. Although the clothing contained some Lastex (a form of rubber), the material was used to enhance movement, rather than to impede it. Earhart stressed that her clothing was for athletic women, or at least, for women on the move. The key to her clothing was practicality. The clothing was without ruffles. The fabric was usually of a washable material, often cotton flannel or a lightweight tweed. The design emphasized the naturally "flat stomach" and slim silhouette of "the athletic girl" by incorporating "deep waistbands" and avoiding "unattractive gaps in the silhouette."[36]

Although women's sportswear already contained pockets, Earhart added and deepened them. One unusual feature was "a pocket in the right sleeve," which could handily carry a log book—or a pack of Luckies! One of her raincoats featured "commodious flap pockets" into which rain hats and other items might be placed.[37]

Her other outfits were practical, as well. One of her tennis outfits was cleverly designed so that a button-down skirt covered up the pair of shorts when the match was over.[38] Amelia Earhart surely understood the difficulties of having to present a suitable appearance in a hurry.

Figure 5. The Earhart label combines flight and fashion.

She also knew that the woman who performed male tasks, such as driving a car, had a wickedly uncomfortable time doing so in traditional female clothing, which hindered movement and unduly exposed parts of the body to the male gaze as they attempted to perform routine tasks. To remedy this situation for the female motorist, Earhart helped design the Skyway coat, made of "zephyr cloth," which "can be pulled comfortably over the knees when sitting down. Ideal when driving a car . . . [the coat could be] quickly managed by gloved hands."[39]

Despite her stated intentions, her most notable achievement was not in designing clothing for the average woman but in helping to produce outfits for other women aviators. "There are a number of costumes designed for women fliers. Tailored slacks to be worn with windbreaker jackets, spirited as to colors, practical and becoming as to cut and fit. Monkey suits or overalls that have zipper back flaps. And the lined overall or flying suit for those who would attempt altitude records."[40] Before the advent of this fashionable and comfortable clothing, female aviators generally wore ill-fitting clothing that had been designed by men, or they froze in skirts in unpressurized airplanes. The back flap was particularly helpful for female flyers, who could not relieve themselves into a bottle or tube as did the men. Earhart and other pioneering women of the air often reeked of urine when they landed after a long flight.[41] Therefore, her female jump suits were a solution for a very practical problem; more important, they also opened the way for women in other industries to have clothing designed and cut for them instead of having to make do with altering men's uniforms.

Earhart was not the only aviator to develop products designed to ameliorate the toll flying took on women's bodies. In 1935, her good friend Jacqueline Cochran opened a cosmetics company named after herself "as a personally owned, unincorporated business and that moisturizer [Flowing Velvet, her best seller] came about because of the problems she had with her own skin when flying at high altitudes and over long distances. . . . And she was out there on other fronts too: custom-blended cream bases for makeups, antiperspirants, hair dyes you could mix yourself."[42] Like Earhart, she tried to get department stores to adopt her products, but only two lesser-known stores—Pogue's in Cincinnati and Halle Brothers in Cleveland—carried them, and even then they did so because Cochran "knew several flying enthusiasts in those stores."[43] In addition to Flowing Velvet, Cochran's biggest hit was her invention of Lipsaver, which repaired the dry cracked lips of test pilots and, most important, of her husband, the business magnate Floyd Odlum! Perhaps because of Odlum's financial backing, Cochran kept her company going well into the 1980s.

In specialized clothing, Earhart remained the premiere name, and her aviation gear made the most lasting impression on the fashion industry as distressed leather flight jackets and vibrant jumpsuits remain popular fashion staples in the 1990s. While reporters were delighted to interview and photograph her for daily newspapers and rotogravure sections across the country, her designs were not accorded serious critical attention in the fashion magazines that truly counted in public opinion, such as *Vogue, Harper's Bazaar,* and *Vanity Fair.* Fashion commentators were more interested in stylistic breakthroughs than in curious gimmicks. The "belted front, flared back, boxy jackets, and normal fitted waist lines" were an established part of the "arrived fashions" in 1934.[44] For example, although her line of raincoats was more practical than previous styles, other companies had made much more dramatic changes. In November 1934, *Vogue* announced, "Rain-coats are so thin that they can be rolled up in a purse when the shower is over, or they are like any other tweed coat and can be worn in the country or in town without that drab feeling that was associated with rain."[45]

When we try to analyze the failure of this fashion venture, the most serious flaw was the timing of the Earhart line. In the depths of the Depression, most women weren't concerned with buying the latest fashion wear. For the average middle-class woman to whom the sportswear line was geared, bigger and more numerous pockets would only emphasize their emptiness. Women who coveted the Earhart label were apt to buy a similar pattern, which was readily available in *Vogue* or other magazines for under a dollar, and imitate the fabric and colors as closely as possible. And though Earhart's adventures signified a certain fashionable daring, women did not dream of emulating Earhart's appearance, for they still remembered her as a rumpled, greasy, and grimy woman emerging from dusty airplanes. Her short tousled hair (she curled it with an iron—it was actually straight) and informal photos that appeared of her in jodhpurs or denims, checked shirts, and knotted scarves made copying her style rather than the softened, made-up version of Hepburn or Dietrich seem too much like cross-dressing. In actuality, women preferred to emulate movie stars. For escapist worship the activities and extravagances of the Vanderbilts, the Duchesse de Chaulnes, the Duchesse de Luynes, Captain and Mrs. Alistair Mackintosh, and the Comtesse de la Falaise were also more exalted illusions.

As much as she needed the money to promote her aviational agenda, Earhart's heart was not in selling clothing to the zestful degree that Cochran promoted her cosmetics (and went on to be named Businesswoman of the Year in 1953 and 1954). Since the market for Earhart's speaking engagements at $250 each had also virtually disappeared in the weak economy, it was too tiring for Earhart to fly all over the country only to promote her clothing line. "Some new exploit and further newspaper coverage would be needed to bring her name into the forefront of the public mind."[46] She found both that exploit and financing by turning her attention to the possibility of first solo nonstop flight from Hawaii to Oakland, California, for a prize of $10,000, which had been offered by several Hawaiian businesses to stress the proximity of their islands to the mainland.[47] That prize and the support of Purdue University eventually helped her to purchase her "flying laboratory"—the Lockheed Electra in which she disappeared near Howland Island on her round-the-world flight on July 2, 1937.

Amelia Earhart clothing disappeared from department stores after only one season, and only three of the many biographies written about her even mention its existence. For many of her biographers and fans the image of her fashionably cloaked in a Skyway raincoat would only detract from the fantasy of her starving while awaiting rescue on a Pacific atoll, wasting away in a Japanese prisoner-of-war camp, or hiding in New Jersey under an alias while American troops combed the Japanese-held Pacific under the guise of looking for her. Like Sappho, Joan of Arc, Marie Antoinette, Mata Hari, Renée Vivien, and countless other female heroines, her apotheosis could only transpire at the moment of her death. Any element of her life that did not directly lead up to her disappearance in 1937 was a momentary distraction, to be skipped over, not contemplated. Therefore, her biographers invested her with a single-minded mission befitting a mythological presence and discarded anything that did not seem appropriate to the development of a heroine—or spy (depending on the viewpoint). That she might be interested in design, that she might be concerned with the physical discomfort caused by contemporary fashion, that she had a vested interest in improving the working conditions of her sister aviators, all seemed beside the point. We want our heroines to be hard—tough-minded like Earhart's famous contemporary and friend Katharine Hepburn—and it would be unforgivable if Earhart cried as her plane ran out of fuel and plummeted downward. We ask them to abandon their femininity in the name of equality and then to prove they are really women after all by getting married, having families, cooking food—in short, proving that they are both men and women at the same time. And so women like Earhart try to go around the world and to the fashion racks at the same time, hoping to be remembered for the former, fearing to be criticized for the latter. And the pattern still exists as popular figures, such as Martina Navratilova, try to succeed with their own clothing lines. So little has changed. We create genderized schizophrenia and then pretend we haven't done so by glossing over the complexities.

Earhart knew that she wasn't going to replace Schiaparelli, and she abandoned an unsuccessful venture. In business ventures, at least, she knew where she couldn't succeed. For historians and for most of her fans, it was just as well: had Earhart been remembered for her clothing rather than her daring, failed attempt to fly around the world at the equator, the world would have been a more difficult place for any woman who wanted to step out where no woman had gone before.

NOTES

Grateful acknowledgment is made to the National Endowment for the Humanities for a Travel to Collections Grant, which allowed me to perform research at the Special Collections Library of Purdue University. The Special Collections Library at the Fashion Institute of Technology in New York City kindly let me use their facilities. I would also like to thank the Summer Grant and the Scholarly Research Grant programs at Pace University for their support of this essay. Citations from Earhart's unpublished material are reprinted with permission of Purdue University Library, Special Collections, West Lafayette, Indiana.

1. Pilot Wilmer Stultz, copilot Louis Edward Gordon, and Amelia Earhart flew from Trepassey, Newfoundland, to Burry Port, Wales, on June 18, 1928. This was the first group transatlantic flight, the first solo having been completed by Charles A. Lindbergh on May 20, 1927.

2. Amelia Earhart Special Collection, Purdue University Libraries, Purdue University, West Lafayette, Indiana, folder IA.

3. *Transatlantic,* June 20, 1928, 15.

4. "Miss Earhart Spurns Fashions," *New York Sun,* June 20, 1928, 10.

5. George Palmer Putnam, *Soaring Wings* (New York: Harcourt, 1939), 79.

6. Doris L. Riche, *Amelia Earhart: A Biography* (Washington, D.C.: Smithsonian, 1989), 187.

7. Amelia Earhart, *The New York Times,* June 21, 1928.

8. Earhart Collection, Purdue University, folder IID.

9. Riche, *Amelia Earhart,* 77.

10. Earhart Collection, Purdue University, folder IF.

11. Ibid., folder 1A.

12. Ibid., folder III.

13. Mary S. Lovell, *The Sound of Wings: The Life of Amelia Earhart* (New York: St. Martin's Press, 1989), 140.

14. Ibid., 140.

15. Jean Backus, *Letters from Amelia 1901–1937* (Boston: Beacon, 1982), 102. All brackets in original except for final pair.

16. Riche, *Amelia Earhart,* 151.

17. Lovell, *The Sound of Wings,* 205.

18. Roland Barthes, *The Fashion System,* trans. Matthew Ward and Richard Howard (New York: Hill and Wang, 1983), 9.

19. U.S. Rubber, "Amelia Earhart Turns from Flying to Designing," Catalog for Amelia Earhart Clothing, 1934.

20. Earhart knew many celebrities, especially in the 1930s when Putnam had sold his publishing firm and had taken a job at Paramount. Earhart attended the Broadway premiere of *The Lake,* one of Hepburn's least successful stage ventures. After Earhart's disappearance Howard Hughes wanted Hepburn to star in *The Amelia Earhart Story,* but the project never materialized. See Anne Edwards, *A Remarkable Woman: A Biography of Katharine Hepburn* (New York: Morrow, 1985), 120, 15.

21. Ibid., 107.

22. Donald Spoto, *Falling in Love Again: Marlene Dietrich* (Boston: Little Brown, 1985), 45.

23. Ibid., 45.

24. Gertrude Bailey, "Amelia Earhart, Our Newest Designer," *New York World Telegram,* December 29, 1933, 16.

25. "'Earhart Couturiere' Tries on Some of Her Own Designs," *Washington Post,* January 5, 1934, 13.

26. U.S. Rubber, Catalogue for Amelia Earhart Clothing, 1934.

27. "'Earhart Couturiere,'" 13.

28. Muriel Earhart Morrissey and Carol L. Osborne, *Amelia, My Courageous Sister: Biography of Amelia Earhart, True Facts About Her Disappearance* (Santa Clara, Calif.: Osborne, 1987), 40.

29. *Vogue,* May 15, 1934, 86.

30. Riche, *Amelia Earhart,* 209.

31. "Connoisseur's Luggage," *Vogue,* May 15, 1934, 100–102. Amelia Earhart luggage fared better than her clothing and still exists today. At the time of her death, the luggage was bringing in a royalty of approximately $850 per year. See Earhart, Probate Case #181709, Los Angeles County, 1949, 1.

32. Susan Porter Benson, *Counter Cultures: Saleswomen, Managers, and Customers in American Department Stores, 1890–1940* (Urbana: University of Illinois Press, 1986), 103.

33. Ibid., 103.

34. Ibid., 108.

35. Alison Lurie, *The Language of Clothes* (New York: Random House, 1981), 131.

36. Bailey, "Amelia Earhart," 16.

37. "Sports Clothes Designed by Amelia Earhart," *New York Herald Tribune,* December 31, 1933.

38. Ibid., 7.

39. Advertisement in *Vogue,* November 15, 1934, 15.

40. Bailey, "Amelia Earhart," 16.

41. At least Earhart wasn't prone to airsickness. In general, passengers were. According to test pilot Ben Howard, "When TAT [an early airline] reached only 75 percent air sickness we thought we'd passed a point in aviation history. . . . People were so sick they used rubber matting instead of carpeting on the floor of the plane. . . . They used to say passengers didn't get out of a plane, they slid out—skated down the aisle" (quoted in Riche, *Amelia Earhart,* 107, ellipses in original).

42. Scott Kale, quoted in Jacqueline Cochran and Maryann Bucknum Brinley, *Jackie Cochran: An Autobiography* (New York: Bantam, 1987), 121.

43. Cochran, quoted in ibid., 123.

44. "Vogue's Chart of Incoming and Arrived Fashions," *Vogue,* September 1, 1934, xii.

45. "Let It Rain," *Vogue,* November 15, 1934, 73.

46. Lovell, *The Sound of Wings,* 206.

47. The $10,000 prize was primarily sponsored by the sugar industry, which was the archenemy of the tobacco industry, since cigarettes were often promoted as a dieting device ("Reach for a Lucky instead of a sweet"). "Since legislation was under consideration in Congress to reduce the sugar tariff, it was clear to some people that Amelia had 'sold her soul' to the sugar interests" (Backus, *Letters,* 163).

Hélène Cixous
Translated by Deborah Jenson

Sonia Rykiel in Translation

My starry jacket: it lives in my closet like a discrete primitive deity. Like an allusion to night. We watch over one another. Sometimes I wear it; sometimes it wears me.

Modestly, my jacket manifests the luminous presence of the night, up above and in my closet. The Great outside is also inside.

Sometimes I wear a warm starry night on my person. Night in a woolen jacket? Why not? Nothing makes one think more of what there is of night in each woman, of what is soft, silently black, brilliantly soft and black. It is the starry bosom, which modestly continues to envelop us.

All this, this world, in this jacket? Yes, because it is so simple. All black with small crystals of strass hung like stars in the mildness of the night. It is not an outfit;[1] no detour, no disguise. Just "night": as a child would design it, with all its attributes, the Great True Night with stars pinned on the great black bosom.

All this to draw attention to the enigma of this garment cut from a simple bit of warm night: there is continuity between world, body, hand, garment. The designing hand of the child: night, the hand stuffed with stars, the hand making a starry jacket. From sky to body, the stars wend their way, in neat formation.

This garment comes from very far away. I had never seen it, I have always known it. It comes from the origins. It comes from the trace of the immemorial origins in the farthest depths of my memory, where memory does not remember itself, has no images, is still nothing more than the movement of life.

This garment comes from an Orient, from an East always beating in the heart of the inside.[2] It goes back to a beginning, emerges on my surface, and it is: East.

What is this internal Orient? Nothing exotic. The most intimate part of myself, the ancient restless and tranquil site, where the body felt itself take its first steps. This garment is native; its model: the body's internal sensation of itself, the secret of the body. Sonia Rykiel designs this sensation.

I go to Sonia Rykiel as one goes to a woman, as one goes home. As one goes to a closet-friend; which is to say: I go inside, eyes closed. With my hands, with my eyes in my hands, with my eyes groping like hands, I see—touch the body hidden in the body.

In moving outward, in expressing oneself in wool, in jersey, in visible forms, the intimate does not *show* itself, does not exhibit itself. There is no rupture with the body hidden in the body. There is continuity. Transmission of the secret, barely perceptible revelation.

Everything is continuous. It brims over the edges; the garment doesn't stop short, doesn't declare its boundaries, doesn't gather in its frontiers. The gentle unbordering of fabrics, the terrestrial fabric, takes place in gradual, light changes of color and substance. Skin of the world.

And the seams? I mean the inside out, I mean the right side out, I mean the right side where it is the inside out that is the right side.

My mother said to me: You put your sweater on inside out again. It's strange.

—It's Sonia Rykiel.

That the seams should remain apparent is the immodesty of writing.

Writing likes its composition to be savored. Ever since the Bible, writing is what lets the inside out show: and there is no more inside out.

The most delicious of meals: first the friend serves you a dish of marvelously complicated preparation, but ultimately the taste is simple. It is one, and it is unique.

So I ask the friend how she did it. First the friend tells me the story of the dish—how she did it, where she bought her slices of lamb, and her oysters.

Then, she sits down at a little table and she writes out the recipe. The recipe retains the taste of the dish, the history of the dish. Now I see how the dish was sewn, and I find it all the more delicious. The dish is entrusted to me.

The dress is entrusted to us.

The nonviolence of these clothes: Sonia's clothes never turn back against the body, never attack it, never seek to put one in one's place. They don't conceal, don't forbid. There are shield–clothes, mirror-clothes, shimmering, dazzling clothes, clothes which both attract and repel the gaze, clothes of the armor species, clothes which remold the body to a precise measure, to perfect composure, clothes which adorn. I have had some. Few. I never liked them. I donned them to go to war.

Sonia's clothes are for peace. For skin which breathes like animals in the field, for the palm. Not loving the gaze. They give themselves to be lived. At Sonia's, as in my home. I enter the tender ancestral tent, and in its peaceful and near shelter, I become friendly, I am her friend and the friend of the world.

It is a question of an alliance, a marriage, an accord: of the arch of the feet with the sand, of the flesh with the water. I enter the garment. It is as if I were going into the water. I enter the dress as I enter the water which envelops me and, without effacing me, hides me transparently.

And here I am, dressed at the closest point to myself. Almost in myself.

In Sonia's boutique there are ornaments, accessories, details that do not come from the body but which exude colors, contemporary painting, the world of representation. For me, these are the supports for simplicity, the easel, the frame from which the night, black, rises.

One day I tried to put on a striped pullover and it didn't work.[3] The stripes crossed me out, crossed the pullover out. I came back to unified colors, to the united, to union.

A garment which is not a noisy manifestation of the street, but a fine manifestation of the world. A bodily insistence: imitation of the unique curve in which the body flows.

I am going to talk about the dress:

The dress by Sonia Rykiel doesn't surprise me. It comes to me, agrees with me, and me with it, and we resemble one another. Between us is the memory of a nomadic fire. The dress dresses a woman I have never known and who is also me.

There is a woman who traverses all women. A woman who exists in all paintings and all countries and all houses; whether she is slight or sumptuous, wide or narrow, she is recognizable by her desire to live, by the impetus which lifts her up, by the grace which moves the monumental body as easily as the minute one.

This woman needs all of her body to embrace life, to do things, to take pleasure.

Undoubtedly it is she who inspires Sonia Rykiel's dress. This dress (there is only one of them) is the proof that someone exists who is called woman, joyfully, always has been, and who knows what to do with all of her body in the world.

A woman who has no angles. A woman who flows in the world, a woman who does not cut herself off from either the world or herself.

By all the pockets of the dress she rejoins the body, she re-creates the circle.

A woman with long curves, like a tree, like a river, a woman who doesn't end, a woman of one slow and continuous movement.

A woman who feels herself living translates herself through all women like the course of a river.

And the dress takes up and pursues the slow course.

I say: the dress. I call every garment "dress." And I only wear pants and pullovers. Yet I hold myself to this inexactitude: because it is into a "dress" that the two pieces translate themselves, into a single enveloping curve in which the apparently separate pieces of the garment melt together. The water opens up, and recloses.

The dress doesn't separate the inside from the outside, it translates, sheltering. Light enchantment of a metaphor that doesn't erase its source.

Sonia Rykiel fabricates the dream of the body: to freely be of a body with the legs, the belly, the thighs, the arms, with the air of the sea, with space.

I said a dress, a single dress. For there is only one of the truth. One dress but full of dresses. A dress which holds innumerable dresses in its bosom.

A musical dress, which gives birth to thousands of notes. A dress which bears a Kyrielle or stream of garments in its folds.[4] Magic of the anagram.

What is there in some names? A Kyrielle of names, of fateful signs, prophecies. There are names which sybillate and play with the ears.[5]

The name Sonia Rykiel, I mean her sonorous dress, is Sa Robe, "Her Dress," full of a range of sounds, signs, of innumerable issue.

There are names condensed like dreams: bouquet of syllables whose opening out sends the hundred sounds bounding back to the cardinal points of the imagination.

What is there in Sonia Rykiel? *Qui elle,* she who? You hear the resonance of she who lives, unconscious bearer of a treasure of sounds, of fabrics, of a *kyrielle* of questions, of dreams, of flashes of foreign languages, of Greek, of Russian, of litanies of linen, of invocations to a Creator—who, it must be said, has showered her with gifts—Kyrie eleison.

I listen seriously to messages in translation. And if Stéphane Mallarmé had been named differently, would he everywhere have inscribed his nostalgia for a strange marriage never celebrated? I wonder.

And there are dresses like dreams full of history, of known unknown persons. Dresses pregnant with dresses and women. In this way the dress, like the dream, is a voyage. A dress which hides in its folds the great voyage in proximity and intimacy.

This dress is a dream of the body, the dream of a voyage of the body within the body, of the child within the mother, of the woman within the woman. That is why one feels good in it.

One feels loved.

This Dress I will call Gradiva. It makes me think of the adorable *Gradiva* by Jensen, the eternal young woman who, after having resuscitated man from among the stones, and herself from among the ashes, aroused in Freud a text as charming as an adored girl.

I call it Gradiva, for like the beautiful young woman in the story, who was dressed in a dress of a thousand folds of river, it contains in its bosom life in the process of reconstituting itself. And in its name it contains the name of the woman full of being Gradiva, "the woman in sum." A sum of woman?

NOTES

1. Cixous uses the French *costume,* "suit," which also means "costume" in the sense of "disguise."—Trans.

2. The term "East" in French, *Est,* differs from the third person singular of the verb "to be" only in its capitalization; Cixous emphasizes the intended overlap of the two meanings by using a lower case *e.*—Trans.

3. The adjective *rayé,* "striped," comes from the verb *rayer,* which also can mean "to cross out."—Trans.

4. The french noun *kyrielle* signifies "stream" or "string."—Trans.

5. The invented verb "sybiller" combines the adjective *sybilant,* denoting a sound with a whistling quality, and the adjective *sybillin,* denoting anything relative to the sybils, women prophets from Greco-Roman antiquity. As applied to language, *sybillin* connotes obscurity. Cixous unites these different meanings.—Trans.

Sonia Rykiel
Translated by Claire Malroux

rom *Celebration*

It's in the fold that all comes into play. As in a dream, it rises and then hides itself, unfolding into a sun, regathering into tiny folds or falling back into still tighter pleats. Open the heart of these folds to find creative genius. The pleat is sewn to conceal inner thought that can play hide-and-seek without a sound.

The beauty of a single fold where it should not be, like memory with all the folds that have already lain there before. And then a precise pleat, not some hybrid frill or flounce present by chance. One of those infinite folds which keep their mystery, bowed like the fold of a red-sealed letter on a silver tray.

Today, creation is in a spin. Stills, sets no longer exist. The frozen image, the time to take one's time, just to get the feeling. Finished. You cannot dwell on a page, you must turn them faster, close the book, put it aside, and open another.

Why? There's never enough time. We must move on, never fall by the way, never a false step, never a crease, ever put right, grasp the occasion, shape it in the mind, work at it and bring it out. That's what a work of art is.

Work? You're kidding: it isn't that either!

Things happen differently. There's beginning, a point which develops, which becomes a line, a color, or a shape to be shaken out, refolded, stroked to match the idea of the creator, his theme.

What excess!

Concept?

Concept is not style, but not far. It is rather an art of living, a space in which all is decided, almost a philosophy. Ideas are the link between creator and recipient, an artificial paradise in which all is organized and fits into a precise system like Meccano with from time to time a part that fails to fit into another and may become the start of another concept. It could be said that a concept is a new idea occurring because we are swamped, choice is too difficult, almost impossible, and the creator, by bringing his image into focus, arouses interest, exposing in a single shortened and folded page, a clear sewn-up deal.

Where's creation in all this?

Produced by a true, an authentic creator who an instant earlier had closed his eyes, the concept is a creation, a harmonic line justified by the very place of the creator within his era.

You bet I can see that woman, the one I have been pursuing for twenty years, the one who tempts me, hiding behind fabrics, baring a shoulder, slipping on her dress inside out, turning it right side out and then jilting me to run after that man who was eyeing her. She is beautiful, elusive, quiet, calm, but when I think I've caught her, she is already gone dancing from one bank to the other, a coin struck on one side with "Woman" and on the other with "Man." She kicks off her shoes, crosses the bridge with outstretched arms and eyes lifted to the sky, wears men's sweaters with tight skirts or ample slacks with close-fitting pullovers, unpicks her hems, dresses warmly in April, lightly in May. One day, she even set "Black is beautiful" in her heart because her glance had met the black eyes of a Negro child.

As in stories of love, eternal love or impossible love, her dress is a plaything like a lover following with his hands the lines of the body without touching it, without coming to rest and who then yields . . .

To get to know oneself . . . or to lose one's heart to a dress designer who would understand the body, the whim of the moment, the color of skin, the softness of complexion, the frailty of the soul.

Figure 1. Original design by Sonia Rykiel.

Figure 2. Original design by Sonia Rykiel.

To give one's body to the fantasies of another, his obsessions, his passions, to surrender heart and soul to a stranger who would adorn the skin with his *idées fixes,* his dreams . . . Aren't we mad to let them move us about, push us around, wrap us up, reproduce us so we are all the same or nearly so, all of a mold with perhaps a difference in the voice, in a gesture . . .

Not knowing how, I was able to do otherwise.

My creation knows no stages, just odd moments, a skirt, a pullover, a gown.

Fashion, like history, parades, all lights turned on it. It spangles and glitters, studded with silver and gold. It sparkles from head to foot, bursting out triumphantly, gloriously, luxuriously, demented flesh, trailing skirt, hooked-up bra, a long string of dummy pearls, regilded shoes, bare legs, bare head, bare chest.

It is said that everything may be read in a face; me, I reckon that all may be read in clothes, but if the face is supposed to be radiant, clothes come alight only when the body moves.

She is transparent, inside and out, as if body and dress were mirrored images of each other, each the consecration of the other.

You are being watched, you know, robbed, betrayed, nothing escaping us, neither sound nor thought. You know that we are lying in wait, that the fatality of creation prompts us to lie, that the ephemeral which is the natural condition of fashion forces us to turn inward that which the previous season faced outward and that even if the basting is strong, the result of real know-how, it is inadequate to propose a lifelong style.

One must be ambiguous and real, ritualistic and vague, present and absent, lying and truthful, but in the pleasure of doing there is the contentment of taking without being noticed.

Fashion unstitches, restitched and starts anew a hundred times over. It is mystery everywhere and yet it is nowhere. It evades, lies but invents, turns its coat because coats must be turned to understand better, like seaming turned either in or out, yet right, well cut with or without hem, must fall . . . right. Troubled by the folds of life's creases which are never in the right place and which it must refold to its plan.

History fails to tell all, as we well know; she wore a red dress with a blue gardenia . . . a dangerous relationship; she had a Persian cat and a silk sofa, another dangerous relationship; she dressed . . . to be undressed, read Léautaud while listening to Stevie Wonder and sipped Champagne with an Italian prince. She wore a ruby on her left hand and an emerald on her right . . . dangerous, sucked peppermint drops and swallowed homeopathic pills . . . dangerous.

She glided through life as if through a work of art and her body, her true body, that which breathed, which lifted her gown, showed signs of pleasure . . . dangerous.

And yet she wondered how to place the brooch on her blouse, powder her back, reverse situations, reveal her cleavage, spread honey on toast, take a bite and offer it to her lover. How to stroll in October air although leaves are still green, having already changed the color of her makeup.

Breasts bared . . . not bared . . . Hide them, show them, unhook, open a little, fasten the button, variations on a theme. Body hidden because previously too exposed. Fashion changes, burns. Tradition demands that . . . we expose no more, we dress, fold, sew, fix, tie. Tradition's not revolution, but revolution . . . isn't really fashion . . .

He who utters the word *fashion* knows not what he says. Lean closer to hear the rustle of fabric, the words of the artist, his passion for dress. Lean even nearer to see that he is not destroying but having new thoughts, repositioning, reworking, reshaping the same form on which he has already thought, positioned, worked, shaped, everything being drawn from the depths of the eternal and essential memory he has of the object already conceived long ago.

The first sweater and the second, the third and the thousandth and that of tomorrow, all related like the pages of the same novel, a distorted unfinished text seeking a companion for the next season, neither too distant nor too near, unbuttoned in the right place, slit on the proper side.

Are we not destroying fashion, chasing it around like this? Every six months, a kick in the behind; it enters through the main portals and is made to exit down the back stairs. It climbs in again through a window, skirts longer, more mobile, closer fitting. It lasts merely the time of a Summer and leaves wider, padded at the shoudlers. It's Winter once more. It's molded, draped to the ground, coat upon coat, absurd. Could we not evolve rather than destroy, work on clothing like one works on a book and avoid, we the creators, being "consecrated" or "desecrated" every half year?

Twenty years ago, I invented an image, a paper woman written in the folds of the fabric, the knitted threads, the colors of the flesh; I bestowed on her

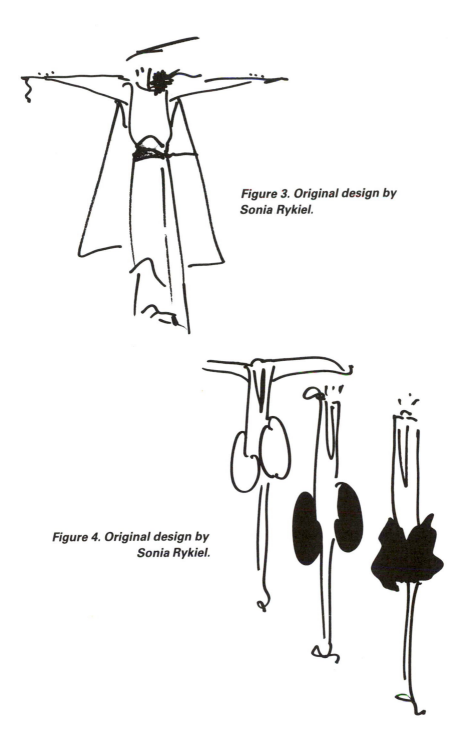

Figure 3. Original design by Sonia Rykiel.

Figure 4. Original design by Sonia Rykiel.

visible signs of luxury, joy, colors, a modern package, a day-to-day destiny, a pure line with hazy outlines, a story.

She ran away and I caught her again; I left and she came back to me.

A novel is a novel only by comparison with another novel. A gown is a gown by comparison with another gown; so I turned it, I sewed its name inside, I pinned it to a wall. In its folds, I sounded all the notes, sought out the differences, folded the print to give it shape. I leaned to the left to sound its heart, on the right I sewed badges, pasted trinkets. I unpicked the hems for freedom and folded the seams so they can be felt, be seen.

I wonder if it is you or I who dictate fashion. If it be not you compelling me to shorten, lengthen, widen, remove the belts, lengthen again, no more red but some yellow and blue and then red again. If you are not there, you, behind me to see that I unstitch the hems or overstitch them, that I sew on beads, spangles, and even flowers, if you don't push me to tighten the waist or lower it onto the hips, to remove the petticoats, add flounces, to show the stitching and to hide it, if one season you revel in luxury, sumptuosity, gilt, and then another season in despair (which is not black but rather a look), if you don't pull me apart to attach, tuck, close or open, draw aside to peep at skin, the luster of the flesh, the texture of the fabric, pull the threads to gather the material, fold the muslin to imitate a book. If it be not I on the couch and you on the chair and that naturally, without appearing to, it's you who dictate fashion.

It is an art to dress, attract the other, capture him. The difficulty of being "natural" or "sophisticated," in "good taste" or in "fashion," modern or "outside of fashion," resemble a Madonna or nobody. In the world of fashion, "Fashion" is refashioned each time but one remains oneself in one's "own world," in one's own style, that's what's difficult. To be at the same time excessive and sober, sincere and false or mad, not to be a mere image but a true illustration of woman. Short-skirted doll, high heels, or long-skirted idol, flat heels, inconstant woman playing her role from day to day.

One can work without problems, simply with drawings, happy pros—I know some of them—but behind the gown, the painting or book, the object exhibited, the perfect object, "beautiful in its perfection," there are in each fold, in each page, traces of work, reflection, scrapping, fresh starts.

It is difficult to build a legend, to create history, hold a name high, consecrate it every six months.

Often I looked at it, that finished gown, I smiled because it was beautiful and had cost me untold suffering.

The creator is out of step, since he must be "before" but at the same time "actual." That he lives in the past also, it's his role, since he must be a witness. But he must see more clearly, further ahead. The creator's paradox is the play between before, during and after, the passing of these three periods, attention to the past, present and future, shaping each one, folding it into the others and then creating the work of art. What counts is style.

Style is the difference between him who gives life to words, gowns, pictures, and him who creates words, gowns and pictures without giving them life.

The style of a work is its folding and unfolding in time.

You stitch, you unstitch, you shape, you unshape, you reshape, you create. To build, construct, invent and destroy, put into place, a moment, a gown, a page, a line. Before, after, to find the beginning of the gown, the part which touches first, which caresses. Author, actor, that which is seen and that which remains, that is work.

I erase, I scratch out, I turn the page. That's luxury. Then I return to my old sweater, my old skirt. That's even greater luxury.

Nothing marked me out for dress designing except a knack of organization, mixing, disrupting, and destroying truth.

Create an illusion, but convincingly, opening out in the fold, flaring out, caress the seams to reveal the body and then fold them in again to play with the slits, the openings. Light, color, shadow, not necessarily black but a gray edged with red like a November sky.

Woman is institution and what's good about institution is to be able to break away from it.

Carol Shloss

Off the [W]rack:

Fashion and Pain in the

Work of Diane Arbus

In a class she gave shortly before her death in 1971, Diane Arbus observed that people are rarely content with their own peculiarities and do not rest until they have created another set. "Our whole guise," she remarked, "is like giving a sign to the world to think of us in a certain way." In her view, human efforts at self-alteration seldom worked, and in the difference between desire and outcome, she saw the essential irony of the universe. "It has to do with the fact that what you intend never comes out like you intend it."[1] She considered that her photography recorded her subjects' desire to create along with the deconstruction of their hopes, as if the photographic moment could be explained by a fundamental tension between "making" and "unmaking" or between the imagination and the pain occasioned by its frustration.

Arbus is famous less for the innovation of her camera technique than for the unflinching quality of her vision. Over and over again, she could stare down the most damaged of human beings; and despite the recent publication of a book about her magazine work,[2] her reputation continues to rest on a series of portraits that first appeared in the Museum of Modern Art's New Documents Show in 1967 and its retrospective of her photography in 1972. Russian midgets, nudists, female impersonators, transvestites, circus performers and retarded people claimed her attention; and although we may never be able to explain the exact nature of her attraction to them, we do know that her forays into the underworld were made, at least partially, in response to her dissatisfied sense of having been overly protected from reality as a child.

The daughter of Gertrude and David Nemerov, who owned Russek's Fifth Avenue, she was brought up on Park Avenue and Central Park West, where even the Depression failed to dissipate a prosperity built on the sale of mink coats. Later Arbus would associate this comfort with psychic isolation and with a "sense of being immune," as if a bourgeois life were not a life but only a series of evasions or coverups.[3]

She included in this dour judgment the world opened to her through the Russeks department store itself, where "[I]t was like being in some loathsome movie set in an obscure Transylvanian country." In her memory, the fur salesmen rubbed "their hands together like shoe salesmen" and she was "treated like a crummy princess."[4] I include these biographical details because they form an interesting pattern in which wealth and fashion are associated with aversiveness, and artifice (or what was perceived as artificial) is conflated with pain. In Arbus's mind, clothing was taken away from its ability to protect and "to confirm and enhance the physical presence of those wearing it" and placed in a private configuration of psychic oppression.[5] For Arbus, fashion could never succeed in being a "vestimentary system" in the way that Roland Barthes conceived it because she realized at a very young age that garments, whatever their form, fabric, or color, could never lead to possession of the beneficient occupations, states, and moods of the world.[6] She understood that the basic promise of fashion—that variations of clothing can produce variations in character or fortune—was false.

Given these predilections to swerve away from artifice and to seek a greater source of authenticity for herself, it is interesting to remember that Arbus began her career as a fashion photographer, working with her young husband, Allan, to create the very images that perpetuated the myth that she privately abhorred. They began their work together in the early 1940s, working first for Russek's, and gradually they expanded to include accounts from Bonwit Teller, *Glamour, Seventeen, Harper's Bazaar,* and (in 1949) *Vogue.*

In writing a retrospective for *MS* magazine about her mother's magazine work, Doon Arbus (b. April 3, 1945) would later claim that it was her father who actually took the pictures, but the memory of the Arbuses' models often contradict her. "It got to be a big joke in the business," Carole McCarlson, a Ford model, recalled. "Diane and Allan huddling under the focusing cloth—because no matter how many people you get under that cloth, only one person can click the shutter! . . . No other husband-and-wife photography team worked the way they did—so tenderly, so closely, in complete collaboration."[7] But even if it is true that Allan Arbus usually clicked the shutter, it is surely the case that both of them understood the "syntax" of high-fashion photography in New York City at that time—a syntax by which each garment was "robbed" of its essentially protective function and expropriated to another secondary "language" that promised to grant all of the attributes of the fashion image to those who bought into the system. The Arbuses did not simply photograph clothing, but clothing-in-action; and in doing this, they contributed to the implicit story told by all of the beauty magazines of this era: to purchase a garment, an accessory, a grooming article, or even sleepwear or underwear was to purchase what surrounds and upholds that item as well.

The first of their photographs to appear in *Vogue,* on May 1, 1949 (figure 1), for example, displayed a young woman wearing a short-sleeved, polka-dot dress, a light, feathery floral hat that surrounds and embraces her face, and white gloves. She is seated in the back seat of a car with an impeccably dressed young man. The two of them are holding hands (indeed their hands rather than the dress center the frame), and both peer out

Figure 1. Allan and Diane Arbus, American Vogue, **May 1, 1949.**

of the window toward something or someone on the sidewalk side of the automobile. We infer that they are in a limousine and that their arrival at an afternoon social event is marked by the gaze of a concierge or doorman. Although a written description of the clothing might be needed to locate the variation of the ensemble that makes it fashionable (is it the scoop neck, the pattern of the cloth, or the length of the hem?), the photographic composition as a whole tells the viewer that attending to such details will bring about the estate of the model: her kingdom precludes loneliness, anomie, and unpleasant subway rides; in it, one will always be accompanied; one will always be expected, and no noise, grime, or abrasiveness will ever spoil the afternoon's costume. The anticipation of the model's face is the anticipation of fashion itself: transformation is within reach.

Indeed, many of the Arbuses' fashion photographs make this conflation (woman + garment = security, esteem) at the same time that they address the issue of metamorphosis itself. A series done for *Glamour* in 1948 features "the plump girl" (figure 2) and "the short girl" practicing "contour camouflage" and "wardrobe prestidigitation" in the successful pursuit of romance in the park:

> The slimming silhouette of unbroken black with tiered peplum cleverly cut to give an illusion of slim hips; surplice-front neckline for a longer look; just-above-elbow sleeves to minimize heavy arms; well-groomed, medium-short hair to further lengthen a short neck. (78)
> Miss Five Feet Five (and under) can give herself a lift, and also create an illusion of height. . . . Her clothes, never fussy, are just a bit shorter than fashion dictates, with slim shoulder-to-hem lines. She wears them with hats sized in proportion, avoids large hats because they tend to dwarf her. (80)

Although it is undoubtedly true that "written fashion" guides the interpretation of each image (threatening torture or malformation [dwarfing] if the rule [dictate] of fashion is ignored), it is also the case that the photographs themselves show that the rewards of such attention to clothing will be the steady gaze of a lover, the unobstructed path through life, and the fecundity of nature itself.

In creating these photographic tableaus, the Arbuses were not being original, but neither were they aberrant. One could say that they tended to speak a certain "dialect" of the language of style. Where other photographers of the forties and fifties (Cecil Beaton, Horst P. Horst, Jacques-Henri Lartigue, Irving Penn) made their mark by exoticism, exaggeration, distortion, or dramatic lighting effects, Diane and Allan Arbus chose the narrative of the happy ending in which ordinary people can make something of themselves; they can alter the plot of their own anonymity and

The plump Girl

Figure 2. Allan and Diane Arbus, Glamour, *July 1948.*

isolation; in fact, they can defy the dictates of their own creation (their bodies, their life circumstances) by a counter-creativity. Made artifacts can suffice to change destiny.

Although one way of analyzing this type of cultural story is to point out that it results from the manipulation of desire by a fashion industry that is driven by greed, the explanation that interests me more focuses on the power material culture seems to offer by speaking to the creative urge itself, for its implicit message is about "making" and about people's need to meet the inner requirements of desire or fear or hunger by having objects (here clothing) that express and accommodate those needs. Although what is offered by the Arbuses' photographs of clothing is usually ready-made (it will come off the rack at Bonwit's or Saks Fifth Avenue), each viewer can imagine that among such items, there will be one that is a "perfect fit"—not only between the body and the garment—but between one's inner self-image and one's ability to project that image out into the world in a sharable form. In this sense, all fashion photographs comfort by reaffirming that garments can act as tools for transforming interior claims into objectified forms.

The magazines for which the Arbuses worked seemed alternately to play with their readers' need to believe in the efficacy of creating an appropriate personal guise and with an equally strong need to acknowledge the hidden mechanisms of their own disguises. The July 1951 issue of *Glamour* offers an example with its article called "Are You on the Cover?" Featuring a series of women ("a girl in her twenties"; "a woman in her thirties"; "a lady in her forties") who were supposedly "discovered" on the streets of New York, the essay uses ordinary people to bridge the distance between the professional model and the aspirations of its readers. "Those who are single, those who are married, and all who work . . . you're there [on the cover] if you have even moments when you dimly suspect you're not making the most of your looks. . . . No magic, not secrets. What we did for them, you can do . . . for yourself" (27). The Arbuses' photographs are carefully composed versions of before-and-after pictures. One woman is on the subway; another is on a bench in Central Park; on succeeding pages they wear evening gowns, furs, and highly stylized makeup to inspire other secretaries and mothers to similar acts of self-improvement—simple but powerful salutes to the body's malleability in the face of the will.

Scattered among such articles are numerous ads that form what we might call an "anti-grammar" or a "liar's abcdarium," for they expose the dissimulation behind the editors' "no secrets, no magic" call to their clientele. Against the seeming reality of self-transformation posed by the magazines' producers, the ad writers and illustrators reveal the fear that the body itself may be intractable and not subject to actual reformation: one may buy a facial mask, a girdle, a wired bra, a new sanitary napkin, but its purchase does not erase bad skin, fat thighs, small breasts, or body odor. The very existence of the products speaks, in fact, to a wild but unstated anguish in the face of genetic material that refuses the will and the imagination, even as the imagination bursts with images into which to pour itself. I will conclude this section by claiming that the distance between our ability to imagine better physical selves and our truculent corporeality is experienced as pain.

In the mid 1950s, Diane Arbus began a series of moves that seemed to change the course of her carrer. In "The Magazine Years, 1960–1971," Thomas Southall points out that she began to take a number of photography courses, especially with Lisette Model, who encouraged her "to become more specific, more daring and more diligent in her work."[8] By 1956 she had, he claims, stopped working with Allan Arbus, although his atelier continued to bear the name Diane and Allan Arbus. It is interesting to note that Southall conflates this process of growth with Arbus's search for a radically new subject matter, as if the world of fashion photography were inauthentic or inadequate to Arbus's talents. "Around this time," he tells us, "she discovered Hubert's Museum, a flea circus located in the basement of one of 42nd Street's penny arcades, with its old posters of carnival performers, its exhibits and the live show put on by sideshow freaks."[9] And it is the case that Arbus moved during this time from recording images of ease and beauty into a demimonde where such beautiful and rewarding circumstances were almost unthinkable. But it is not true, even if the types of people Arbus photographed changed, that she retreated from the issues raised by fashion photography. Indeed, the images she created out of her wanderings with the camera seem to arise out of an implicit dialogue with *Vogue* and the family of Condé Nast publications, and seem, in the end, to speak the same language of signs.

One of the semiotic systems that indicates a line of continuity in Arbus's work is her obsession with masks, false fronts, and the need to announce inauthenticity. Where the fashion magazines she had worked for seemed to woo their readers with appeals to honesty ("no magic") and then to undercut that approach by revealing their own "fibs," Arbus worked always to reveal the artfulness of surfaces. Rather than photograph "the comfortable suburban home" or "the smart New York townhouse," she was drawn to the façade that could not fail to be recognized as such. The face of a house constructed for a Hollywood movie, the Manhattan apartment building *trompe l'oeil* that seemed to bring a lake and trees into the lobby, the castles of Disneyland, all were constructs that seemed in some way to comfort her with their obvious duplicity. "As a kid," she had said, remembering her well-protected lifestyle, "I was confirmed in a sense of unreality."[10] Later in life, she seems to have associated the "madeness" of culture with that former sense of falsity, and as a consequence, she wanted to use her camera for exposure, for showing the false front to be empty of content beyond the will to deceive. In this way, her photography called attention away from the artifact and toward the desire that had called it into being. It served as a sort of tribute to the human impulse behind all creativity—the will to extend the self into the world through made objects—and at the same time, a judgment about the fragility and inefficacy of that effort: no one is fooled. The house is empty; the lake is not there.

But of course it was by precisely this kind of effort that her previous photography had been achieved. By gathering together models, garments, makeup, and scenery, she had once affronted her viewers with a similar *trompe l'oeil*: the clothing displayed did not belong to the mannequin and the scenes of romance the models enacted were equally fabricated. Seen in relation to this previous camera work, Arbus's "new" post-1956 photographs can be understood as an answer to the fashionable world and as a comment on her own role within it. She had been the artificer whose maneuvers she would now expose.

If we continue to look at the photographs in Arbus's 1972 retrospective in this way, we can see the versatility of her exposé. Like the sanitary-napkin advertisers who called their product "Fibs" or the maternity dress ads that announced "heaven only knows," she took her stance as an "anti-grammarian," whose opus would deconstruct the illusions she had formerly colluded in making. From this perspective, her photographs seem to be united less by their focus on "freaks" than by the issue of alteration and suitability that they confront. To what extent can the imagination find resources to effect the presentation of self that it envisions? In what ways do we judge that alteration, that surge of creative energy in the face of given circumstances to be culturally acceptable or "suitable"? Her nudists, midgets, transvestites, and twins all serve to address these questions, and we find, in looking at them, that they are almost invariably "fashionable." In fact they seem so obsessed with fashion that we could say that they are the readers whom *Glamour, Harper's Bazaar,* and *Vogue* had sought to influence. They are evidence of the human proclivity to project itself into the made world or to create a guise. "When I look in the mirror . . . I don't know myself!" [The New DuBarry Success Course]. "I have made myself into something 'other.'"

Again and again, we see in these photographs people who refuse the engulfment of their bodies by creating a front: they adorn themselves with "glamorous" artifacts or they assume the physical postures of the "beauty" culture. Two quite different girls seem to have bought the same bathing suit because it is currently in style. A man, feigning femininity, apparently knows exactly which bra, garter belt, and stockings to wear, almost as if he were posing for The Firstone Contro ad: "It keeps its shape and yours—even after countless washings because Contro is the only elastic vitalized with vitalin, the magic rubber vitamin." "Dancing or dusting, it moves with you yet holds your contour firm."[11] He seems to know, too, from the model's gyrations (she is dancing, not dusting) that it is appropriate to display oneself to the camera in one's underclothes. Another man in drag (figure 3) seems to know that he has achieved the proper "pomp" for his wig, since it resembles a hat ("roses scaling a tall cloche") designed by Adolfo Ayres for Neiman-Marcus (figure 4).[12] Still another man, pretending to be a woman, has mastered the classic female posture for naked sexual display: one of his arms extends straight down the side so that the hand can hold the thigh; the other arm is bent so that the hand can rest on

Figure 3. Diane Arbus, "Two men dancing at a drag ball, N.Y.C. 1970."

Figure 4. Vogue, March 1960.

the waist. His legs are placed tightly together with the weight on one leg only so that a hip juts out to emphasize his shapeliness. His shoulders are twisted slightly away from the camera so that the head must be turned coquettishly to the body's side to give full face to the photographer (figure 5). It does not matter that he may have seen this posture in something like a Colgate commercial for "Veto" deodorant (figure 6), for he seems to understand that it is the body and not the product (which is "soft as a caress . . . exciting") that is saying "*Yes* to Romance."

The body language of high fashion is something that many of Arbus's subjects have mastered: they know how to tip the torso forward to display their breasts; how to apply lipstick to widely smiling lips and how to mold artificial eyebrows and eyelashes. They have learned the art of simulating a relaxed posture in a homelike environment and they know when leopard-printed clothing is in vogue and when it is appropriate to convert to "changeable ocelot spots."

Many of Arbus's critics have noticed the intensity of the collusion that seemed to exist between her and her subjects, and she herself spoke of the familiarity she experienced when photographing them. "There are always two things that happen," she claimed. "One is recognition and the other is that it's totally peculiar. But there's some sense in which I always identify with them."[13] To many people, this identification has seemed as if it were the key to some dark psychological proclivity in the artist. They seemed to want to know how a well-bred young woman from Park Avenue could feel kinship with these extreme, marginal people, and then to posit that these sideshow subjects expressed the photographer's own sense of marginality and psychic displacement.

While this may be true at one level, there is also a more direct way to understand Arbus's ease with them, and that is simply to notice that they have learned how to pose in a "fashionable" way. Whatever their life choices or sexual preferences, Arbus's subjects possessed a common language, or at least a familiar responsiveness: as they stood ready to display themselves in whatever guise pleased them, she, in turn, knew how to photograph their projected image. Another way to express this idea is to say that their encounters, no matter how singular to a middle-class audience, were already mediated by her familiarity with what was in *Vogue* or *Harper's Bazaar*. "Bazaar," a locus of display for selling merchandise, and "bizarre," the exotic or weird person or circumstance, were more alike than Arbus may have consciously discerned.

Why is it, then, that Arbus's photographs often seem so disquieting even when we recognize the coded behavior that they record? One reason that I return to in my own thinking is that they are testaments to the failure

Figure 5. Diane Arbus, "A naked man being a woman, N.Y.C. 1968."

Figure 6. Glamour, June 1948.

of "the vestimentary system," for they show us garments on bodies for which they are entirely unsuitable, and they reveal, through their settings, that possessing fashionable attire does not lead to romance, security, or social esteem. In short, these photographs expose the falseness of the equation: off the rack = off the wrack. In Arbus's post-1956 work, made artifacts (which Elaine Skarry eloquently refers to in another context as "perceived-pain-wished-gone")[14] clearly do not lead to beneficient states of affairs but remain themselves: wired bras or wing-tipped glasses or leopard-skin dresses that sit on tired or flabby or sexually confused flesh without securing the alteration in circumstances that the fashion images of these artifacts had promised. One of the deep ironies of fashion photography is that it seems to tell us that we can escape from the fate of our own corporeality, that we have at hand tools adequate to the task of self-transformation. Pain can be "wished-gone" and then we can "make-it-gone." In fashion photography, the clothing seems almost to circumvent the body and to point directly to the glamorous aspects of the world which will open to those who dress well. One of the most profound truths of Arbus's later work is its demonstration of the extent to which our bodies remain beyond craft.

What we experience as disturbing, then, is not simply the photographer's choice of subject; we are not made uncomfortable by the outcast status of Arbus's circus performers, transvestites, and retarded people per se. Rather, we are shocked by the conjunction of their physicality and their desires. We see in them both a spiritual investment in artifice and, despite this, a failure to remake their images—a failure that is obscured in fashion photography because of the beauty—or at least the nonintrusiveness—of the models' bodies and the contrived nature of the photographic settings. What may seem suitable on a slender, well-proportioned woman seems radically unsuitable on a squat senior citizen with eyeglasses or on a retarded person, and certainly on a man in drag. Yet all of them are announcing through their "get-up" the wish to materialize their imaginations through clothing. They are no different from Arbus's previous fashion models except for the (now) obvious discrepancy between the interior of their consciousness—made manifest through the cut of their garments and their choices of fabrics and accessories and makeup—and their literal embodiment. The writing of fashion has failed to erase or alter the anterior writing of the flesh itself.

It is this exposure of intention-plus-the-impotence-of-intention that I see as the heart of Arbus's post-1956 photographic project. She forces us to see the basic mystery of sentience: the hoped-for sharability of experience that is represented by our "guise" or by the garments we choose as projections of our desires and the genetic endowment which traps us in isolation. As Elaine Skarry has said, "The notion that everyone is alike by having a body and that what differentiates one person from another is the soul or intellect or personality can mislead one into thinking that the body is shared and the other part is private when exactly the opposite is the case."[15] When someone is photographed wearing a decent white blouse with a button-down collar on a college campus, the image directs our attention to the appropriateness of conjoining modest feminine attire with the ease and achievement that the campus represents. When triplets wear white blouses with button-down collars, their bodies disrupt the cultural equation (clothing = worldly circumstances) and make us face the very frontiers of culture. It is not that they lack fashion, but that, being fashionable, they show us the place beyond which fashion, as a cultural system, cannot go. No one can share, even with the help of looking at their chosen appearance, the mystery of genetic sameness multiplied. Like so many of Arbus's other subjects, they speak to us from a place that is beyond culture's ability to signify even while they participate in common signifying systems.

Arbus was, I think, obsessed by this mystery of embodiment. It was what she alluded to when she said, "There's a quality of legend about freaks. Like a person in a fairy tale who stops you and demands that you answer a riddle."[16] And her photographs extend this "riddle" to her viewers. They confront us with a "site of wounding," with the irreparable "damage" of the body's isolate existence in time and space and hence with knowledge that we normally categorize as private or stigmatized.

Fashion photography leads us away from this privacy by emphasizing the power of cultural codes to direct our imaginations into the sharable world of made artifacts. They speak eloquently about our imagination's desire to extend itself into the world of commonly understood cultural meanings and through them to participate in recognizable signs of beauty and esteem. The images in *Vogue* and *Glamour* appeal because they acknowledge our longing for Otherness and tell us that it can be appeased.

The photographed bodies of Arbus's stylish freaks give the lie to the cultural strategy of these magazines. They speak back to and deconstruct their facile manipulation of desire. If we think of culture as a whole as humanity's collective "perceived-pain-wished-gone," then Arbus's images teach us by visual signs the same lessons that are taught by injury or any other kind of physical aversiveness: the extent to which individual sentience remains beyond the power of cultural intervention. "And that's what all this is a little bit about," Arbus said, "that it's impossible to get out of your skin and into somebody else's. That somebody else's tragedy is not the same as your own."[17]

Notes

1. Diane Arbus, *Diane Arbus* (Millerton, N.Y.: Aperture, 1972).
2. Diane Arbus, *Diane Arbus: Magazine Work* (Millerton, N.Y.: Aperture, 1984).
3. Arbus, *Diane Arbus,* 5.
4. Patricia Botsworth, *Diane Arbus: A Biography* (New York: Avon, 1984), 12.
5. John Berger, *About Looking* (New York: Pantheon, 1980), 33.
6. See Roland Barthes, *The Fashion System* (New York: Hill and Wang, 1983).
7. Botsworth, *Diane Arbus,* 80.
8. Thomas Southall, "The Magazine Years, 1960–1971," in *Diane Arbus: Magazine Work,* 153.
9. Ibid., 153.
10. Arbus, *Diane Arbus,* 5.
11. *Harper's Bazaar,* June 1948.
12. *Vogue,* March 1960.
13. Arbus, *Diane Arbus,* 1.
14. Elaine Skarry, *The Body in Pain* (New York: Oxford, 1985).
15. Ibid., 256.
16. Arbus, *Diane Arbus,* 3.
17. Ibid., 15.

Mary Ann Caws

*a*n Erotics of Representation:

Fashioning the Icon with Man Ray

> Photography has invented a new method: to space, it presents the image exceeding it. . . . When everything called art had gotten really rheumatic, the photographer lit thousands of candles with his lamp, and the sensitive paper absorbed by degrees the black taken from some ordinary things. He had invented the strength of an illumination at once tender, cool, and greater than all the constellations destined to our visual pleasure. A deformation mechanical and precise, unique and fitting is made smoothly, filtered like a mane of hair by a comb of light.
>
> **—Tristan Tzara, Preface to Man Ray, *Les Champs déliciency*, original album of photographs**

To fashion a recognizable and memorable icon, you have to get a conscious handle on the object. Among fashion photographers, Man Ray, the American who turned himself into a French fashion and fashioner, is distinguished by his postmodernist intelligence and manner. The knowing wit of his photographs, as well as his original conception of remaking the model for the viewer, demands—as I have argued elsewhere—a certain complicity of the person modeling.[1] But it also demands a *specific* reformulation of the art of observing, which I want to take up here and now. We are looking, in these pictures, at an icon-maker skilled in such handling of representation; it is our own looking skill we have to refashion.

Man Ray's signature way of fashioning and iconizing does not concern only the pose of the model, but also, and even in particular, how it refers out beyond itself. I want to examine this reference in several different images: what is so crafty about Man Ray's representations and references, how the artful is made to look natural, and how the natural takes on an artful manner. In each case I am considering here, the references both implied and evident transform the pictured object into a subject of interested contemplation, representing more than it initially did.

Manipulative Handling

Man Ray's handling is "manipulative" in the most literal way: hands-on arranging (*manus:* "the hand") of each image, which, as Tzara points out, "exceeds the space" it takes up. Only the first kind I will discuss bears any resemblance to what we are likely to think of as the "fashion photograph," being an enhancement of the figure chosen by a prop that is specifically glamorizing. Thus the object and person are combined into one fashioned and fashionable thing.[2]

Take, for example, Juliet Man Ray wearing different sorts of headdress or necklace, the prop, however minimal, emblematic of beauty itself. By isolating some minimal prop and stressing it to its limit, Man Ray manages to combine simplicity with excess. Juliet may be wearing a Marajo hat, her face framed by it and by the exotic flavor it imparts: the caption, probably put upon it by one of its collectors, explains about the headdress that its straw and pieces of shell were taken from the Marajo Indians, living on an island shaped like an egg in the mouth of a snake that is the Amazon River. "The island is larger than France," continues the caption, and "these people are the greatest artists of the region." So her beauty is enhanced by the art of the *other,* representative now both of geographical region and of local art. The human is adorned by the natural, reconstructed for this specific enhancement.

In a superb picture of this type, simply entitled *Juliet with Scarf and Necklace* (figure 1), Juliet's outline is blurred, and bent back on the diagonal, as if in action; we are not looking just at the photographer's embellishment of a human figure, but at an emblem of beauty beribboned and yet free. Streaks of light run strangely and becomingly up and down her body, and her feet are encased in beribboned sandals; yet the whole composition is

e:
se
of

*. Juliet, Nude (1945), gelatin silver print, 13¾ × 10¹¹⁄₁₆
f the J. Paul Getty Museum, California. Copyright
'ADAGP-Paris/ARS-USA.*

d from
fashion–
so highly
to hint at
the whole
arge of the
raud used to
ature is quite

otograph; they
ke a body part
ge but strangely
uite naturally, just
ence.³ From there,
Mirror floating by
elf.
e recognize instantly
ying objects, welding
nis picturing of Picabia

so indicative of freedom that there is no sense of being tied down, even by the glamour of the image.

In the painterly *Juliet, Nude* (figure 2), Juliet stands sideways to the viewer, graceful in the double drapery of the towel around her hair and the piece of clothing held in front of her, extending below her left arm. The white towel is knotted loosely behind, like a gigantic ribbon whose ends fall down her back. The construction is quoting from Ingres' bathing nudes, turned away from us in the same way. The sight line flows from the turbaned towel down the back and behind the slight protrusion of the shoulder blade, forward to the draped cloth in front of the figure, in a serpentine sweep at once liquid and "natural," slightly swaying toward the front. Nudity, drapery, modesty are knotted together in a graceful twist like the towel. The picture reads like a classic icon of a bathing beauty. In one of these prints, a silver print gorgeously, richly illuminated ("treated") with colored pencils, the knot of the white towel is breathtakingly delicate, giving the natural nudity a majestic stance.

Many other photographs of Juliet pluck their adornments from natur she might wear snail earrings and a floral motif for a hat; but of all th pictures, it is the toweled nude turned away that serves as the very ico naturalness.

HIGH FASHIONING

When the image is rendered in stark isolation, an emblem divorc what it emblematizes, we are looking at iconization, with a high ing of surprise. The point would be that Man Ray's signature is visible in any case that in order to *do* a photograph, he has onl the slightest give and take between the model and the world an thing bears looking at, bearing also in itself a metonymic c whole. He needs no props to bring about what Antonin A call the "miraculizing" of what the artist touches. The sig simply: "Man Ray Fecit." Man Ray Did This.

So, for instance, Lee Miller's lips will take up an entire p exist without the rest of her, a metonymy of herself, sailing across the sky if we look long enough. In a stra predictable transformation, recognizable, they float by as if some red velvet sofa were to take up celestial resid it goes on, famously, like the eye of Magritte's *Fals* ith clouds across it, to stand for Surrealist vision its Man Ray's crafting of the photographic image, in which he sticks the figures to their identi h bizarre overtones. Thus, we remember and his steering wheel, or then Méret Oppenheim standing nude beside her printing wheel, with printer's ink on her hands, as if she were printing her own figure, fashioning her own image.[4] She is wielded by the picture-maker even as she seems to be printing herself. Tzara is pictured with his monocle, Duchamp with his larger glass: all these images with the identifying object serve as instant identifications, as style itself.

When the observer bears in mind all these instant identifications, Man Ray's magnificent and minimal constructions of and with Kiki de Montparnasse, Lee Miller, or Juliet Man Ray take on an entirely different mode of self-presentation. They are already inscribed in a body, a corpus used to being imposed upon, read against, fashioned.

FASHIONING THE NATURAL

A picture of Kiki de Montparnasse with ferns (figure 3) manages to *unite* the natural object and the female body, as if they were speaking to each other. Kiki posing nude among the ferns and grass, with the shadow of

Figure 3. Man Ray, Kiki, Nude (1927), gelatin silver print, 6¹³/₁₆ × 5¹/₁₆ inches. Collection of the J. Paul Getty Museum, California. Copyright 1929, Man Ray Trust/ADAGP-Paris/ARS-USA.

the fern against her arm like a bracelet above the elbow, laughing, and another fern playing a fig leaf, feathering gently over her left thigh. A protrusion of phallic rock sticks out to the right of her head. . . . Like a laughing Botticelli, with leaves in her mouth, joyous.[5] This joyous outdoor Kiki embodies nature itself, or the myth of naturalness, loud with sheer animal joy. She is fashioned here in a way both primitive and knowing, and makes a direct appeal.[6]

So far, none of these images reads like an imposition of the photographer, but rather, like the conversations of body and surround, like the photo of Henry Miller and a nude posing behind him, who has the outline of a leaf with its striations, but transparent, over each eye, the nose, the forehead. Made into an African statue, she is as primitive and cultured as Kiki among the ferns, bare in the forest.

Between Nature and Art

Man Ray's treatment of Elsa Schiaparelli in a draped white dress with short-croppped jacket of feathers and a light cast on her short-cropped feathery hair (figure 4) works a transformative magic: this bird/woman is caught in profile, the feathers of hair and jacket fluttering downward to the drape upon the dress, as she looks away from the camera and into space. Like a fleeting object of cultural desire, she is constructed as so wrapped in feathers that she is about to take flight, a creator of fashion taking off into nature.

Charged Objects: Illuminations and Impositions

Entirely different in feeling is the image of Kiki posed in one of the frames for *Retour à la raison,* her bare torso striped with the reflection from the curtain by the window.[7] The sense is both natural, but like an animal—tiger-striped—and cultural, since the reflection is of a constructed object. This woman is made animal by the imposition of the photographer's design.

We might compare with this form of imposition one no less striking, that of Duchamp with the frame of his glass placed over his face. Just as striking, in the series of photographs called *Electricité,* there is laid over a nude female with a hazy surface, standing in a bathroom, a sharp white tubular line, its very distinctness outlined against the softness of her skin as it is pictured. This is handling with cruelty in the sense of Antonin

Figure 4. Man Ray, Elsa Schiaparelli *(1934), gelatin silver print, 4¹/₁₆ × 2¾ inches. Collection of the J. Paul Getty Museum, California. Copyright 1936, Man Ray Trust/ADAGP-Paris/ARS-USA.*

Artaud's "Theatre of Cruelty," part of his *Theatre and Its Double,* since it reads like an imposition of necessity.

In another photograph of the same *Electricité* series (figure 5), also from 1931, a few stripes of white of different thickness are projected—like tubes of neon light—across two nude female bodies. This quite special juxtaposition—one whiter and smaller, in front, fitting against a darker, larger, taller one with just her shoulder lit—together with the electric *impositions* of a highly erotic kind, set up the already charged feeling of the scene. The head of the smaller body is turned away, just the neck showing its arch above the breasts. The current would seem to run between the two bodies, both charged with this bright ribboning, like an affair of love and light.

The romanticism of electricity is emphasized by Man Ray's accent, in other photographs, of the glamour of light—for example, a light bulb in

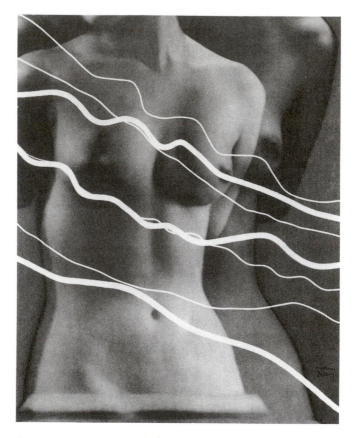

Figure 5. Man Ray, Electricity *(1931), photogravure, 10¼ × 8¹⁄₁₆ inches. Collection of the J. Paul Getty Museum, California. Copyright 1931, Man Ray Trust/ADAGP-Paris/ARS-USA.*

the sky shedding white flakes, in the form of a constellation. This adornment of the natural by the electrical is charged to the limit: what is iconized is both the body and the lighting, like some reference of photography to itself.

This universe speaks loudly and high of relations in the surrealist world and framework, of the delight at bodily exhibition, even of the bodies of objects—it is fashioned carefully, and contained without scandal. There is no apparent struggle between model and fashioner, or between the objects pictured. Impositions and juxtapositions are made, complied with, and whatever resistance there might be is not allowed to be in evidence.

A naked body is visible under the left side of a glass circle, part of a lamp. The play is again upon illumination, although when we first look at the body, not reading the shape of the translucent outer circle, just taking pleasure in the play of glass against flesh, translucent layers against dewy surface, until we realize it is indeed part of a lamp. Part of the joy of reading the sometimes complicated images of Man Ray is the realization we come to about them, slowly. They *develop* in our minds, their artifice becoming natural in our view.[8]

Icons Posed and Wrapped

The celebration of the female image calls for multiple techniques. One sometimes has the feeling that Man Ray used them all, during his periods of genius. Of which he had many.

One of the most successful glorifications of a female face and its features is the implicit comparison with the religious: thus, Genica Athanasiou will be pictured with her head thrown back, her black hair gleaming against the light backdrop, for all the world like some Byzantine icon (figure 6). We can almost see her head outlined as with a halo, her face solemn and

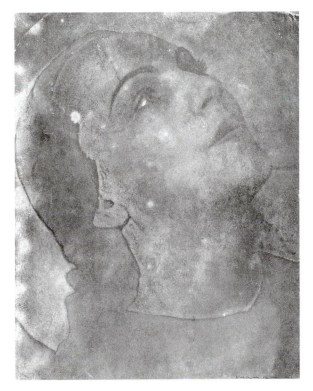

Figure 6. Man Ray, Mlle. Anthanasiou (1933), three-color carbon transfer print, 10⅝ × 8³⁄₁₆ inches. Collection of the J. Paul Getty Museum, California. Copyright 1935, Man Ray Trust/ADAGP-Paris/ARS-USA.

gorgeously turned to the side, not to face us. Worshippers do not want to, do not need to see face on. The many photographs of Genica Athanasiou, whether her head is lifted on the diagonal or thrown back, always capture that slightly haughty expression, sanctifying her with her own pose, as representative of art as Kiki laughing outside is of nature.

More poses, easy to make and take. Nusch Eluard was posed in 1935 by Man Ray against a background so soft it feels, to the sight, like velvet. It was for Eluard's poems called *Facile,* or *Easy.* Love seemed easy then, and the body was chiseled against the ground. Easy, and carved in deep. We grew used to that; such is the carry-over expectation from the lovely "easy" pose that when we see Rosa Covarrubias sitting in front of her mirror, a large spit-curl perfectly in place, dressed only in her slip (itself slipping off one shoulder), and with a towel casually caught between her legs, all the other easy and beloved images come back, with their own accessory objects. Eve with a scrap of a towel, just a suggestion of a suggestion. But bringing all the others back creates a network of Man Ray images, remembrances of his eye and hand, that do the work of the narrative. Juliet even is posed like this sometimes, a blonde wig over her hair, nude, with a transparent cloth between her legs.

It is not all easy. A ghastly and no less iconic imposition comes from 1936, appropriately called *Restored Venus* (figure 7). She is just a torso, wrapped in heavy cord, packaged like something Christo would wrap, immobilized like something out of the Marquis de Sade, for beating or then sending like one of Derrida's *Envois. The lady is very smooth;* yet she has, of course, no head about her and cannot protest, no legs and cannot flee, no arms and cannot take revenge.[9] She is in fact a statue, which does not reconcile the female viewer to the cording of her body.

No one is posing here as a natural. The reference this time is to the Venus of Milo and the Victory of Samothrace; they are not yet restored to life, but the rope scaffolding is there for restoration. Tied up, and ready to go.

FASHIONING THE READER

We are led into the iconization of the image, as it is posed and imposed on, wrapped ready to go. As happens with the model, we as onlookers are seduced into collaboration with the photographer's sight. What, in Man Ray's pictures, captures the onlooker as well as the model? It is, on occasion, just the sense of that collusion and collaboration that is ongoing in the image itself. As an early example, take the frequent collaboration of Man Ray and Marcel Duchamp, developing in 1920.

Figure 7. Man Ray, **Restored Venus** *(1936), gelatin silver print, 6½ × 4½ inches. Collection of the J. Paul Getty Museum, California. Copyright 1938, Man Ray Trust/ADAGP-Paris/ARS-USA.*

Against the ascetic, unsmiling, and beautiful face of Marcel Duchamp is superimposed the white frame of his Large Glass (figure 8). His eyes look out through the rectangular shape, as though imprisoned by his own glass. Who has chosen the pose here? Whose *is* the imposition here? It is as if Duchamp's *Glass* had been imposed upon its creator, used by Man Ray to frame him. But he is plainly willing, as he collaborates in the pose of himself. In another shot of the same frame and framer, Duchamp is lying down, his hands grasping the hemisphere of the glass in repose; Man Ray then cuts out that image, carefully cutting around the hands, placing it upon a piece of paper, in a further cropping and collage.

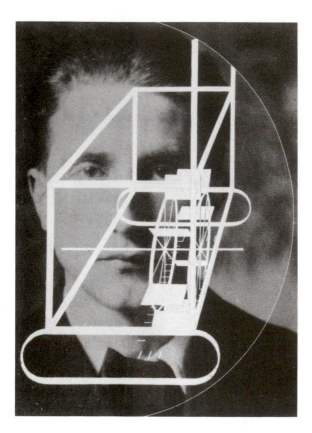

Figure 8. Man Ray, Duchamp with his "Large Glass" (1917–1923), gelatin silver print, 6⅝ × 4⅝ inches. Collection of the J. Paul Getty Museum, California. Copyright 1925, Man Ray Trust/ADAGP-Paris/ARS-USA.

Man Ray's well-known photograph of Marcel Duchamp with a star cut out in the center of his hair can be seen to imply ironically that this is a Star; it also says that Man Ray was here with his camera, one star photographing another. Already in Man Ray's shot of Marcel, there is a larger-than-life characterization of a figure as myth, of a great conceptual artist as subject/object.

The case is especially complicated in the doubling of the character of Marcel Duchamp as Duchamp in drag, physically and mentally; as Rrose Sélavy, always photographed by Man Ray.[10] All three Rrose Sélavy shots of 1920 have a lot to say. "Eros is life," reads her name, as she poses in various fashions, impersonated by Marcel, most remarkably as a high-fashion model behatted and perfumed, in the classic pose of *Marcel Duchamp as Rrose Sélavy* (figure 9). Here, as in the other pictures, Marcel EROS ITSLIFE himself/herself appears in drag, heavy circles around the eyes, thick eyebrows, and a hat bordered with a design easily describable as chic. There have not been many more seductive poses—something about the offness of the image is instantly attractive. Marcel's wig is

*Figure 9. Man Ray,
Rrose Sélavy (1920),
gelatin silver print,
8¹¹/₁₆ × 6¹⁵/₁₆ inches.
Collection of the J.
Paul Getty Museum,
California. Copyright
1922, Man Ray
Trust/ADAGP-Paris/
ARS-USA.*

rough, and the continuity of texture between its rough hair and the hat border is to be *felt*. The light falls on the back of the fur, and on the cheek directly above gives the impression of luxury and of ease, slightly leaning to the side—as if it were not quite as seductive to be straight. The insolence of "her" gaze unsettles, beside her blonde wig.

More than unsettling, this image is an icon of disquiet. Between her little finger and the others, there is an erotic gap, and even the fur collar of her coat lies a trifle sideways. Things are tipped, unbalanced, insolently begging to be questioned. This is a deliberately mystifying Marcel(le), transfigured into a Rrose. Her ambiguities posed here resemble those of Duchamp, as witnessed by his celebrated door at 13 rue Larrey that opened out and in at the same time. If you closed it here, it opened there, disproving Musset's statement, albeit a theatrical one: "A door has to be opened or closed."

Marcel/Marcelle did not, as Rrose Sélavy, have to be in drag or not; she was, in Belle Haleine, for example, with the sultry face and necklace, with the perfume bottle opening to the right and slightly protruding erotically, sensually, already a quintessence of Eau de Violette instead of Eau de Toilette, veiled and watery, like something shimmering in moiré. The edges of the stopper are striped, like hair elegant on either side, and the face looks lovingly at us. In this sultry perfumed scene, even the letters of RS are reversed, Eros and Sélavy leaning on each other back to back, in one of the steps of a frozen tango: to the beat of Eros That Is Life.

Man Ray's most celebrated photography always retains about it this sense of ambiguity, of pose chosen by photographer and willing sitter, capturing both of them within in a collaboration itself seductive of the onlooker, forcibly in cahoots with the pair, or then left out entirely. The out-of-sight references are often what draws the onlooker into the picture by implication: as seen here, the myths of nature (birds and country landscapes), and art (ancient statues and Byzantine icons), and early on, of doubleness, in gender and representation. The point of Man Ray's photographs is not an *excluding* or *exclusive* point: it is rather an implication beyond itself, into a another space. Knowledgeable viewing, being, as it were, in cahoots with the photographer, is preferable to being cropped out.

Man Ray fashioned into icons his imagination modeling itself through his posing figures: Rrose Sélavy is the height of a fiction *à deux,* the double creation of Marcel and Man. What Man Ray created was more than style—it was a whole erotics of representation, in which the observer is involved.[11] In his associations, isolations, and impositions, he not only iconizes the subject, but refashions seeing itself.

NOTES

My warmest thanks to the Getty Center for Art History and the Humanities for their welcome and their help during the development of this photographic essay; in particular, to Gordon Baldwin of the Photographic Study Center, for his discussions of fashion photography, and to Jacklyn Burns of the Getty Museum's Rights and Reproduction Center.

1. See "Ladies Shot and Painted: Female Embodiment in Surrealist Art," in Mary Ann Caws, *The Art of Interference,* (Princeton: Princeton University Press, 1989), 111–134. This essay is also available in Susan Suleiman, ed., *The Female Body in Western Art* (Cambridge: Harvard University Press, 1985, 1986), 262–287, and in *The Expanding Discourse: Feminism and Art History,* ed. Norma Broude and Mary D. Garrard (New York: HarperCollins, 1992), 381–395. I do not deal in this essay with the observer's collaboration in the erotics of representation, which is my topic here.

2. Often the object exists without the person, and with a glittering presence. Such depersonalized glitter emanates from a metal bracelet with no wrist inside, and a superb metal necklace with points glittering but no neck within it. Another rayograph shows the necklace in white, with the same points: "Jewel for Elsa Trio-

let," it reads, and the date is 1928. It is the jewel we see, and not Elsa. *What matters is craft*. Elsewhere, sequins float in some liquid, attached to no material, simply twinkling like little dots, needing nothing but themselves. This is high-fashion solipsism—the ornament glistening alone, in personless fashion. These images disturb: they are perhaps the best testimony to Man Ray the Surrealist.

3. This sofa, like two velvet lips to sit on, originally adorned the house of the Surrealist collector Edward James.

4. In "Ladies Shot and Painted: Female Embodiment in Surrealist Art," I analyze the problematics of the female pose in surrealism specifically, with Man Ray and Magritte's renderings in particular. This disquieting work is one of the key reference points, in both its cropped and original versions. It is no simple spinning wheel we are concerned with here, and this is no ordinary spinning of a yarn.

5. Dated as 1927, the image in fact likely comes from an earlier moment, since their relationship ended in 1926.

6. A rainier outdoor Kiki was filmed by Man Ray for the poem of Desnos called *L'Etoile de mer,* where—through a filter—we see her face under a cloche hat, as she walks with a companion along a stream.

7. For the background of this shot, see Billy Kluver and Julie Martin, *Kiki's Paris: Artists and Lovers 1900–1930* (New York: Abrams, 1989). The image of her body striped with shadows "was combined with images of ordinary objects like salt and pepper grains, pins, and thumbtacks placed directly on the unexposed film in May Ray's 'rayofilm,' *The Return to Reason*" (24).

8. Man Ray was fully conscious of his artifacts/artifice. About one of the rayographs of the 1921–1928 series, containing a lamp, one of a pair of dice, and the top of a cello, the whole bathed in radiance, he remarks to Nusch Eluard when he sends it: "In this little corner," he says, "there are all sorts of games, and objects to pass the time when you are alone—even the Queen of Spades is hidden there, and comes out of hiding only when her double comes with a slick transparent umbrella, like a peeled peach" (signed "Man"). The beautiful features of Nusch as the Queen of Spades form one part of the quadrilateral.

9. In "Seeing the Surrealist Woman: We Are a Problem," my introduction to *Surrealism and Women,* ed. Mary Ann Caws, Rudolf Kuenzli, and Gwen Raaberg (Cambridge: MIT Press, 1991), I analyze in similar terms ("Headless. And also footless. . . . Give them their head, they had one") Man Ray's untitled image of a woman's torso tightly wrapped in moiré silk, her arms akimbo.

10. In the name of Rrose Sélavy, Robert Desnos the Surrealist poet also wrote some of his poems—she really got around.

11. Some of Man Ray's best critics show him as creator, as hunter of the image. I am thinking of a text by Timothy Baum, for *Man Ray's Paris Portraits 1921–39,* for the Middendorf Gallery, called *Cachet Man Ray*. Hide Man Ray, "cachez Man Ray," hide Man Ray . . . and an album of his photographs for *Vanity Fair* in 1922, called, significantly, *Les Champs délicieux*—like *Les Champs magnétiques,* that first surrealist text by Philippe Soupault and André Breton.

Maureen Turim

Seduction and Elegance:

The New Woman of Fashion

in Silent Cinema

Long before she emerged as a "flapper" in the late twenties or adopted the streamlined elegance of thirties, the "modern woman" of fashion made initial appearances in earlier silent cinema. She dressed for the part in elegant clothing whose connotations came to include a self-conscious sexual desirability, a knowing seduction. This paper traces the history and the permutations of that fashionable entrance of feminine modernity. I focus on American cinema from 1902 through 1926, from the first references to modern fashion, through the "Gibson Girl" image, to more self-assured and even avant-garde models of female sexual modernity. I place this analysis in an international context, for the social changes in female fashion and sexuality in the United States are intricately interwoven with those of Europe.

When looking at America at the turn of the century, the question of "The Victorian" imposes itself, for it is common to speak of this period as one of transition from Victorian mores and fashions to more modern ones, culminating with the Jazz Age, the Roaring Twenties, and the flapper as images and evidences of transcendent modernity. In this formulation, earlier Puritan ethics and moral presumptions are revitalized in the nineteenth century by middle-class British values. Yet we might well ask, what do we mean by the "Victorian" as a set of values or influences on turn-of-the-century American culture? We are hampered in answering this question by the relative paucity of comparative study of Victorian British and nineteenth-century American culture, although such study would seem necessary; similarities are more assumed than interrogated, and often influence is considered unilaterally that of Britain upon the United States, rather than the inverse. "The Victorian," in this large and vague sense, means the "cult of true womanhood," defined as a proscriptive domestic sphere, and a concomitant ideology stressing the pursuit of propriety, decorum, self-sacrifice, and social as well as maternal nurturing.[1] This often translates into the Victorian being seen as a repressive or censoring force exerted over sexuality and freedom of expression.

In "Modern Sexuality and the Myth of Victorian Repression," Christina Simmons directs us to Michel Foucault's *The History of Sexuality,* in which he critiques the normative view of Victorian repression; with irony, Foucault describes the "received idea" of the Victorian:

> But twilight soon fell upon . . . [the] bright day, [when bodies made a display of themselves] followed by the monotonous nights of the Victorian bourgeoisie. Sexuality was carefully confined; it moved into the home. The conjugal family took custody of it and absorbed it into the serious function of reproduction. On the subject of sex, silence became the rule. The legitimate and procreative couple laid down the law. The couple imposed itself as model, enforced the norm, safeguarded the truth, and reserved the right to speak while retaining the principle of secrecy. . . . [P]roper demeanor avoided contact with other bodies, and verbal decency sanitized one's speech.[2]

In presenting this norm, Foucault acknowledges some truth to it, as well as exceptions others have made, such as Steven Marcus in his work on the "other Victorians."[3] Foucault's work does not allow us to take the "repressive hypothesis" for granted. No longer can we see the nineteenth century as simply an age of sexual repression, but one in which regulation indicates a preoccupation with sexuality. As Simmons states, "The Victorian prescription of restrained sexual activity and modest sexual speech did not mean the absence of 'repression' of sexuality but rather focused psychic attention on it."[4] In her view, the myth of Victorian repression in the U.S. context is in part created by "white liberal commentators on sexual life in the 1920s and 1930s" who wished "to describe old behaviors and shape new ones."[5]

Many paradoxes and ambiguities surround such hypotheses. Scholars are now finding it increasingly hard to separate the history of a period from the readings and received ideas passed on in historical writings of that period and the years immediately following. As concerns women and questions of gender, the paradoxes surrounding this history are even greater. This age of "repressive" sexual mores and euphemistic polite speech is associated with female empowerment, in relation not only to Victoria's reign itself but also to the increasing influence of women in nine-teenth-century society. Women, both in general social interactions and in social reform movements, are seen as furthering repressive mores, at the same time that their place within the home is being idealized in Victorian essays and literature. When you add to this picture the irony that many women both in their fiction writing and their political work were begin-ning to criticize these roles, the clarity of the picture of Victorian woman's sexual attitudes dissipates, and no singular, unified image emerges.[6]

Even after calling the notion of Victorian repression into question, Simmons returns to such a phrase as "By the early twentieth century, Victorian conventions based on these sexual concepts [of continence and moderation] were breaking down," thus at least wavering on her own earlier confidence in this same essay on Foucault's proclamation of the myth of repression.[7] Foucault himself never addresses the appropriateness of "Victorian" as a term for a general history of sexuality that would in-clude not only the United States but, presumably, all of continental Eu-rope. Simmons follows him and many other historians in using the term "Victorian" for American nineteenth-century culture.[8] The slipperiness of historical and geographical reference in this generalized use of the Victo-rian is not often noted. So even if we follow Foucault and Simmons, sub-stituting a differential means of regulation for the repressive hypothesis, we need to ask if a distinctive formation, or mentality, determining such regulation in Victorian Britain remains. We are still left with the connected problems of how the nineteenth century refined this regulation to produce the impression of restrictive norms, and how the term "Victorian" drifted away from its designation of a period and a nation to mean a general evacuation of the display and self-consciousness of sexual desire from so-cial space. It seems that much of this is traceable to assumptions about Puritan values and practices that are themselves erroneous, and that link Great Britain and Colonial North America as common puritan cultures.[9] Obviously the terms "Puritan" and "Victorian" have become a shorthand code for sexual repression. In questioning them, I wish to look at how assumptions of singular, pervasive value systems are misleading both his-torically and theoretically, leading us to read periods of complex social upheaval in mores and culture as simple substitutions of one set of values for another "modern" one. It is toward this goal that such writers as Fou-cault and Simmons have paved the way.

For those of us interested in fashion and its implicit repression, regula-tion, expression, or stimulation of attitudes toward women and sexuality, Foucault's study of sexuality raises yet another problem. Intriguingly, it neglects both the discourses about and the material manifestations of fashion. We have to look elsewhere to gauge how the determination of women's appearance was seen as an attempt to define the social function of women.[10] In so doing, we see that much remains to be investigated in the assumed repressive notion of "the Victorian."

In fashion terms, the Victorian meant the covered female body, clothed in markers of a femininity that masks its sexuality. Practically, this entailed the predominance of plain neutral colors—black, navy blue, tan, white—high collars and long sleeves, usually adorned by discreet lace. Clothing is less embellishment than uniform, composed of either a shirtwaist, a dark skirt and white blouse, or a suit. Victorian dress inverts the color restrictions of sumptuary laws, as if the bourgeoisie were at last reclaiming an ironic justice by relegating the upper class to its prior outcast palette; upper-class status is now associated with dark, neutral or subdued colors, and white. The epitome of such decorum is the fashion set by Queen Victoria's mourning dress.

Shirtwaist development is a way of understanding the conjunctions of fashion, industrialization, and women's movements. According to Nancy Wolloch,

> The shirtwaist business was a relative newcomer to the garment trade. Starting only in the 1890's, waist making developed rapidly after 1900. Its growth was connected to another development, the rise of the woman office worker. The shirtwaist was the emblem and uniform of the new white-collar woman wage earner—the salesgirl, stenographer, switchboard operator, and office clerk, as well as the schoolteacher. Similar to a man's shirt, but of thinner cloth, the shirtwaist was usually pleated in front, with a row of tucks, and buttoned in the back. The shirtwaist dress, made by the same manufacturers combined the blouse with a long dark skirt.[11]

Significantly, five million American women were wage earners by the turn of the century, according to Wolloch. This means one out of five women was employed, a quarter of them in manufacturing; half of these were employed in the manufacture of cloth and clothing, including shoes, gloves, hats, stockings, and collars, primarily as machine operators, trimmers, and finishers. If women's use in production in the garment industry grows in parallel with women's role in consuming fashion, it is not just a case of working-class women producing luxury goods for the upper class, as much artisanal manufacture had been. Mass production turns workers into consumers; even in Lewis Hine's photographs of women workers in the sweatshops, we see the women dressed in proper attire. The 1909 shirtwaist strike photograph of AFL president Samuel Gompers addressing strikers and sympathizers at Cooper Union shows women (most likely the upper-class reformers who had started the Women's Trade Union League) in the foreground wearing the elaborate feathered hats of the period, and all women in shirtwaists and suits. This strike is a major milestone in both women's and labor history for precisely the coalition it mobilized, although the settlements produced mixed results.

Another way of understanding the social context of late nineteenth century fashion is to see in what ways Victoria is drawn as a model in America. In examining the function of the woman's magazine *Godey's Lady's Book,* Mary Ryan suggests how direct reference to the Queen herself shapes an American ideology of womanhood confined to its separate sphere, and an ideology of gendered social roles. She quotes Godey's editorial pronouncement that "Victoria we consider the representative of the moral and intellectual influence which woman by her nature is formed to exercise," although the magazine envisioned women ruling only on "the throne of the heart," limited to domestic space. "From their little kingdoms, however, women were assured that they could dictate national morality, preside over the tone of American culture as surely as Victoria reigned in England."[12] We might look further into what this use of Victoria by the magazine implies about the indirect way in which Victorian social values are assimilated in the U.S.; the British monarch is appropriated as an oblique symbol of female power, in a manner that only indirectly speaks to her influence on British national culture as monarch. Masked, however, is any direct plea for American readers to adopt the values preached by Victorian etiquette manuals; the implicit argument for Victorian values is made without exploring the question of applicability of those values to quite different American contexts.

In *Gender and the Politics of History,* Joan Scott argues that historians have failed to look at the contradictions in and contestation of the cult of true womanhood.[13] Although this might be unfair to historians who have considered precisely how class and race affected the definition and application of principles of true womanhood, it suggests the continuing need for greater theoretical examination of the nineteenth century as a period marked by both competing discourses and regional variations. Even as Victorian dress seemed to demand a restriction of sartorial codes to moderation of decorative and suggestive elements, the introduction of various connotations of the elegant, the attractive, the beautiful, and even the seductive never left the world of fashion. Rather, fashion, especially in the latter half of the century, was simultaneously engaged in mass industrialization of its production and expansion of its markets into the growing middle and working classes.

We should remember that Parisian haute couture first began in the latter part of the nineteenth century; in fact, it can be said to have been born in the midst of the Second Empire when Worth opened the first design house. Worth made the kind of elaborate gowns that previously could be made only by dressmakers. In the Belle Époque, high fashion quickly became stratified as industry and the manufacture of the fashion house expanded. The most expensive and richly decorated crinoline gowns of the period, fitted to a severely corseted bodice, could only be bought by the rich. Yet frills and flounces also marked the Sunday dress of the European working class. Leisure time and class ascendancy became marked for women by the ability to adorn themselves as shining, floating billows sheltered by parasols.

In the United States this fashion was often ordered directly from Paris, but it was also copied by the American manufacturers who were emerging at the turn of the century. The copied dresses had looser bodices and were both less frilly and more tailored than the French originals, but they still retained connotations of grace and dignity. These dresses and the innovative skirt-and-blouse ensembles were retailed in department stores and even mail-order houses to middle-class and working women. Despite their more comfortable look, they continued to depend on the S-shaped corset. Thus, constriction remained the prerequisite for an image of dignity and respect.

We also need to consider how suffrage and women's rights advocates were themselves redesigning womanhood. In some instances, their discourses critiqued the "cult of true womanhood" and in others coincided with certain notions of propriety and respect, but for entirely different reasons. In both cases, this is evident in attitudes toward fashion. It was important for advocates of a sanctified domesticity to proscribe dress that befitted the restriction of women's roles to wife, mother, and social helpmate, eliminating any connotations of the overtly flirtatious. Some of the same sorts of changes in women's dress, however, were also advocated by early feminists seeking to emancipate women from subservience to male wishes. In Charlotte Perkins Gilman's 1915 magazine, *The Forerunner,* she writes, "The girl growing into youth and womanhood finds nothing to check the doll-and-baby influences, or the imitative instinct. . . . Only in dress, and almost wholly in the dress of women is it possible to dictate to half the adult population as if they were a lot of hypnotized dummies."[14] Gilman's disdain for fashion contrasts with Elizabeth Cady Stanton's earlier strategy of urging women "to be as bold in the arena of the discourse on the vindication of rights as they were in the display of their bodies."[15] From both early feminists we see a keen awareness that women's relationship to a fashion system has psychoanalytic and ideological implications for defining women's subjectivity. If American feminists have called at many points for fashion reform as part of a project of social and political liberation, rarely have they been as completely aligned with a repression of the beautiful, the elegant, and the seductive as the images film and media have created of their positions. If Griffith's 1913 film *The Reformers* visually mocks the plain dress of the Reform movement, actual photos of these groups show a much more stylish embodiment of female activists.

A third factor in stipulating limitations on the decorative and sensual embellishment of clothing was religious. The heritage of Puritanism survived in modified form in many of the dominant Protestant movements. Utopian movements all had their own version of plain dress, handmade, utilitarian apparel. In the period we are addressing, the Quakers and Mormons continued to exert considerable influence. New immigrant populations from eastern Europe and Italy often followed religious restrictions that echoed elements of American religious dress codes. There were also large-scale efforts to dress the Native American tribes in European clothes; this reveals how feathers, nudity, and face paint gathered their connotations of "primitive" and heathen, and how their return in the realm of middle-class fashion marks a "return of the repressed."

Still, American high society put a premium on elegance and embellishment. The elite of the antebellum South had developed dress, architectural, and furnishing codes into their own odd mix of rococo and neoclassicism, ordering much of their goods directly from France, Germany, and eastern Europe; clearly the articulation of such fashions had everything to do with slavery as an institution. For southern ruling-class whites to maintain their racist delineations, such signs of culture and refinement became useful in naturalizing constructed identities. After the Civil War, southern Reconstruction, meant to overturn these identities, gave way to their reconstitution. Both *The Clansman* and *Birth of a Nation,* as well as the book and film versions of *Gone With the Wind,* mythologize just such impulses to retain this splendor of corporeal decoration as emblematic of the pride of the white South. By transforming respectively Flora Cameron's leftover cotton bolls into an ersatz ermine collar, and the velvet draperies of the besieged and broken plantation, Tara, into Scarlett's ravishing day costume for her visit to Rhett in prison, both films present the individual heroine's refashioning of her former dress codes as a symbolic gesture at restoration of white supremacist pride, a gesture to be coupled with landowning and entrepreneurial hegemony.

For the northeastern United States, Continental Europe set the fashion, particularly France, but also the major cities of Italy, Germany and Austria with their emphasis on theater, opera, ballet and dining at restaurants and cafés, for which the middle and upper classes appeared appropriately and fashionably dressed. France and the rest of continental Europe played a large role in at first modifying, then overwhelming the restrictive aspects of Victorian dress and puritanical restraint. Elegance was the model; if, even in Britain, the Victorian age did not foreclose such bourgeois activities and the pursuit of quiet splendor, in America, the attraction of continental sophistication for an upwardly mobile bourgeoisie was enormous. In New York, Boston or Philadelphia, the society pages were preoccupied with fashion as the emblem of wealth throughout the half-century preceding World War I. With Edward VII's 1901 ascendance to the throne in Britain, his affinity for the Belle Époque in France helped end much of what lingered as an Anglo-American attempt to differentiate itself from the continent.

In film culture, the evidence of such ambivalences were coupled with a shifting class appeal that has been hotly debated in recent film histories. The attempt to gain for the nickelodeon an increasingly middle-class clientele is often cited as the shift from more bawdy and uncensored subjects to ones in which narrative and sartorial elegance replace the direct seduction of female display and even nudity. Although there is certainly a historically documented move toward upscale audiences, there is also some ambiguity about where and when the precise stages of the shift took place. From the beginning, what has been called the cinema of attractions depicted women in distinct costumes according to type. In U.S. nickelodeon views, women appeared in such roles as the artist's model and the belly dancer. For example, Edison's *Lola's Turkish Dance* features a costume that makes the most of kinetic vision through both pelvic thrusts and twirling gestures. To this we can contrast the street views where women are documented in their daily attire; here women appear in proper upper- and middle-class dress that marked its elegance for daywear with a long, detailed suit jacket and skirt and large hat. A less wealthy or warmer-wear version often comprised a long skirt coupled with a white blouse, impeccably detailed and pressed. But in these views, women are a part of the cityscape, taken for granted. It is intriguing that the early views do not include image-newsreels of women's fashion, which only begin in 1910.

When we meet the prostitute, we find her dressed in an only slightly gaudier version of the conventional attire, but this tendency toward overstatement is tempered by her lack of funds and access to fashion, because prostitution did not truly allow her to transcend her lower-class status. The similarity of her dress to that of other lower- and middle-class women is taken in charge by several film narratives. Two films that Noel Burch cites as representing the working-class immigrant, *The Female Crook and Her Easy Victim* (Biograph, 1905) and *How They Rob Men in Chicago* (Biograph, 1902), point out how disreputable women frequent social spaces virtually disguised.[16] In the former film, the Female Crook sitting at a table slips drugs into the drink of the man who joins her table at a cafe, then robs him once he has succumbed to the sleeping potion. In the latter film, the woman acts as seductive foil on the street, while her accomplice picks the interested victim's pockets. Despite their behavior, these women dress in modest and fashionable dress.

In contrast, the reputable poor are seen in traditional eastern European peasant dress, if not rags. This can be seen in the famous shot in Griffith's *Musketeers of Pig Alley* (1908), in which characters played by Lillian and Dorothy Gish cross each other on the street. Yet this shot reminds us that its like is relatively rare. The cinema of attractions sometimes documented the parts of the city its first viewers inhabited, but was more likely to show the more elegant areas to which they perhaps aspired, especially the changes in the cityscape that were identified with modernization and monumental architecture. For this reason, women about town are depicted in some version of modern and sophisticated attire.

With the development of longer narratives, costuming became crucial and distinctive. Apparently, the earliest costumes for women in U.S. films were borrowed; actresses reportedly supplied their own clothes. Although designers as such didn't appear until the twenties, fashion became a significant element of film narration much earlier.[17]

The opposition that develops in American culture can be characterized as that of the "New Woman" versus the "Old-fashioned Girl," types that will be seen not only in opposition, but as composites in film narratives. The "Old-fashioned Girl" was modest, devoted to family, virginal, obedient, trusting, and a most heroic victim. The "New Woman" was seeking a good time, romance, work, class ascendancy, and fine clothes.

A combination figure of the "Old-fashioned Girl" and the "New Woman" was found in the "Gibson Girl."[18] She developed as the fantasy of artist/illustrator Charles Dana Gibson. The Gibson Girl is an ideal type who is fashionable and yet modest. She is an image of health, rather than overt wealth, although we know that the pursuit of physical well-being was limited to those of means and of leisure; health becomes another means of indicating wealth and class.

We see the narrativization of the oppositions in D. W. Griffith's *The Gibson Goddess,* a Biograph film of 1909, where the leisure space of the seashore provides a discourse on the reception of fashion, voyeurism, and female identity. The film starts with a telling shot, one worth analyzing in detail, for it establishes in visual terms the opposition between the old-fashioned and the attraction of the fashionable. A title announcing "At the seaside resort almost any lady can draw the mashers" introduces a shot of men grouped around a lone woman in a very plain dark skirt, light blouse, hair parted in the middle, all crowded to the left of the frame; when a carriage enters in the right background of the shot, the reason for this unusual framing becomes clear. It allows the contrasting fashionable woman to descend from the carriage into the shot, showing off an over-sized straw hat and a suit with stripes on the sleeve and around the hip of the jacket, adornments enough to attract all the men away from the plainer woman, following our fashion plate as she exits in the foreground toward the camera. Two more women, also in more old-fashioned dresses, pre-viously hidden by the crowd of men, now share their indignation with the plainly dressed woman as the shot ends. What is clear is that the details that make one woman the object of attention and desire are of minimal yet significant difference. Seen together all four women share a common style. If the fashionable woman is clearly more elegant and up to date, she is no less modestly covered than the others.

Throughout this eleven-shot film the men continue to follow this woman as she retires to her room to change, then reappears in her even more elegant seashore costume, avoiding them and only seeking a refuge to read alone. Chased off a bench, then the resort pier, she cannot be left in peace even on a primitive fishing pier to which her elegant suit, com-plete with parasol and trimmed with buttons asymmetrically descending along the breast line to the hip, make a dramatic contrast. Much of the pleasure of this film is dependent on watching this costume move during her hurried escapes from the men the film terms "mashers." Her next strategic move is to use her sense of fashion aggressively. She returns to change clothes again, after bemoaning her fate with the line, "Oh why did they have to call me the Gibson Girl?" The surprise is that this time she changes into a bathing costume, although she subsequently covers it with a full-length cape. Then, returning to the resort pier, as always followed by the eager men, she sheds her cape, showing off the flirtatious ruffles of her bathing costume. As each would-be beau bows to offer his respects, he notices her baggy and unattractive leggings, and each in turn is so re-pulsed and shocked by the ideal being degraded that he takes off. Only one remains to garner what the title tells us is "fidelity's reward" as he strolls along past the others arm in arm with the Gibson Goddess who has in this final shot revealed shapely legs in form-fitting bathing tights.

There might be a tendency to read such images from the present vantage point as quaintly Victorian, but I would rather emphasize the struggle with modernity they represented in 1909. Here is a woman portrayed as seeking to define her own space. She wishes to escape the voyeuristic gaze and unwelcome advances of what the film terms "mashers," but not through the more old-fashioned solution of concealing her sexuality or remaining only in protected interiors. Yet she cannot simply dress to please herself, if her self-representation conforms to an image that signals a message contrary to autonomy and solicits precisely the attention she wishes to avoid. The compromise is to play a joke on the male crowd, to tantalize and repulse in a single sweep of the gaze, the once-over from head to foot; only once she has tricked the majority does she gain the power to choose her companion selectively and to wear fashions with impunity. This represents a dilemma in which female wit needs to outsmart the threat of male dominance; that this is represented as possible only by choosing the proper male companion is not surprising in a context where female autonomy is perceived as the underlying threat posed by suffrage and the women's rights movement.

Over and over again in Griffith's work we find the representation of values in conflict concerning fashion and social space.[19] Consider four Griffith Biograph films made from 1910 through 1912 in which the discourse on fashion plays a prominent role: *Gold Is Not All* (1910), and *Those Awful Hats* (1910), *The Painted Lady* (1912), and *The New York Hat* (1912). A determined contrast of classes structures *Gold Is Not All,* with crosscutting as well as montage compositions within some shots juxtaposing the manners and fates of a wealthy couple with the poor. Although the finery is established as visual attraction, the narrative didactically suggests that wealth is detrimental to the pursuit of happiness, with the elegant wife finding herself deserted after ten years have passed. Complaint about hats at a movie theater is the comic subject of *Those Awful Hats;* an industrial crane is brought down from the top of the frame to remove the grandiose accessory that threatens to block the screen, even as the women in the film within the film are seen sporting similar fashions. The imperative of modern allure for women is linked to madness in *The Painted Lady;* here a woman who is so pure as to eschew face powder finds herself taken in by a swindler who romances her despite her refusal to follow fashion. When she shoots him during his attempt to rob her father, she becomes delusional, repetitively powdering her face and meeting an imaginary beau at their former trysting place. *The New York Hat* concerns a dying mother leaving her daughter the female legacy of a fancy hat, although she does so indirectly through money and a note left with her minister; his purchase for her daughter then intimates scandal amongst his shocked parishioners. Marriage of the girl and the minister at the film's end sanctifies desire for beautiful adornment. Taken together, these films suggest the uneasy integration of high fashion into modern life; the films seem nervously obsessed with fashion as object and motor of social change and seek in various ways to ironically contain and recontextualize fashion accessories. If they can't be physically removed, they can be integrated and sanctified;

the most curious narrative offers ironic warnings about madness and the evil of seduction that follow *even* from the refusal of face powder. It suggests the moral contamination even of an unrealized desire.

This work to contain the explosive power of female fashion continues into Griffith's features, such as *True-Heart Susie,* where the heroine must accommodate modernity and compromise her outdated appearance, if not her old-fashioned sensibility. The film depicts the persistence of Susie and William's true romance despite William's attraction to and subsequent marriage to a "milliner from Chicago," a flapper. Still, this interlude of competition marks an intriguing shift in ideology concerning the emergence of the modern woman, a trust in past values that is depicted, at least temporarily, as misguided. As we shall see, the context in which this flashback is placed demonstrates that the past and its charms are simply outmoded and ineffective. This temporary negation of nostalgia must finally be circumvented by a compromise that reestablishes the values of the past in a less naive context.

After Susie is shown watching William walk by with his new flapper fiancée, she returns home to mimic the modern fashion in the hope of regaining William's attention. The camera tilts down her body with a "once-over" gaze following her attempt to look stylish, which is still quite conservative compared to the dress of her competition. Although the film appears to be championing the old-fashioned, it inscribes its heroine in an evaluative, fetishistic gaze, its visual strategies contradicting the moralism of its thematic didacticism. We then see Susie's subjective flashback to an earlier scene at the soda fountain, which a title anchors as Susie's memory of William's earlier remarks at this site disparaging painted ladies. The flashback causes Susie to return temporarily to her less fashionable attire, only to realize that trusting in this memory dooms her to failure, for she does not succeed in deflecting William's interest in the modern woman.

The motor force of the narrative is the social force of modernity represented here by changing appearances and sexual roles. By killing off the flapper, the film negates the modern woman in her most explicit form. Susie adapts her own "true-heart" nature, however, by acquiring some aspects of a modern style, thus reconciling nostalgia with the intrusive inevitability of change. The film closes with a dominant sense of continuity with past values despite intervening transgressions and slight compromises.

It is intriguing to see many of the same elements of *True-Heart Susie* reworked in another Griffith melodrama, *The White Rose,* years later. Again, a series of three flashbacks is used in another tale of a romantic triangle between a minister and two women; in *The White Rose,* however, the flapper, Bessie "Teazie" Williams (Mae Marsh), is the heroine and the narrative is structured to build a sympathy for her that was lacking for the "modern woman" in the earlier film. It is a variation on the same tale whose elements are a taboo or moral norm, a violation of that taboo, and a redemption and reconciliation that modifies slightly the absolutes of the taboo while maintaining the same value system that structured the taboo in the first place. The persistence of the emotional symbolism, the accumulation of objects and memory images, serves to align the audience with Bessie, to imbue the flapper with a traditional Victorian sensibility despite her modern appearance.

"Lilian Gish: The Apotheosis of the Victorian Heroine" is the title Sumiko Higashi gave to her assessment of Gish's roles in the Griffith melodramas of 1915–1921.[20] Yet prior to 1915, we find in the Biograph films the notion of the "Old-fashioned Girl" already interrogated by the imposition of modernity. The virginal little girls portrayed by Gish, Blanche Sweet, and Mary Pickford are already in the process of coming of age; even Mary Pickford's dresses eventually were designed for her by Lanvin of Paris, as depicted in a 1920 *Ladies' Home Journal*.[21] Lanvin's design, however, retains the lines of youthful innocence that built Pickford's fame.

In contrast to Griffith's films, we find the shift into high-fashion extravagance in films by Cecil B. DeMille, among others. This transition from one costuming aesthetic and ideology to another is intriguingly posed by the work of Clare West, one of the first designers employed in Hollywood. She began her career with the two-year project of designing *Intolerance,* where her Babylonian slave-market costumes introduced a fleshy allure (using full-length body stockings) in a biblical context; then she became DeMille's designer for several films, collaborating with set designer Paul Iribe. West's work on *Intolerance* and the DeMille films are often presented as an aspect of Hollywood's seeking designers to compete with *Cabiria* (1913) and other epics of the Italian cinema, including the more avant-garde works. Already, Griffith's *Judith of Bethulia* (1913) presented a tale of significant seduction from the *Apocrypha* in which Blanche Sweet was draped in a sheath with a slit hem.

There is some confusion among sources on the West-Iribe collaboration: sometimes he is given sole credit for design, while elsewhere Iribe is credited with Gloria Swanson's dresses alone and West with designing for the rest of the cast. This may be read as a nervousness about crediting women designers. It also points to Iribe's original attraction for Hollywood, for previously he had made his name as a sketch artist for the French fashion designer Paul Poiret. Poiret, whose dresses minimized curves formerly emphasized and eliminated molding undergarments, was a major force in introducing the modern look in Paris. His "hobble skirts" had tight hemlines around the ankles, which constricted mobility, but also gave women an emphatically sexy hip movement, especially when viewed from behind. This skirt, incidentally, was the subject of a joke in the modern story of Griffith's *Intolerance,* when the poor woman played by Mae Marsh ties a string near her ankles to mimic the latest fashion.[22]

As Peter Wollen points out, as early as 1911 Poiret was pursuing a style of Orientalism parallel to that of Leon Bakst and Henri Matisse.[23] Hollywood became intent on borrowing from the avant-garde and the imagery of decadence. The cinema's fascination with orientalism is manifestly illustrated by DeMille's *The Cheat* (1915), where both costumes and sets provide an exotic background for this most directly sexual of melodramas. It is notable that the Vamp, in the form of Theda Bara in *A Fool There Was,* was also introduced in 1915.

Nowhere is the submergence in the imagery of decadence more evident than in DeMille's *Male and Female* (1919). The modern scene, the haut-bourgeois drawing room, is doubled by its narrative antithesis, as constituted by the primitive, when the members of this wealthy family are shipwrecked on a tropical island. Such tropes are typical of British melodrama and comedy in which the inversion of classes serves to undercut the rigidity and naturalization of class distinctions. Here this class message is transformed and somewhat muted, however, as the film seems designed to explicate and legitimize the codes of female decorative and seductive attire.

To see how this works, let's look at a few significant scenes. Take, for example, a contrast built in the introduction between "Tweeny," the maid, and her employers, Lady Agatha and Lady Mary Lasenby. Tweeny's look at Lady Agatha's stockings is one of envy; the voyeuristic gaze here is presented not as male desire and possession, but as class envy articulated as the desire to have the elegant clothes of the rich.

The film's famous bath sequence is equally complex in its staging of desire and power as luxury. An intertitle justifies the scene's excess by praising "the ancient art of bathing," supposedly rare in this modern context. Yet simultaneously the bath scene visually ridicules the excesses of such luxury accomplished through both servants and modern machinery, even as it inscribes this particularly modern bathroom with intense fantasy. We see the tension in discourse between disdain and wish fulfillment. Further, this scene only presents nudity as a "tease" behind elegantly draped fabrics.

Once the shipwreck occurs in *Male and Female,* the world and its class hierarchies are turned upside down. Yet as the women compete for the former butler's attention, the island increasingly supplies them with adornments such as flowers, beads, and grass fringes, intimating that such self-decoration is natural, occurring in the most primitive form of self-constitution.

This is reinforced with a fantasy illustration of the "Christian-slave" poem read "aloud" in the film. The fantasy is set in Babylon, allowing the costume even more exoticism. The long-train elegant costume of this fantasy, like the bath scene, provides a transhistorical, cross-cultural justification of embellishment. DeMille seeks such points of reference to embroider his film's fantasies; the doubled and trebled temporal settings help the films indulge and condemn in a manner that makes no sense except if we understand it through the psychoanalytic trope of denial.

The Ten Commandments (1923) constitutes a return to the strategy of *Intolerance* made eight years earlier; again, the biblical story serves as cover, sanctifying the exploration of the sensual, the decorative, the flamboyant. In this case, the antithesis of the modern scene is the ancient scene of the Jews' exodus from Egypt and the conflict between Moses and Aaron, which precipitated the delivery of the Ten Commandments. This double temporality has the ancient acting as a foil to the emergence of the modern; the exodus is told first, then encased as the biblical lesson the mother of the modern story is reading to her two sons.

In the biblical opening scenes, it is the Egyptians who first display the sensuality of fashion while the Jews are dressed in the rags of slaves. We see extravagant costumes on Ramses III and his son, the row of women who attend his court, the dancer who distracts him after Moses' threat of a most devastating tenth plague. In Ramses' costume we see a combination of nakedness, jeweled adornments, and the long train of his cloak.

We might note here how female sexuality is construed in relation to male and homosexual sexuality. Significantly, the biblical, the primitive, and the oriental allow the male bodies in power to be dressed and indeed undressed in these films in ways that are unimaginable in settings or narratives that did not provide such coded motivation. Male homosexual appeal here is striking, as if the celebration of male nudity exceeds the heterosexual contexts. The references in these films are similar to patterns of orientalism and primitivism others have traced in their impact on modernism in painting and the arts.

Later, in the scenes of Moses and Aaron that lead to the Golden Calf orgy, the Jews adopt the decadent costumes earlier associated with the Egyptians. The orgy scene provides the most erotic imagery in the film. It is to such lustful images of hair being stroked over the statue of the calf, and couples and even threesomes having gestural sex, that the law, the commandments, respond.

The censor seems to dictate that the modern story take over as echo and narrative transformation. The modern story echoes the Old Testament moralism, tempering it with New Testament forgiveness. It is also a duel of two love triangles as two brothers, Danny and John, fall in love with the same woman, Mary, of whom their fundamentalist mother disapproves. Her unrelenting opposition and strict biblical interpretations drive Danny and Mary to elope. When Danny becomes a corrupt developer while John is a humble carpenter, the Christ imagery takes over what had been writer Jeannie Macpherson's attempt to critique the overly zealous. The emergence of a new triangle with Danny, nouveau riche wife, Mary, and a "Eurasian" mistress lead to a conflict of costumes, as I want to call the climactic scenes.

Both women show up at the church-construction site in elegant coat-dress ensembles, elaborate versions of Venus in furs. Before multiple deadly confrontations finish off all but John and Mary, the film explores the imagery of exposed skin, leading to the plague of leprosy that links parts of this film. Leprosy first occurs in the Old Testament context of the scenes of the Golden Calf, then later in scenes of Christ healing the leper. In the present-day story, we are told that the Eurasian lover escaped from a leper colony in packages of jute that Danny imported to make his concrete cheaply. Clearly a metaphor for venereal disease, the symbol of leprosy appears where we might feast our eyes on flesh and fashion. Once again, the discrepancy between narrative moralism and visual display points to a period of historical transition; the visual regime has become infinitely more powerful than the narrative one meant to contain and forbid it.

The Golden Bed shows us another aspect of the West-Iribe designs for DeMille. Like *Gold Is Not All* and the modern tale of *The Ten Commandments, The Golden Bed* is a morality tale about the corruption of the soul in seeking wealth and physical luxuries. Yet it is also more clearly an exploration of female seductiveness and power. Here the sumptuous sets and costumes take on a life of their own, notably with long trains that turn the male into a virtual page, picking up the woman's dress so that she can make the next move. A fantasy of European royalty mixes with orientalism to produce women as a modern object of desire.

Throughout this article, I have asked what sort of fantasies surrounded modernity as it was being experienced in the social and industrial realms. The specifics of fashion and film bring the issues of the dissemination of modernism within popular culture to the fore; rather than merely investigating the influence of avant-garde theater, dance, and film on popular representations, I want to show that the primitive, the ancient, and the exotic were mined simultaneously in both avant-garde and popular culture for inspiration in the present.

In closing, I will look at Alla Nazimova and designer Natacha Rabatova's *Salomé* and *Camille* as paralleling the DeMille and Iribe productions. Their work can be seen as examples of how the avant-garde's "infiltration" into the American film industry came via the entrée of fashion and design as signs of female sexuality.

For *Salomé* (1922), Nazimova and Rabatova draw on the Aubrey Beardsley illustrative lithographs for Oscar Wilde's play; retaining the decadent edge of Wilde's rendering of the seductive Salomé's fetishistic desire of parts of the Prophet Jokanaan's body, the film concentrates attention on visual detail in Salomé's costuming. She appears in a series of white costumes, luminous and provocative. For her opening love proclamation, she is adorned with a globelike headdress in which white balls bobble from spikes that radiate in all directions, coupled with a bubble skirt and fish-scale tights. For her dance of the seven veils she wears a tight thigh-length strapless sheath, while each "veil" is a long white runner connected to other women in white costumes. Later she appears in a long cape with full train, the most directly reminiscent of the Beardsley illustrations.

Costuming takes the same prominence in *Camille* (1924), where a title announces that the "Basque and Crinoline of other versions" will here give way to a "Camille of today" constituted by a tight lamé skirt and halter top on which a camellia centrally figures. This costume is completed by a long-sleeved lamé shawl and a long train, threaded through Camille's fingers. This self-conscious modernization of Camille via clothes design hints at a strategy that displaces a narrative of female self-sacrifice and creates one in which the spectacle of female seductive power becomes a celebration of modernity. This is an extension of the West-DeMille collaboration carried to an extreme; the design is the point and the celebration of elegance informs the ideology. The movement of the narrative through interludes with nature in everyday dress, and Camille's demise, after she effaces her love for Armand for his good, do little to carry an audience through any identification with these alternatives as noble and redeeming gestures. The narrative discourse is outweighed, even caricatured, by visual elegance given such primary importance.

As DeMille himself stated in a *Theatre Magazine* interview, "I believe I have had an obvious effect upon American life. I have brought a certain sense of beauty and luxury into everyday existence, all jokes about ornate bathrooms and de luxe boudoirs aside." For American women, this effect on everyday life meant an effect on their lives. I have argued that this period of silent cinema be seen as a transitional one in which key figures shaped seduction and elegance into the focal point of a narrative discourse on female representation. Seduction mixes appeals, such as the "primitive" and the "oriental," with the Modern. It reveals flesh, but mere disrobing or nakedness is less the goal than the design of the veil. For seduction here calls on connotations of elegance drawn from codes of royalty. Decoration and embellishment become essential elements of self-presentation.

If this image is ultimately condemned in several of these films, if Mary in *The Ten Commandments* is cleansed while Sally Long is killed, for example, these condemnations are not to be taken too seriously. Seduction and elegance are here on the verge of yielding to a new concept, "glamour," in which Hollywood will play a determining role in setting the fashion for the world.

I have argued that a close look at costuming in this transitional period reveals not an abrupt shift from repressive Victorian mores to the sexual celebration of the flapper, not a movement from strict repression to licentious sexual liberation, but rather a history in which female representation is clothed in sexuality in a complex manner. Narrative structures often contradict the power of costume presentation, condemning or transforming heroines for their style and their mores, while obviously celebrating the sexual allure of such style for the audience. What emerges in cinema through the influence of designers, including those whose creations are truly avant-garde, is a new form of elegant and sensual female representation that realigns the discourse on what constitutes womanhood.

NOTES

1. Barbara Welter, "The Cult of True Womanhood, 1820–1860," *The American Family in Social-Historical Perspective,* ed. Michael Gordon (New York: St. Martin's Press, 1978).

2. Michel Foucault, *The History of Sexuality,* trans. Robert Hurley, 2 vols. (New York: Vintage, 1980), 1:10.

3. Steven Marcus, *The Other Victorians: A Study of Sexuality and Pornography in Mid-Nineteenth-Century England* (New York: Basic Books, 1966).

4. Christina Simmons, "Modern Sexuality and the Myth of Victorian Repression," *Passion and Power,* ed. Kathy Peiss and Christina Simmons (Philadelphia: Temple University Press, 1989), 156.

5. Ibid., 157.

6. See Nina Auerbach, *Women and the Demon: The Life of a Victorian Myth* (Cambridge: Harvard University Press, 1982); Christina Crosby, *The Ends of History: Victorians and "The Woman Question"* (New York: Routledge, 1991); Lloyd Fernando, *"New Women" in the Late Victorian Novel* (University Park: Pennsylvania University Press, 1977); *Victorian Women's Fiction: Marriage, Freedom and the Individual* (Totowa, N.J.: Barnes and Noble, 1985).

7. Simmons, "Modern Sexuality," 158.

8. As an example of how "Victorian America" is used by historians, see John S. Haller and Robin M. Haller, *The Physician and Sexuality in Victorian America*

(Urbana: University of Illinois Press, 1974); Ronald G. Walters, *Primers for Prudery: Sexual Advice to Victorian America* (Englewood Cliffs, N.J.: Prentice Hall, 1974); and Stanley Cohen, *The Rebellion Against Victorianism: The Impetus for Cultural Change in 1920s America* (New York: Oxford University Press, 1991).

9. See John D'Emilio and Estelle B. Freedman, *Intimate Matters: A History of Sexuality in America* (New York: Harper and Row, 1988). Two works that make a link between puritanism and Victorian values are Florence Maly-Schlatter, *The Puritan Element in Victorian Fiction* (Zurich: A. G. Bebr. Leeman and Co., 1940; reprinted by Norwood Press, 1978), and John Owen King III, *The Iron of Melancholy: Structures of Spiritual Conversion in America from the Puritan Conscience to Victorian Neurosis* (Middletown, Conn.: Wesleyan University Press, 1983).

10. Some previous writing that discusses the means through which the social function of women is defined by appearance includes Anne Hollander, *Looking Through Clothes* (New York: Avon, 1980); Jane Gaines and Charlotte Herzog, eds., *Fabrications: Costume and the Female Body* (New York: Routledge, 1990); and Maureen Turim, "Fashion Shapes: Hollywood, the Fashion Industry and the Image of Women," *Socialist Review* 71 (1983): 83–95.

11. Nancy Wolloch, *Woman and the American Experience* (New York: Alfred A. Knopf, 1984), 202–203.

12. Mary Ryan, *Womanhood in America: From Colonial Time to the Present* (New York: New Viewpoints, 1975), 114–115.

13. Joan Scott, *Gender and the Politics of History* (New York: Columbia University Press, 1988).

14. Quoted in Wolloch, *Woman,* 203.

15. Elizabeth Cady Stanton, *Eighty Years and More: Reminiscences 1815–1897* (New York: Schocken Books, 1971).

16. Noel Burch, "What Do Those Old Films Mean?" (U.K./France: Channel 4/FR3/P1 Productions, 1985).

17. Elizabeth Leese, *Costume Design in the Movies* (New York: Ungar, 1978), 10–14. See also entries on the earliest designers for feature productions: Ethel Chaffin, 35; Lucille (Lady Duff Gordon), 75; and Claire West, 124.

18. Martha Banta, *Imaging American Women: Idea and Ideals in Cultural History* (New York: Columbia University Press, 1987), 211–218.

19. For further discussion of space in Griffith, see Thomas Elsaesser, ed., *Early Cinema: Space Frame Narrative* (London: BFI, 1990); Tom Gunning, *D. W. Griffith and the Origins of American Narrative Film: The Early Days at Biograph* (Urbana: University of Illinois Press, 1991); and Joyce E. Jesionowski, *Thinking Through Pictures* (Berkeley: University of California Press, 1987).

20. Sumiko Higashi, *Virgins, Vamps and Flappers* (St. Albans, Vt.: Edens Press, 1978), 1–26.

21. Brian Holme, ed., *The Journal of the Century* (New York: Viking, 1976), 99.

22. Miriam Hansen refers to this scene to discuss patterns of narration and address from a feminist perspective in *Babel and Babylon: Spectatorship in American Silent Films* (Cambridge: Harvard University Press, 1991), 151.

23. Peter Wollen, "Fashion/Orientalism/The Body," *New Formations* 1 (Spring 1987): 5–37.

Douglas Kellner

*M*adonna, Fashion, and Identity

For the past decade, Madonna has been a highly influential fashion and pop culture icon and the center of a storm of controversy. She is the best-selling and most discussed female singer in popular music, one of the great stars of music video, a hard-working movie actress, and, most of all, a superstar of pop culture. "Madonna" has become a site of contestation and controversy, adored and abhorred by audiences, critics, and academics alike. Most of the polemics, however, are contentious and fail to grasp the many sides of the Madonna phenomenon. While some celebrate her as a subversive cultural revolutionary, others attack her politically as an antifeminist cultural conservative, or as irredeemably trashy and vulgar. Against such one-sided interpretations, however, I shall argue that Madonna is a genuine site of contradiction that must be articulated and appraised to adequately interpret her images and works, and their effects.

My argument is that Madonna's image and reception highlight the social constructedness of identity, fashion, and sexuality. By exploding boundaries established by dominant gender, sexual, and fashion codes, she encourages experimentation, change, and production of one's individual identity. Yet by privileging the creation of image, looks, and fashion in the production of identity, Madonna reinforces the norms of the consumer society that offers the possibilities of a new commodity "self" through consumption and the products of the fashion industry. I argue that grasping this contradiction is the key to Madonna's effects, and interrogate the conditions under which the multiplicity of discourses on Madonna, and contradictory readings and evaluations, are produced. Madonna pushes the most sensitive buttons of sexuality, gender, race, and class, offering challenging and provocative images and texts, as well as ones that reinforce dominant conventions. Madonna is her contradictions, and I shall take pleasure in the following pages in immersing myself in the Madonna phenomenon to explore her highly volatile and charged artifacts.

FASHION AND IDENTITY

Ultimately, Madonna is interesting for cultural theory because her work, popularity, and influence reveal important features of the nature and function of fashion and identity in the contemporary world. Fashion offers models and material for constructing identity. Traditional societies had fixed social roles and fixed sumptuary codes, so that clothes and one's appearance instantly denoted one's social class, profession, and status. Identity in traditional societies was usually fixed by birth, and the available repertoire of roles was tightly constricted to traditional social functions. Gender roles were especially rigid, while work and status were tightly circumscribed by established social codes and an obdurate system of status ascription.

Modern societies eliminated rigid codes of dress and cosmetics, and beginning around 1700 changing fashions of apparel and appearance began proliferating.[1] Although a capitalist market dictated that only certain classes could afford the most expensive attire, which signified social privilege and power, in the aftermath of the French Revolution fashion was democratized so that anyone who could afford certain clothes and makeup could wear and display what they wished. Previously, sumptuary laws forbad members of certain classes from dressing and appearing like the ruling elites.

Modernity also offered new possibilities for constructing personal identities. Modern societies made it possible for individuals to produce—within certain limits—their own identities and experience identity crises. Already in the eighteenth century, the philosopher David Hume formulated the problem of personal identity, of what constituted one's true selfhood, even suggesting that there was no substantial or transcendental self. The issue became an obsession with Rousseau, Kierkegaard, and many other Europeans, who experienced rapid change, the breakdown of traditional societies, and the emergence of modernity.[2]

In modernity, fashion is an important constituent of one's identity, helping to determine how one is perceived and accepted.[3] Fashion offers choices of clothes, style, and image through which one could produce an individual identity. In a sense, fashion is a constituent feature of modernity, interpreted as an era of history marked by perpetual innovation, by the destruction of the old and the creation of the new. Fashion itself is predicated on producing ever new tastes, artifacts, artifices, and practices. Fashion perpetuates a restless, modern personality, always seeking what is new and admired, while avoiding what is old and passé. Fashion and modernity go hand in hand to produce modern personalities who seek their identities in constantly new and trendy clothes, looks, attitudes, and behavior, and who are fearful of being out of date or unfashionable.

Of course, fashion in modern societies was limited by gender codes, economic realities, and the force of social conformity, which continued to dictate what one could or could not wear, and what one could or could not be. Documentary footage from the 1950s in artifacts such as the 1982 ABC documentary *Heroes of Rock* showed parents, teachers, and other arbiters of good taste attempting to dictate proper and improper fashion, thus policing the codes of fashion and identity. Crossing gender codes in fashion was for centuries a good way to mark oneself as a social outcast or even to land in jail or a mental institution.

The 1960s exhibited a massive attempt to overthrow the cultural codes of the past, and fashion became an important element of the construction of new identities, along with sex, drugs, and rock 'n' roll, phenomena also involved in the changing fashions of the day. In the 1960s, antifashion in clothes and attire became fashionable, and the subversion and overthrowing of cultural codes became a norm.

During this period, pop culture became a particularly potent source of cultural fashions, providing models for appearance, behavior, and style. The long-haired and unconventionally dressed rock stars of the 1960s and the 1970s influenced changes in styles of hair, dress, and behavior, while their sometimes rebellious attitudes sanctioned social revolt. More conservative television programming, films, and pop music provided mainstream models for youth. During the past two decades, cultural conservatives have been reacting strongly against 60s radicalism and fashion and youth culture have become battlefields between traditionalists and conservatives and cultural radicals, attempting to overturn traditional gender roles, fashion codes, and values and behavior.

High school in particular is a period in which young people construct their identities, attempting to "become someone."[4] High school has been a terrain of contradiction for the past several decades. While some parents and teachers attempt to instill traditional values and ideas, youth culture is often in opposition to conservative culture. Although the 1980s were a predominantly conservative period, with the election of Ronald Reagan and a "right turn" in U.S. culture, the images from popular music figures sometimes cut across the conservative grain.[5] Michael Jackson, Prince, Boy George, and other rock groups undermined traditional gender divisions and promoted polymorphic sexuality. Cyndi Lauper reveled in offbeat kookiness, and Pee Wee Herman engaged in silly and infantile behavior to the delight of his young (and older) audiences. Throwing off decades of cool sophistication, maturity, respectability, and taste, Pee Wee made it OK to be silly and weird, or at least different.

ENTER MADONNA

It was during this period that Madonna first came to prominence. Her early music videos and concert performances transgressed traditional fashion boundaries, and she engaged in overt sexual behavior and titillation, subverting the boundaries of "proper" female behavior. Thus, from the beginning, Madonna was one of the most outrageous female icons among the repertoire of circulating images sanctioned by the culture industries. Although there were no doubt many farther-out and more subversive figures than Madonna, their images and messages did not circulate through mainstream culture and thus did not have the efficacy of the popular. The early Madonna sanctioned rebellion, nonconformity, individuality, and experimentation with fashion and lifestyles. Madonna's constant change of fashion, image, and identity promoted experimentation and the creation of one's own style and identity. Her sometimes dramatic shifts in identity suggested that identity was a construct, that it was something that one produced and could be modified at will. The way Madonna deployed fashion in the construction of her identity made it clear that one's appearance and image helps produce what one is, or least how one is perceived.

Thus, Madonna problematized identity and revealed its constructedness and alterability. Madonna was successively a dancer, musician, model, singer, music video star, movie and stage actress, "America's most successful businesswoman," and a pop superstar who excelled in marketing her image and selling her goods. Consciously crafting her own image, she moved from boy toy, material girl, and ambitious blonde to artiste of music videos, films, and concerts. Her music shifted from disco and bubblegum rock to personal statements and melodic torch singing, then, with the aid of her music videos, to pop modernism. Madonna's hair changed from dirty blonde to platinum blonde, to black, brunette, redhead, and multifarious variations thereof. Her body changed from soft and sensuous to glamorous and svelte to hard and muscular sex machine to futuristic technobody. Her clothes and fashion changed from flashy trash to haute couture to far-out technocouture to lesbian S & M fashion to postmodern pastiche of all and every fashion style. New clothes and a new identity for all occasions and epochs. As it turns out, Madonna's fashion moves generally caught shifts in cultural style and taste and thus achieved the status of the popular, becoming important cultural icons and influences.

While there are certain continuities in Madonna's development that I shall be concerned to explicate, there are also at least three distinct periods that can be (roughly) equated to shifts in her music production, her deployment of fashion and sexuality, and her image. I shall accordingly attempt to delineate these periods to articulate the contours of what has become known as the "Madonna phenomenon." My focus will be on Madonna's images and cultural production, their impact on their audiences, and her cultural effects over the past decade. Although I shall deploy the standard methods of cultural studies featuring textual analysis and reception of texts by audiences, I argue that a generally neglected component of cultural studies—political economy and the production of culture—is an important key to the Madonna phenomenon.[6] For Madonna's success is largely a marketing success, and her music, videos, and image (although not all of her films) are triumphs of extremely successful production and marketing strategies. Madonna has made the right connections, has worked with talented music and video producers, has a phalanx of professional business managers and publicists, and has for the most part brilliantly produced her own image and sold it successfully to her audiences.

Thus, I shall focus on reading Madonna's work as a cultural text, using the methods of textual analysis with some look at audience reception and the actual production and distribution of the work. I begin by examining her early work and how she became a pop star and then go on to examine the troubled period of her mid- to late-1980s work, concluding with an examination of the more complex and modernist productions of the late 1980s and early 1990s.

Madonna I: The Boy Toy

In 1983, Madonna released her first album, *Madonna,* and two of the songs ("Lucky Star" and "Holiday") became hits. Her early music and songs are rather conventional popular dance music aimed at a teenage market. But Madonna was an especially flashy performer and began to attract notice at this point with music videos of her top hits, which were featured on MTV, a relatively new channel that was to play a key role in her career. The music video "Lucky Star" features her as an especially voluptuous sex object, energetic dancer, and innovative fashion trendsetter. The video opens with a black-and-white sequence: Madonna is wearing black sunglasses, which she slowly pulls down, revealing sultry eyes intensely focusing on the camera (and viewer). The sunglasses, of course, were symbols of the punk generation out of which Madonna emerged and would later become a symbol of the cyberpunk movement as well (as Bruce Sterling claims in the introduction to his anthology *Mirrorshades*). Their deployment suggested that Madonna would reveal something of herself in the video, but that she knew her performance was an act and that she would maintain her control and subjectivity. The final sequence returns to black and white and shows Madonna pulling the shades over her eyes as the screen fades to black.

At the end of the brief opening sequence, the screen dissolves to white, and a color sequence shows Madonna dressed totally in black. As the music slowly begins, she writhes in an erotic pose, the camera cuts to a freeze frame of her face, she winks, and the video cuts to Madonna dancing and cavorting with two dancers. Eschewing the narrative frame of most music videos of the day, Madonna presents instead a collage of images of her body. The video shows her energetically dancing, alone or with the two dancers, striking erotic poses, and showing off her body and clothes. Madonna is dressed in a tight and short black skirt with a black leotard underneath. She wears a loose black blouse that lightly covers a black veiled lace body shirt underneath. One sees around her waist the famous "unchastity belt"—later marketed by her Boy Toy line of fashion—with a large buckle and chains around the waist. Madonna has a large black bow in her hair and a large star earring, with smaller crucifix earrings. Completing the outfit are black bobby socks and short black boots.

Madonna's fashion at this stage constituted a subversion of conventional codes and justified wearing any combination of clothes and ornaments that one wished. Of course, Madonna herself became a model of teen fashion and the infamous Madonna "wannabes" slavishly imitated every aspect of her early "flashy trash" clothing and ornamentation. She linked fashion to exhibitionism and aggressive sexuality, connecting fashion revolt with sexual rebellion. Thus, Madonna legitimated unconventional fashion and sexual behavior, endearing her to an audience that felt empowered by Madonna's flouting of traditional standards and codes.

Her other early rock video hit, "Borderline," depicts motifs and strategies that would make Madonna a lucky star. The video narrative images weave two sequences together to illustrate the love song. In color sequences, Madonna sings, flirts, and seduces a Hispanic youth, while in a black and white sequence an Anglo photographer snaps pictures of her and courts her. In one black and white sequence, she sprays graffiti over lifeless classical sculptures, a modernist gesture of the sort that would later typify Madonna's music videos. The lyrics once again promise a utopia of sexual ecstasy ("You keep on pushing my love over the borderline"), and the music has upbeat dancing rhythms that enable Madonna to exhibit her energy and talent as a dancer. In this video, Madonna wears several different outfits, and her hair ranges from dirty and messy blonde in the Hispanic color sequences to beautifully fashioned glamorous blonde in the black-and-white sequences.

Offering herself to males of various colors, Madonna broke down racial barriers to sexuality. This was also a clever marketing strategy, inviting white, Hispanic, and black youth to fantasize that they too can have or be Madonna. In her first music videos Madonna is already deploying fashion, sexuality, and the construction of image to present herself both as an alluring sex object and as a transgressor of established borderlines. On one hand, the video validates interracial sex and provides all-too-rare images of Hispanic barrio culture. Yet the two contrasting narrative sequences convey the message that although you might have a good time hanging out with Hispanics, it is the white photographer who will provide the ticket to wealth and success. But she ends up with the Hispanic youth, and the narrative valorizes multiple relationships, for the Madonna character continues to see both guys during the narrative sequences, projecting the fantasy image that one can have it all, crossing borderlines from one culture to another, appropriating the pleasures of both cultures and multiple relationships.

The video also puts on display the contrasting fashion codes between upper-class culture and Hispanic culture, identifying Anglo culture with high fashion, high art, and luxury. By contrast, Hispanic culture is equated with blue jeans, pool halls, and less-expensive and stylish clothes and ornamentation. A later Madonna video, "La Isla Bonita," however, utilizes fantasy images of Hispanic fashion as an icon of beauty and romanticism. Such "multiculturalism" and her culturally transgressive moves (such as explicit sexuality and interracial sexuality) turned out to be highly successful marketing moves that endeared her to large and varied youth audiences.

Madonna became a major pop culture figure with the beginning of her concert tours in 1985, and she began consciously marketing her own image and a wide range of fashion accoutrements, which she sold under the Boy Toy label. *People* reported: "At concerts her per capita sales of T-shirts and memorabilia are among the highest in rock history. 'She sells more than Springsteen, the Rolling Stones or Duran Duran,' says Dell Furano, the concession merchandiser for her tour. At her San Francisco date, $20

T-shirts sold at the rate of one every six seconds." She began marketing "Madonna-wear," which she described as "sportswear for sexpots." The line included "a $25 lace tank top, a $30 sweatshirt, $20 pants and a medium-priced ($30) tube skirt that can be rolled down for public navel maneuvers."[7]

Although an upscale version of Madonna-wear was also marketed, as were Madonna makeup kits, her image also encouraged thrift-shop down-scale fashion for the Madonna look: underwear worn outside skirts, loose T-shirts, cheap bracelets, earrings, chains, and crucifixes also provided appropriate decoration. Indeed, the Madonna look became known as "flash-trash," so that almost any teenage girl could afford to look like Madonna and share her attitudes and styles. Madonna fashion made it possible for teenage girls to produce their own identity, to make their own fashion statements, and to reject standard fashion codes.

During the Virgin Tour, Madonna wore a brightly colored jacket and tight micro-miniskirt, a sparkly lingerie harness, black lace stockings that stopped at the knee, and an array of ornaments, including crucifixes, a peace medallion, and bracelets. Prancing around in spiked boots, her belly button exposed, Madonna would take off the jacket to reveal a lacy purple shirt and black bra, accenting a lush and accessible sexuality. For the hit song "Like a Virgin," Madonna appeared in a white wedding dress and screamed, "Do you want to marry me?" to which the girls and boys both answered, "Yesss!" Thrusting her hip as she sang, "You make me feel like a virgin," she unfolded a belly roll as she intoned, "touched for the very first time." This highly sexual rendition of the song mocks virginity, but also makes fun of sexuality by ironizing its codes and gestures. Her play with sexual codes reveals sexuality to be a construct, fabricated in part by the images and codes of popular culture, rather than a "natural" phenomenon.

Madonna's deployment of fashion and sexuality during this early phase is more complex than it appears at first glance. Although it is easy to dismiss the early Madonna's posturing as that of a shameless sex object, boy toy, and material girl who reinforces traditional gender roles, a closer reading of her music videos produces another picture. For instance, her music video "Material Girl" (1984) seems at first glance to be an anthem of Reaganism, glorifying shallow materialism and celebrating greed and manipulation ("The boy with the cold hard cash / Is always Mr. Right . . . cause I'm just a Material Girl"). On this reading, the song is a replay of Marilyn Monroe's "Diamonds Are a Girl's Best Friend" and is advocating the same calculating and shallow materialist attitudes.

Although Madonna has assumed a Monroe-like look in this video and does deploy some of the fashion and poses of Monroe's 1950s hymn to bourgeois materialism, a closer look at the music video provides some different perspectives. In one reading, which Madonna herself advanced, the video shows the "material girl" rejecting her wealthy suitors in favor of a poor working boy. When confronted with the critique that she was celebrating crass greed, Madonna responded, "Look at my video that goes with the song. The guy who gets me in the end is the sensitive guy with no money."[8] On this account, Madonna turns down the guys courting her in the music and dance sequences for the poor but sincere boy shown in the "realism" sequences.

A closer reading raises questions, however, as to whether the "poor boy" in the video, played by Keith Carradine, is really "poor" and whether Madonna doesn't actually get a very rich and successful guy in the video. The narrative images reveal the Carradine character to be a studio mogul who cleverly poses as a sincere poor boy who wins Madonna's heart. Thus, in "Material Girl" Madonna is all things to all people and has it every way: for conservatives of the Reagan years, she is a celebrant of material values, the material girl, who takes the guilt away from sex, greed, and materialism. For this audience, she is Marilyn Monroe reincarnated, the superpop superstar, the super ideal male fantasy sex object and female fantasy icon. For romantic idealist youth, however, she is the good girl seeking love who chooses true love over material temptations. Yet in the music video narrative, she gets both love and a successful guy.

Moreover, the video "Material Girl" problematizes identity and decouples the link between expensive clothes, wealth, and position. Carradine wears a brown work shirt and pants, and this is perfectly acceptable, the video suggests, indicating that fashion and identity are up to the individual, not to societal codes. Madonna's images and music videos thus legitimate individual choice in appropriating fashion and producing one's image. Yet the most attractive images in the musical production numbers do celebrate high and expensive fashion, diamonds, and other costly ornaments as keys to a successful image and identity. And it could be that the powerful images of wealth and high fashion, reinforced by the musical lyrics, do endorse bourgeois materialism over romance and individual choice.

A high level of ambiguity, irony, and humor permeates Madonna's work and image. Her use of fashion is humorous and ironic, as are many of her videos and concert acts. The items marketed in her Boy Toy and Slutco lines are often humorous, as are the very titles of the lines themselves. Indeed, the much maligned term "Boy Toy" itself is ironic and allows multiple readings. On one level, Madonna is a toy for boys, but on another level boys are toys for her, the Boy Toys are there for her toying around and the unchastity belt comes off at her whim and desire. Indeed, "Material Girl" shows the guys as Madonna's toys and her dance numbers with men during the Virgin Tour concerts shows them as her underlinings, accessories that she toys with and totally dominates.

Crucially, the early Madonna projects in her videos and music an all-too-rare cultural image of a free woman, making her own choices and determining her life. The early Madonna image of a free spirit floating through life on her own terms is perfectly captured in her role as Susan in Susan Seidelman's *Desperately Seeking Susan* (1985). The message here, consistent with Madonna's other early work, is that one can fundamentally change one's identity by changing one's fashion, appearance, and image. Madonna herself would dramatically exemplify this philosophy in her two succeeding stages, in which she radically altered her image and identity.

MADONNA II: WHO'S THAT GIRL?

Madonna had arrived. In 1985, her records had sold 16 million singles and albums. She had number-one pop hits, "Like a Virgin" and "Crazy for You," and by the time she was twenty-six, Madonna had produced seven Top Twenty singles in seventeen months. (It took Barbra Streisand seventeen years to have that many.) Madonna made a successful film debut in *Desperately Seeking Susan,* and her Virgin Tour established her as one of the hottest figures in pop music. She was featured on the cover of *Time* magazine and was profiled in *People, Newsweek, Rolling Stone,* and other popular magazines. Her first album, *Madonna,* eventually sold over three million copies, and her *Like A Virgin* album racked up 4.5 million copies in domestic sales, with 2.5 million more worldwide by 1985. Moreover, Madonna *knew* she was a superstar and plotted her moves accordingly.

Needless to say, Madonna deployed fashion and sexuality to produce the image that would mark her mid- to late 1980s stage, characterized by continued megasuccess as a record producer with best-selling albums and music videos, another successful concert tour ("Who's That Girl?"), a much discussed and eventually failed marriage with movie actor Sean Penn, and two movies that flopped with critics and audiences (*Shanghai Surprise* and *Who's That Girl?*).

The first visible change in image had to do with her weight and body shape. The early Madonna was soft and a bit chubby, but rigorous exercise and diet transformed her body. She also changed her hair and fashion styles, utilizing more glamorous haute couture fashion, while frequently changing her hair arrangements. In many photographs and in the 1986 film *Shanghai Surprise,* Madonna appeared more and more like Marilyn Monroe, with glamorous, wavy, fluffy blonde hair. She also emulated the look of other classic movie stars, such as Lana Turner and Marlene Dietrich. In her rock videos "Cherish" and "Papa Don't Preach," Madonna sported short, cropped blondish hair (à la Jean Seberg in *Breathless*); she wore garish platinum blonde hair in the 1987 movie *Who's That Girl?,* which reprised the figure of the 1930s Hollywood screwball comedy heroine. The video "Like a Prayer" featured Madonna with her natural dark hair, and she also appeared in red hair and various shades between light and dark in the videos, photos, and documentary footage of the period from 1986 to the late 1980s.

During this period, Madonna adopted more traditional fashion and attitudes and tried to appear more respectful of traditional gender roles. Trying to make her doomed marriage with Sean Penn work, Madonna appeared in romantic love songs videos (for example, "True Blue") singing of the joys of devotion, commitment, and true love. Madonna decided to shed the trampy sex kitten look and boy-toy image for a more conventional feminine appearance. As *Forbes* put it, "She began singing in a deeper, more serious voice, and in a video from her third album wore honey-blonde hair and a demure flowered dress. In July 1987 she got herself on the cover of *Cosmopolitan* as a glamorous blonde, and in May 1988 she graced the cover of *Harper's Bazaar* as a prim brunette. Her *True Blue* album of that period sold nearly 17 million copies, and she sold more albums among the over-20 crowd than ever."[9]

Madonna's 1987 "Who's that Girl?" tour, captured on the videocassette *Ciao Italia!,* disclosed her to be twenty pounds lighter and highly athletic. For years, she had been dieting, exercising for hours each day, and even lifting weights to build up her body. The tour featured her energetic dancing, with break dancer accompaniment, intricate lighting effects, seven or eight costume changes for the star, and dramatic shifts of image and mood throughout the show. Wearing a skimpy black corset at the start of the show, Madonna played to her sex-kitten image, but then shifted to the romantic sentimental mode of *True Blue* album. But after wearing a 1950s prom dress to reflect the innocence of the song "True Blue," she put a black leather jacket over the dress for "Papa Don't Preach," while the words "safe sex" were flashed on a huge screen at the back of the stage.

Mocking "Material Girl," Madonna wore a ridiculously tacky outfit and sang the lyrics with a high-pitched Betty Boop twang to ironize the lyrics.

In "La Isla Bonita" she adorned a Spanish-style cabaret dress; she wore an international mélange of clothes in "Holiday," which signaled the celebratory and wholesome attitude she was trying to promote. Eschewing the bawdy sexuality and sexual repartee that marked her earlier Virgin tour, and which would return in even more extreme forms in the later Blonde Ambition tour, Madonna is relatively restrained in her deployment of fashion and sexuality and exhibits more traditional images of women.

Her album *Like a Prayer* (1989) also revealed her to have matured psychologically and musically. The songs deal with the pain of the breakup of her marriage with Sean Penn, repressed guilt over her mother's death, conflicts with her father, and the pain and difficulties of growing up. The music video of the title song brings out more strikingly than previously the religious motifs from her Catholic upbringing. In her earlier videos and image construction she utilized crucifixes as *part* of her fashion attire; the music video of "Like A Prayer" is built primarily around religious images and themes. The video fuses religion and eroticism in a narrative celebrating love, both spiritual and carnal. The refrain, "In the midnight hour, I can feel your power, Just like a prayer, you know I'll take you there," could either refer to religious or sexual ecstasy. Madonna brings out the latent eroticism in the Catholic religion and uses it for striking aesthetic and moral purposes.

The narrative of the music video depicts an innocent black man wrongly accused of a crime that the Madonna figure observes. She goes into a church, dreams of making love to the statue of a black saint, and then rescues the innocent black to flamboyant images of gospel singing, burning crosses (representing the evil of Klan bigotry), candles, and other religious iconography. For the dream/fantasy sequence of the video, Madonna wears a black slip that signifies sleep and the oneiric, eroticism, and the powerful symbolism and aesthetic effects of the color black. The imagery promotes integration and harmony between blacks and whites: Madonna sings with a black choir in a black church, kisses one black man and saves another. The video thus projects a powerful image of goodness and morality, doing the right thing.

In the music video of "Express Yourself" (1989), which is perhaps the culmination of her second period, Madonna produces a highly complex modernist text that pushes the buttons of gender, sexuality, and class. The video opens with images of a futuristic city in the air, supported by machinery below, drawing on the iconography of Fritz Lang's modernist film classic *Metropolis*. Madonna suddenly emerges standing up on a giant swan. Addressing herself to a female subject (a rather rare move), Madonna proclaims: "Come on girls, do you believe in love? Well, I've got something to say about it, and it goes like this." The lyrics of the song affirm self-expression, doing your best in all things ("Don't settle for second best, baby"), and overcoming obstacles to one's goals. The song employs the imperative mode, and Madonna defiantly shouts "Express yourself!" at key junctures in the song. While a verse indicates that "What you need is a big strong hand to lift you to your higher ground," it is clear from the subtext, and the images that accompany the music video, that the "big strong hand" should be your own, and not the typical male helping hand.

Indeed, Madonna is constantly inverting relations of gender power and domination in the video, putting on display the socially constructed images of women and exhibiting the male fantasies that produce such images of women and sexuality. Utilizing as a frame for the video Lang's *Metropolis,* Madonna inverts the liberal humanist theme of the film, as Morton argues.[10] Lang's film represents conflicts between workers and capitalists in a futuristic city, as well as between father and son, men and women. At the end, all conflicts are overcome in naive images of total reconciliation. Madonna's video, by contrast, presents stark and powerful images of the differences between capital and labor, men and women. Images near the end of the video of two men fighting suggest the irreconcilability of the opposing interests of class and (one might extrapolate) gender and continual struggle between the classes and sexes as the fate of the human species.

Or, one might read the images of the men fighting as a feminist critique of male violence and brutality—a reading supported by the text as a whole. The video presents a panoply of traditional patriarchal representations of women, beginning with Madonna standing on top of a swan and later holding and becoming a cat, sliding across the floor and licking a plate of milk. In the most controversial images of the video, Madonna appears as a woman in bondage with an iron collar around her neck and chains around her body. It is crucial to note that this image is presented as the fantasy of the capitalist in the video who puts on his monocle to feast his eye's upon Madonna in bondage shown on a video screen. The images here are obviously playing on the notion of cinema and the male gaze and its reading as the projection of males who fantasize the objectification of women. From this perspective, Madonna is putting on display the ways that male fantasy and power objectify women, fantasizing them as in bondage, as animals, as beautiful objects for male lust and domination.[11]

Within this display of male images, however, Madonna suddenly emerges in a suit, with a monocle, and grabs her crotch, signifying her assumption of the male position of power and control. At one point, she rips open the jacket to disclose her breasts and to reveal that the male image is just a construction, a subject-position that anyone can occupy. By implication, images of women are also subject positions, produced by male power, that women may choose to occupy, or may choose to vacate in favor of male subject positions—or something altogether different. This deconstructive reading suggests that "Express Yourself" puts on display the artificiality of images of gender and suggests that individuals can choose their own images and self-constructions. The lyrics of "Express Yourself" indeed order individuals to produce their own identity and to construct their own selves.

MADONNA III: BLONDE AMBITION

After the breakup of her marriage in 1989, Madonna continued to explore the boundaries of the permissible in the representations of sexuality and gender, entering upon the stage of her work where she would systematically challenge conventional representations of sexuality. During the 1990s, Madonna produced a series of complex modernist music videos that expanded the boundaries of the art form and even led MTV to ban one of her productions, "Justify My Love," in 1990 and to play "Erotica" only rarely in 1992. Madonna had obviously developed from young sex object on the move to mature woman, prepared to control her own destiny.

During her most recent period, marked by a series of highly controversial rock videos, the Blonde Ambition tour and the 1991 film of the tour (*Madonna: Truth or Dare*), the 1992 album *Erotica* and book *Sex,* Madonna has been recognized as a top pop superstar and even "America's shrewdest businesswoman." In the 1990s, her use of fashion was even more eclectic, drawing on some of her earlier images, which she frequently quoted and sometimes parodied. Madonna also became political during this period, making statements on behalf of AIDS victims, the homeless, saving the rain forests, and women's rights; in 1990 she even made a "get out and vote" video, threatening to spank those who refused to vote.[12] In 1992, she supported Bill Clinton for President.

It was probably her rock videos of the late 1980s and 1990s, in which Madonna most created wide cultural controversy, that attracted the attention of academic critics and cultural theorists. Along with Michael Jackson, she is one of the first video rock superstars and is arguably the supreme master, or rather grande dame, of the form. "Open Your Heart," "Like A Prayer," "Express Yourself," "Justify My Love," "Vogue," and "Erotica" are modernist masterpieces of video art. Breaking the rules of music videos, which deploy expressive images to illustrate the lyrics, Madonna's best music videos contain a multilayered structure of images that require an active viewer to generate the sometimes complex meanings proliferating in the play of the music, lyrics, and images.[13] Densely crafted feasts of images, her music videos can be enjoyed on several levels by different audiences: teen girls and boys can process the music and images in different ways according to their own fantasies; more sophisticated music and cultural critics can enjoy grappling with polysemic modernist texts; and students of popular culture can attempt to discover why and how Madonna is popular.[14]

In the 1990s, Madonna has employed fashion and image to attempt to produce an identity as an artist. Her rock videos became increasingly complex, or attempted to expand the boundaries of the permissible in terms of male and female gender roles, overt sexuality, parody of religion, and modernist ambiguity. Fashionwise, she sometimes returned to the sexy and flamboyant attire of her early stage, but mixed it with haute couture, futuristic technofashion, S&M chic, and a postmodern pastiche of various fashion styles, subverting oppositions between high and low fashion, much as postmodern art explodes established modernist cultural hierarchies between high and low culture. Yet, arguably, Madonna deployed the typically modernist strategy of shock in her outlandish use of fashion, sexuality, and religious imagery, especially in her rock videos, which are highly complex cultural texts that allow a multiplicity of readings.[15]

Throughout the Blonde Ambition tour, Madonna played out this deconstructive drama, frequently wearing men's clothes, grabbing her crotch, and declaring she was the boss, thus occupying male positions. She also had her male dancers wear fake breasts, women's clothes, and submit to her power and control. The message was that "male" and "female" were social constructs that could be deconstructed and that women could occupy male positions, roles, and behavior and vice versa. Yet, as I shall argue in the conclusion of this essay, Madonna does not subvert relations of domination or offer alternative images. Like conservative deconstruction, Madonna puts on display binary oppositions that constitute our culture and society, demonstrates their artificiality, and questions the prioritizing of one of the oppositions over the other, without putting anything new in its place. Thus, she tends to place women, primarily herself, in positions of power and authority, which are aggressively exercised over males.

To deconstruct traditional gender oppositions and relations of power and domination, Madonna uses irony, humor, and parody to push the sensitive buttons of "masculine" and "feminine" and to provoke reaction to the overthrowing of traditional images and stereotypes and their exchange and mixture in the genders of the future, which would presumably be multiple rather than binary. There was indeed always a strong mixture of irony and satire in Madonna's work from the beginning, and her concert performances became increasingly campy, as was the dramatization of her life on the road in *Truth and Dare*.[16] Her performance of "Material Girl" in the Blonde Ambition tour, for instance, is pure camp, with Madonna and two female singers sitting on a raised platform in hair curlers and bathrobes, singing the song with false accents, out of tune and in high-pitched voices. The image puts on display the labor and ridiculous activities that women go through to make themselves "beautiful" and mocks the ideal of the "material girl" (of course, on another level Madonna herself is the extreme example of almost superhuman labor and expense to make herself "beautiful," a contradiction that pervades her work and that I shall return to).

Most of her most recent music videos are highly aestheticized, using modernist techniques in the construction of compelling images. The orgy scenes in "Justify My Love" are highly abstract and theatrical, and "Vogue" deploys posed images to celebrate pure camp ("Strike a pose! Vogue! Vogue!"). Indeed, "Vogue" parodies fashion conventions—modeling, posing, photography, and objectification—but vivifies them by identifying voguing with a gay dance phenomenon and then cultural celebrity.

The video opens with parting feathers, signifying artificiality, and then presents a montage of posed images with her dance troop assuming fashion poses. Two servants voguing while they work suggests the desirability of voguing and image creation throughout the spheres of everyday life. The frame centers on Madonna—who orders "Strike a pose!"—and a set of images shows her ensemble obeying. The lyrics sing of escape from everyday life through voguing, transforming oneself into a more desirable image, "You're a superstar, that's what you are!" Voguing, the lyrics suggest, is open to anyone ("It doesn't matter if you're black or white, a boy or a girl") and produces aesthetic self-transcendence for all ("Beauty is where you find it"). But then the static images, derived from the fashion industry, are transposed into the gay dance style documented in *Paris Is Burning* and infused with erotic energy. And finally, Madonna's pantheon of privileged images ("Greta Garbo and Monroe . . . Bette Davis, Rita Hayworth gave good face") is illustrated by images of Madonna herself striking poses in the guise of those celebrities.[17]

"Vogue" contains images of corsets and bras and the inside/outside fashion deconstruction that one observes in Madonna's videos and concert performances, in which bras, corsets, and panties are worn outside blouses, skirts, or suits, suggesting that all fashion is artificial. Her images suggest that corset, bras, and other standard female attire are symbols of women's submission to cultural standards, which might as well be worn outside to make the bondage transparent. On the other hand, these icons of women's oppression to fashion standards are rendered erotic in Madonna's iconography, showing how one can transform signs of oppression into signs of mockery and libidinal enjoyment.

Madonna's modernist deconstruction was disseminated via an aesthetic of shock and excess defined by her fashion, attitude, and behavior. There were, of course, market reasons why one might adopt such strategies: they create an image, call attention to oneself, and sell. Madonna's continuing to go beyond herself and to push the boundaries of the permissible utilize modernist aesthetic strategies of excess, shock, spectacle, and theatricality. In the Blonde Ambition tour, Madonna produced a futuristic look, wearing far out technofashion, suggesting new syntheses of technology and the human. Her blonde hair tied back severely, a microphone unit strapped to her head, and her body adorned with bustiers and futuristic clothes designed by Jean-Paul Gaultier, Madonna appears as another species, a new technobody, designer-fashioned for the next century.

The Blonde Ambition show also features male dancers with fake breasts, suggesting the emergence of a new species in the technofuture, which subverts previous boundaries between men and women. Grabbing her crotch throughout the show, a defiant Madonna presents herself as an icon of power and sexuality. The dance numbers also exploit far-out fashion and explicit sexuality to constitute her identity as an iconoclastic figure of the transgressor against established conventions. She, like the successful modernist artist, thus establishes new norms by breaking the old ones.

Her 1992 album *Erotica* and book *Sex* indicate, however, that Madonna may be falling into a trap that could render her boring and predictable. The songs in her album and music video "Erotica" deploy some of the same images and blatant sexuality as "Justify My Love" and her earlier sexual provocations, and do not break any new ground. *Sex* is something of an embarrassment, with low-quality pictures on shabby paper with an aluminum cover and metal binding that easily breaks (so I was told by a bookstore manager who showed me several broken books that had been returned). The pictures of S&M in particular are boring and predictable, and the text, supposedly recounting Madonna's sexual fantasies, is also trite and unerotic. Fashion is deployed in these works to shock and provide libidinal excitement, but by now such imagery is rather commonplace.

But in the best of her music videos, Madonna emerges as a modernist boundary buster. Her concept of art celebrates self-expression, experimentation, pushing the limits of taste, and crossing the borderline into new areas of experience and representation. Madonna has continued to push pop culture beyond previous boundaries and to subvert established rules, conventions, and limits. Her deployment of fashion and sexuality in particular shatters previous rules and conventions and establishes her identity as an iconoclastic modernist. On the other hand, so far her modernist moves have been extremely successful from a commercial point of view, and Madonna emerges as clever businesswoman as much as artiste.[18]

CONCLUSION

The Madonna phenomenon suggests that in a postmodern image culture identity is constructed through image and fashion, involving one's look, pose, and attitude. For Madonna, postmodern identity-construction is change, constantly redeveloping one's look and striking outrageous and constantly different poses. Fashion and identity for Madonna are inseparable from her aesthetic practices, from her cultivation of her image in her music videos, films, TV appearances, concerts, and other cultural interventions. A genuinely complex and challenging phenomenon like Madonna, however, puts in question and tests one's aesthetic categories and commitments.

Madonna has been theorized as "postmodern" because of her strategies of simulation and pastiche, her implosion of gender, racial, and sexual boundaries, and her use of irony and camp. Yet boundary deconstruction, irony, and camp are arguably modernist strategies, and Madonna is constantly deploying self-consciously modernist strategies, presenting her work as serious and transgressive art. In the 1990 *Nightline* interview and the 1991 film *Truth and Dare*, Madonna describes her work as "artistic," claiming that she refuses to compromise her artistic integrity. She also wants to continue "pushing buttons," being "political," going beyond established boundaries, and creating new and innovative works of art—all self-consciously modernist aesthetic values and goals.[19] Thus, while one might interpret Madonna as "postmodernist" in the light of her uses of Baudrillardian categories of simulation and implosion, one should also be aware of the ways in which Madonna can be read as modernist.

Although some have attacked Madonna as being antifeminist and a disgrace to women, others have lauded her as the true feminist for our times and as a role model for young women. Camille Paglia, for instance, has celebrated Madonna as "a true feminist," and a role model of the strong, independent and successful woman, who successfully affirms her own power and sexuality and defies conventional stereotypes.[20] I too have stressed the extent to which Madonna reverses relations of power and domination and provides strong affirmative images of women. But one could argue that Madonna merely transposes relations of domination, reversing the roles of men and women, rather than dissolving relations of domination. In her concert performances, her dancers are mere appendages whom she dominates and controls, overtly enacting rituals of domination on the stage. In the HBO Blonde Ambition tour video of 1990, for example, she constantly places herself in positions of power and control over the male (and female) dancers. In simulated sex scenes in the tour, Madonna was usually on top and in her infamous masturbation/simulated orgasm scene in "Like A Virgin," the male dancers first fondle Madonna and then disappear as she writhes in an exaggerated orgasm.

In response to this criticism that she only inverts the dominant order, one could argue that Madonna is constantly ironizing relations of domination, putting their mechanisms on display, and, as I argued in my reading of "Express Yourself," subverting them by disclosing the artificiality, constructedness, and reversibility of relations of power and domination. Yet in her "real" everyday relations with her cast, friends, and family in the documentary *Truth or Dare* (1991), she also constantly positions herself as the mother of her troupe and constantly affirms her power over them, often admitting in interviews that she is a "bitch" and "control-freak." Before each performance, she says a "prayer," much like a football coach prepping his crew to go out and win the big one (in one sequence, she concludes by ordering her minions to go out and "kick ass"). In both work and leisure scenes in *Truth or Dare*, Madonna is clearly in charge, and the opening song of the HBO documentary of the concert showed her with a whip in hand, proclaiming "I am the boss!"

One could, of course, argue that the film *Truth and Dare* is itself a put-on that deconstructs the very genre of a film documentary by undermining the opposition between backstage and onstage.[21] In Madonna's entourage, backstage is onstage, the omnipresent camera catching every nuance and Madonna and many of her circle playing to the film being shot. Yet one could argue that the many images, scenes, and comments of her family, tour ensemble, friends, and fans captures aspects of the "truth" of Madonna and present perspectives on the "real" Madonna. For what is "Madonna" other than the effects she produces and generates, the public persona that she assiduously constructs? The one thing that comes through repeatedly, reinforced by her many interviews and music performances, is that Madonna is in charge, that she is a control freak, that she totally dominates everyone around her. As for Nietzsche, the will to power is at the center of Madonna's universe, and Madonna represents herself as the subject of this will, as the center of power and all-powerful subject. Whereas it is salutary that she presents images of powerful women overcoming male domination, and these images might help to empower women, they do not overcome the dynamics of power and domination in our society. Nor do they present an alternative to the relations of domination and oppression that currently structure everyday life in contemporary societies.

Someone who cultivates an aesthetic of shock and excess, as does Madonna, is certain to offend and to become a target of criticism. Madonna, however, thrives on criticism, which, along with her deployment of fashion and sexuality, helps her produce an identity as rule-breaker and transgressor. Her breaking of rules has progressive elements in that it goes against ruling gender, sex, fashion, and racial hierarchies, and her message that identity is something that everyone can and must construct for themselves is also appealing. Yet by constructing identity largely in terms of fashion and image, Madonna plays into precisely the imperatives of the fashion and consumer industries that offer a "new you" and a solution to all of your problems by the purchase of products and services.[22] By emphasizing image, she plays into the dynamics of the contemporary image culture that reduces art, politics, and the theatrics of everyday life to the play of image, downplaying the role of communication, commitment, solidarity, and concern for others in the constitution of one's identity and personality.

Madonna is thus emblematic of the narcissistic 1980s, a period not yet over, in which the cultivation of the individual self and the obsessive pursuit of one's own interests was enshrined as cultural mythology. The imperative "go for it!" echoes through the 1980s, and Madonna went for it and got it. Yet in becoming the most recognizable woman entertainer of her era (and perhaps of all time), Madonna produced works that have multiple and contradictory effects and that in many ways helped subvert dominant conservative ideologies. Yet her work has become increasingly complex, and it is precisely this complexity, as well as her continued popularity, that has made Madonna a highly controversial object of academic analysis in recent years. Madonna allows many, even contradictory, readings which are grounded in her polysemic and modernist texts and her contradictory cultural effects. At dull gatherings, mention Madonna and you can be sure that there will be violent arguments, with some people attacking and others passionately defending her. Whether one loves or hates her, Madonna is a constant provocation who reveals the primacy of fashion and image in contemporary culture and in the social constructedness of identity.

Notes

1. Elizabeth Wilson, *Adorned in Dreams* (London: Virago, 1985).

2. Following Marshall Berman, I am interpreting modernity as an epoch of rapid change, innovation, and negation of the old and creation of the new, a process bound up with industrial capitalism, the French revolution, urbanization, and social and cultural differentiation. "Modernism," from this perspective, denotes a series of artistic practices that attempt to produce innovation in the arts in form, style, and content, which begin with Baudelaire in the mid-nineteenth century and continue through Madonna. See Marshall Berman, *All That Is Solid Melts into Air* (New York: Simon and Schuster, 1982).

3. See Wilson, *Adorned in Dreams.*

4. Philip Wexler, *Becoming Somebody* (London and Washington, D.C.: The Falmer Press, 1982).

5. See Douglas Kellner and Michael Ryan, *Camera Politica: The Politics and Ideology of Contemporary Hollywood Film* (Bloomington: Indiana University Press, 1988), and Douglas Kellner, *Television and the Crisis of Democracy: Contributions Toward a Critical Theory of Television* (Boulder, Colo.: Westview Press, 1990).

6. Contemporary cultural studies focus on textual analysis and/or audience reception alone, generally ignoring the political economy and production of culture. In his study of Madonna, for instance, John Fiske writes: "A cultural analysis, then, will reveal both the way the dominant ideology is structured into the text and into the reading subject, and those textual features that enable negotiated, resisting, or oppositional readings to be made. Cultural analysis reaches a satisfactory conclusion when the ethnographic studies of the historically and socially located meanings that *are* made are related to the semiotic analysis of the text" (*Reading the Popular* [Boston: Unwin Hyman, 1989], 98). I believe, by contrast, that analysis of the political economy and production of culture is an important component in cultural studies that has been downplayed and even ignored in the recent boom in cultural studies. For my argument for a multiperspectival cultural studies, see Kellner, "Toward a Multiperspectival Cultural Studies," *Centennial Review* 26 (1992): 5–41.

7. *People,* May 13, 1985.

8. *People,* March 13, 1985.

9. *Forbes,* October 1, 1990.

10. Melanie Morton, "Don't Go for Second Sex Baby!," in *The Madonna Connection,* ed. Cathy Schwichtenberg (Boulder, Colo.: Westview, 1992), 220–243.

11. A similar deconstruction of the male gaze is present in the 1986 music video "Open Your Heart." The scenario showed Madonna working in a peep show, with sleazy men ogling her. She appeared somewhat distanced and cool; thus the video

could be read as putting on display the modes of male voyeurism through which the objectification of women's bodies takes place. On this reading, Madonna refuses in the video to allow herself to be an object of male desire; the viewer who wishes to watch her in this mode is rendered uncomfortable by being put in the subject position of sleazy, voyeuristic males. Thus, although the video offers Madonna's body as a spectacle, as an object of voyeuristic pleasure, the framing of the images makes difficult fetishistic viewing by identifying voyeurism and the objectification of the female body as part of a social process that exploits woman for the entertainment of pathetic voyeuristic males.

Susan Bordo counters that the video nonetheless reinforces the spectacle of women's objectification, that the viewer "is not *really* decentered and confused by this video," despite the "ambiguities it formally contains," and that the narrative context is "virtually irrelevant" ("'Material Girl': The Effacements of Postmodern Culture," in Schwichtenberg, *The Madonna Connection,* 272–290). In fact, viewers see the video differently, and although the images of the video may reinforce voyeuristic viewing of objectified women's bodies, as Bordo suggests, the narrative context and juxtaposition of lyrics and images may disrupt, in modernist fashion, voyeuristic viewing. Like "Material Girl," the video of "Open Your Heart" may have contradictory effects and appeal both to cultural critics and those feminists who evaluate deconstruction and subversion, as well as to men who like to gaze upon women's bodies and women who gain pleasure in identifying with objectified females; lucky Madonna, whose polysemic texts attract a wide range of readings and audiences.

12. Madonna started giving AIDS benefits in the late 1980s and her album *Like a Prayer* contained AIDS/HIV information and safe-sex advice. In the 1990s, however, she became more overtly political for a variety of causes and began referring to herself as a "revolutionary."

13. I use the term "modernism" in the traditional sense of cultural practices that break established rules, attempt to produce innovative forms, generate polysemic texts with multiple meanings, and that require an active audience/reader to produce meanings from the material of the text. A more recent "postmodern" take on modernism reduces the modernist tradition and practices to a high cultural elitism, enshrined in canonical texts in which modernist rebellions are transformed into new academic cultural norms. Against the modernist canons, postmodernist texts and practices subvert the modernist separation of high and low cultural forms, reject the attempt to produce monumental texts that break with tradition and that are expressive of an author's subjectivity, and often quote and pastiche previous works and forms. Many critics have interpreted Madonna as a "postmodern" artist. See E. Ann Kaplan, *Rocking Around the Clock: Music Television, Postmodernism and Consumer Culture* (New York and London: Routledge, 1987); also Fiske, Bordo, and many of the contributors to Schwichtenberg's *The Madonna Collection.* This reading, however, covers over the classical modernist aspects of her cultural practices. Indeed, Madonna exhibits the instability of distinctions between modernist and postmodernist cultural practices. Thus, I shall indicate in the following pages that Madonna deploys practices and forms that could be described as both "modernist" and "postmodernist."

14. Once again, we see how Madonna's "subversive" artistic practices also coalesce with a successful marketing strategy. Thus Madonna can easily be inter-

preted in terms both of complex aesthetic practices and crass marketing strategies, and her works can thus be read either as works of art or analyzed as commodities. In fact, they are both, and a multidimensional reading should interpret both sides of the Madonna phenomenon.

15. If one conceives "postmodern art" to be a fragmented display of disconnected elements in a flat, superficial play of surface without any depth or meaning (as Fredric Jameson, *Postmodernism: Or, The Cultural Logic of Late Capitalism* [Durham, N.C.: Duke University Press, 1991] and others would have it), Madonna is emphatically not "postmodern." Rather, both her more realist videos and modernist videos convey meanings and messages, but in the more modernist music videos, like "Express Yourself," the meanings are often elusive and difficult to grasp. The modernist strategy of adopting shock techniques has been a constant in Madonna's work, and although she deploys camp, irony, and humor, her subject matter and themes are often quite serious. So in a sense, Madonna is more modernist than postmodernist, although her work also embodies postmodern themes and aesthetic strategies.

16. On camp, see Susan Sontag, who defines it as an "unmistakably modern" (note: not "postmodern") sensibility, characterized by love of the unnatural, artifice, exaggeration, irony, involving play with cultural forms and images, involving a high level of theatricality and travesty—an excellent characterization of Madonna's aesthetic strategies. See *Against Interpretation* (New York: Dell Books, 1969), 277ff.

17. Madonna has been attacked for "poaching" images and phenomena, like voguing, from gay culture and transposing their meanings to popular culture. Black critics attacked her for drawing heavily on black music in her work and then leaving out references to blacks, or people of color, in her pantheon of images in "Vogue." One could argue, however, that Madonna has done as much as anyone to "normalize" gay and lesbian sexuality and is indeed idolized by many in the gay and lesbian communities. Likewise, she could respond to her black and other critics of color that she has done as much as anyone to promote black (and Hispanic) music, dancers, singers, and musicians, while attempting to break down color lines and barriers between the races. She could also answer that her pantheon in "Vogue" is arguably a gay male pantheon that includes precisely those whom she cites. But one could also argue that Madonna ultimately privileges whiteness and that the people of color around her simply highlight her distinctive whiteness. Moreover, her videos and concert performances replicate white superiority and power, showing Madonna totally in control of, overshadowing, and dominating everyone else. In any case, the complexity and sensitivity of issues of race, gender, sexual preference, and class that Madonna takes on demonstrate a courage to tackle controversial topics that few popular music figures take up.

18. In April 1992, it was widely reported that Madonna had signed a $60 million deal with Time Warner, to market her albums, music videos, and films, thus providing her with large royalties, development money, and the opportunity to promote the work of young artists. Madonna said that she envisaged the contract as an opportunity to produce a group of collaborating artists that would constitute an "artistic think tank," a cross between the Bauhaus, which revolutionized art, architecture, and design in Germany in the 1920s, and Andy Warhol's factory, which brought together artists from film, music, painting, fashion, and other con-

temporary arts (*New York Times,* April 20, 1992, B1). *Forbes* reported that during 1991–92, Madonna earned $48 million, making her, once again, one of the most highly paid performers of the period (September 28, 1992).

19. In the 1990 *Nightline* interview, Madonna defends "Justify My Love" as art, as "artistic expression," by saying, "I think that's what art is all about, experimenting, but it is an expression, it [sexual fantasy] is my artistic expression." She also admitted to "pushing the limits of what's permissible." In *Truth or Dare,* she talks about refusing to compromise the "artistic integrity" of her work when threatened by police in Toronto who wanted her to tone down her concert masturbation scene. In a later discussion in the film, she indicated that she would continue "pushing buttons," exploring the limits of the permissible, and being political. Finally, in a 1992 *USA Today* interview, she described herself as "revolutionary," the ultimate category of modernist theory and politics (October 9, 1992, D1).

20. Camille Paglia, *New York Times,* December 14, 1990, B1. Paglia's labeling of Madonna as "true feminist" underscores the dogmatism and essentialism that characterisizes her work. For Paglia, there is a "real feminism" and Madonna is it—as opposed to a multiplicity of models of feminism. Moreover, it is Paglia who denotes what "real feminism" is, enabling her to savage sundry versions of "false feminism." Likewise, she theorizes the essentially and genuinely "feminine" and "masculine," binary opposites which she believes provide a metaphysical foundation for culture.

21. Deirdre E. Pribram, "Seduction, Control, & the Search for Authenticity: Madonna's *Truth or Dare,*" in Schwichtenberg, *The Madonna Connection,* 193–219.

22. *Entertainment* magazine, in a special issue on fashion (September 4, 1992), estimates that it could cost $377,012 to cultivate the Madonna look if one adds up the expenses from a year's collection of clothes, jewelry, makeup, and services. The early Madonna, by contrast, legitimated mix-and-match fashion in which anything goes. Madonna's transformation of her fashion strategies and body images thus reflects increased immersion in consumer culture and a growing commodification of her image.

Kaja Silverman

*f*ragments of a
Fashionable Discourse

The image of a woman in front of the mirror, playing to both the male look and her own, has become a familiar metaphor of sexual oppression.[1] Despite this cautionary emblem, I would like to reopen the case on self-display via a brief consideration of dress and adornment, which, as I will attempt to demonstrate, turns upon a much more complex circuit of visual exchange than might at first appear.

The history of Western fashion poses a serious challenge both to the automatic equation of spectacular display with female subjectivity and to the assumption that exhibitionism always implies woman's subjugation to a controlling male gaze. As a number of fashion critics have already observed, ornate dress was primarily a class rather than a gender prerogative during the fifteenth, sixteenth and seventeenth centuries, a prerogative that was protected by law.[2] In other words, sartorial extravagance was a mark of aristocratic power and privilege, and as such a mechanism for tyrannizing over rather than surrendering to the gaze of the (class) other. Moreover, the elegance and richness of male dress equaled and often surpassed that of female dress during this period, so that insofar as clothing was marked by gender, it defined visibility as a male rather than a female attribute.

It was not until the eighteenth century that the male subject retreated from the limelight, handing on his mantle to the female subject. During the second half of that century, the voluminous clothing and elaborate wigs of the nobleman slowly dwindled into what would eventually become the respectable suit and *coiffure à la naturelle* of the gentleman, while female dress and headpieces reached epic proportions.

Quentin Bell attributes the new modesty in male dress to the rise of the middle class, and the premium it placed upon industry. He argues that whereas in earlier centuries wealth was associated with leisure and with lavish dress, it came in the eighteenth century to be associated with top-management work, and thus with sartorial sobriety. However, because leisure was still a way of life for the middle-class woman, it became her "responsibility" to display her husband's wealth through her clothing:

> The nobleman, like the lady, was a creature incapable of useful work; war and sport were the only outlets for his energy, and a high degree of conspicuous leisure was expected of him. Equally, it was important that he should in his own person be a consumer . . . But now . . . idleness was no longer the usual sign of wealth. The man who worked was not infrequently in receipt of a larger income than the men who drew rents off him; an industrious life no longer implied a poor or laborious existence, and therefore ceased to be dishonorable. It was sufficient, therefore, that a man should demonstrate by means of his black coat, cylindrical hat, spotless linen, carefully rolled umbrella, and general air of refined discomfort that he was not actually engaged in the production of goods, but only in some more genteel employment concerned with management or distribution. . . .
>
> But the demands of conspicuous consumption remain. Men might escape them, but woman could not. . . . [On] all public and social occasions it was [woman's] task to demonstrate [man's] ability to pay and thus to carry on the battle, both for herself and her husband.[3]

Bell offers a plausible explanation of the economic and social determinants responsible for the elimination of sumptuousness in male dress, and its intensification in female dress, but he fails to address the psychic consequences of these changes, or their implications for sexual difference. He accounts for the greater lavishness of female clothing exclusively in terms of class, reading it as the obligatory demonstration of the bourgeois woman's financial dependence upon her husband—as a mark, that is, of her subordinate monetary status. (However, at one point earlier in the same book Bell describes the sartorial transformation quite differently, at least hinting at the possibility that it inflicted greater losses upon the male than upon the female subject: "It was as though the men were sacrificing their hair, and indeed all their finery, for the benefit of women."[4] I am more than a little intrigued by this fleeting avowal of male castration, particularly when it is further elaborated with respect to baldness: "Ever since the days of Elisha men have been deeply sensitive to the crowning injustice of nature; the wig gave them a century and a half of immunity. Dignified, not too unpractical in its later stages, above all discreet, it was one of the most flattering contrivances ever invented, and yet it went.")[5]

In his classic study, *The Psychology of Clothes,* J. C. Flügel also attributes the changes in male dress during the eighteenth century to a shift in class relations. As a result of that shift, he suggests, masculine clothing ceased to proclaim hierarchical distinction and became a harmonizing and homogenizing uniform, serving to integrate not only male members of the same class but male members of different classes. However, Flügel is ultimately much more concerned with the psychoanalytic than with the social ramifications of what he calls "The Great Masculine Renunciation," arguing that it worked to inhibit the narcissistic and exhibitionistic desires that were so flamboyantly expressed through aristocratic sumptuousness in preceding centuries. He concludes that since the eighteenth century these desires have been obliged to seek out alternate routes of gratification, and have consequently undergone the following vicissitudes: (1) sublimation into professional "showing off"; (2) reversal into scopophilia; and (3) male identification with woman–as–spectacle.[6]

The exhibitionistic bases of the first of these vicissitudes, professional "showing off," are perhaps most evident in the case of spectator sports, where expertise is virtually synonymous with corporeal display, and where viewing pleasure tends to be vicarious rather than overtly erotic. However, the frequency with which the word "performance" is used to designate masculine success in a wide range of other professional fields indicates that it serves a compensatory function there as well.

The second of these vicissitudes, scopophilia, has of course been closely interrogated by feminists, but they have considered it to be primarily a defense against castration anxiety, and a means of mastering the female subject. Flügel's model indicates that scopophilia may also betray desires that are incompatible with the phallic function—that it may attest to a shared psychic space over and against which sexual difference is constructed. It thus maps out an important area for further feminist work.

The last of these vicissitudes, male identification with woman–as–spectacle, has not received the same amount of critical attention, although it would seem the most potentially destabilizing, at least insofar as gender is concerned. Flügel remarks that this identification may take the culturally acceptable form of associating with a beautiful and well-dressed woman, or the much more extreme and "deviant" form of actually adopting female mannerisms and dress (that is, of transvestism). I would maintain that it also coexists with other classically male "perversions," helping to determine the choice of a fetish, and structuring even the most conventionally heterosexual of voyeuristic transactions.

One thinks perhaps most immediately in this context of the figure of

Scotty (Jimmy Stewart) in *Vertigo*, who manifests such an extraordinary attachment to the particularities of Madeleine's gray suit, black dress, and blonde hairdo. This is by no means an isolated example. From *Some Like It Hot* and *Jezebel* to *Death in Venice, Diva,* and *The Bitter Tears of Petra Von Kant,* cinema has given complex expression to the male fascination with female dress, a fascination that is always inflected in some way by identification.

More surprisingly, so has the novel. Perhaps because it arose out of the same historical moment as the Great Masculine Renunciation, that textual system has from its inception taken a passionate interest in women's clothing. In novels like *Pamela, Madame Bovary, Sister Carrie, Remembrance of Things Past,* and *Lolita,* what purports to be a voyeuristic preoccupation with a female figure often becomes the pretext for endlessly rummaging through her closets and drawers. I cannot help but wonder, for instance, for whom he is really shopping when Humbert Humbert spends a whole afternoon buying dresses with "check weaves, bright cottons, frills, puffed-out short sleeves, soft pleats, snug-fitting bodices and generously full skirts" for Lolita[7]—or when Marcel decides after prolonged deliberation to order not one, but four priceless Fortuny gowns for Albertine. What Angela Carter observes about *Women in Love* holds true for dozens of other French, English and American novels: "If we do not trust the teller but the tale, then the tale positively revels in lace and feathers, bags, beads, blouses and hats. It is always touching to see a man quite as seduced by the cultural apparatus of femininity as Lawrence was, the whole gamut."[8]

By characterizing the sartorial transformation that occurred at the end of the eighteenth century as a "Great Masculine Renunciation," Flügel seems to imply that exhibitionism plays as fundamental a part within the constitution of the male subject as it does within that of the female subject—that voyeurism, which is much more fully associated with male subjectivity than is exhibitionism, is only a secondary formation, or alternative avenue of libidinal gratification. Lacan suggests the same in *Four Fundamental Concepts of Psycho-Analysis.*

What tends to be most widely remembered about the Lacanian account of subjectivity is the emphasis it places upon primary narcissism (that is, upon the decisive role of the mirror stage, which aligns the child's image with the first of the countless images around which its identity will coalesce). However, what is equally important, although less frequently remarked, is the function performed by the gaze of the Other, both at this founding moment and upon the occasion of all subsequent self-recognitions. The mirror stage is inconceivable without the presence of an other (most classically the mother) to provide scopic as well as "orthopedic" support, and to "stand in" for the Other. Her look articulates the mirror image, and facilitates the child's alignment with it. In order for the child to continue to "see" itself, it must continue to be (culturally) "seen." Lacan compares this visual mediation to photography:

> . . . in the scopic field, the gaze is outside, I am looked at, that is to say, I am a picture.
> This is the function that is found at the heart of the institution of the subject in the visible. What determines me, at the most profound level, in the visible, is the gaze that is outside. It is through the gaze that I enter life and it is from the gaze that I receive its effects. Hence it comes about that the gaze is the instrument through which light is embodied and through which . . . I am *photo-graphed*.[9]

At issue here is what Lacan calls the "inside-out structure of the gaze," whereby the subject comes to regard itself from a vantage external to itself—from the field of the Other.[10] The naive subject—the subject trapped within the illusions of Cartesian consciousness—imagines that it is seeing itself see itself, an experience that testifies to the involuted structure of the gaze, if not to the gaze's ultimate exteriority. In fact, the subject sees itself being seen, and that visual transaction is always ideologically organized.

If we accept this formulation, then it necessarily follows that the male subject is as dependent upon the gaze of the Other as is the female subject, and as solicitous of it—in other words, that he is as fundamentally exhibitionistic. The Great Masculine Renunciation must consequently be understood not as the complete aphanisis of male specularity, but as its disavowal. In mainstream fashion, as in dominant cinema, this disavowal is most frequently effected by identifying male subjectivity with a network of looks, including those of the designer, the photographer, the admirer, and the "connoisseur." However, the paradox upon which such an identification turns, as the visual fascination that accumulates around the figure of the fashion photographer in Antonioni's *Blowup* or Berry Gordy's *Mahogany* would suggest, is that it can only be negotiated through spectacle. It requires the male subject to see himself (and thus to be seen) as "the one who looks at women."

I think in this respect of a 1947 photograph by Richard Avedon that shows two men admiring a woman wearing an example of Dior's New Look, while the eyes of a third are involuntarily drawn to the camera, hidden from our view (see figure 1). Our vision is thus pulled in two radically different directions by the photograph. On the one hand, we are caught up in the circulation of the New Look between the designer (Dior),

Figure 1. Renée, The New Look of Dior, Place de la Concorde, Paris, August 1947. Photographed by Richard Avedon. (Copyright © 1947 by Richard Avedon Inc. All Rights Reserved.)

the fashion photographer (Avedon), and the two passing admirers—a three-way exchange that works to disavow male exhibitionism. On the other hand, our attention is riveted by the look that falls outside this phallic exchange, the look that acknowledges that it is also being watched, and that in so doing foregrounds the specular bases of male subjectivity. Avedon's snapshot literalizes the metaphor of the gaze as "the instrument through which light is embodied and through which [the subject] is photographed."

Having thus firmly evacuated all three passers-by from the position of the gaze, the interpreter might well be tempted to substitute for them either the figure of the absent designer, or that of the invisible photographer, both of whom seem definitively "outside" the picture. This would be a mistake. Although the gaze is constantly anthropomorphized and individualized in this way, it proceeds from the place of the Other, and is an effect of the symbolic order rather than of human vision. Moreover, although certain subjects, machines, and institutions are always "standing in" for the gaze, it is finally unlocalizable. All this is another way of saying that despite their own visual productivity, the designer and photographer are still obliged, like the female model and the male passers-by, to see themselves from the place of the Other. And since the male subject, like the female subject, has no visual status apart from dress and/or adornment, what they see is at least in part a vestimentary "package."

Clothing and other kinds of ornamentation make the human body culturally visible. As Eugenie Lemoine-Luccioni suggests, clothing draws the body so that it can be culturally seen, and articulates it as a meaningful form.[11] Lemoine-Luccioni's point may be supported by examples from both literature and film. The eponymous heroine of Theodore Dreiser's novel *Sister Carrie* is presented as the quintessence of desirability, yet her physical features are never described. Her body is evoked exclusively through her meticulously described wardrobe, which, like the cut-out clothes of a paper doll, imply in advance a certain shape and stance. Similarly, the body of Charlotte (Bette Davis) in Irving Rapper's *Now, Voyager* conforms so closely to the outlines of her clothing that she can be transformed from an unsightly spinster into a beautiful sophisticate simply by substituting a fashionable suit, hairdo, and pair of high-heeled shoes for the horn-rimmed spectacles, shapeless housedress, and oxford shoes she previously wore.

Even our visual access to the *undressed* body is mediated by the prevailing vestimentary codes. In *Seeing Through Clothes*, Anne Hollander argues that throughout the history of Western art, the (female) nude has always assumed the form dictated by contemporary fashion:

The placement, size, and shape of the breasts, the set of the neck and shoulders, the relative girth and length of the rib cage, the exact disposition of its fleshy upholstery, front and back—all these, along with styles of posture both seated and upright, are continually shifting according to the way clothes have been variously designed in history to help the female body look beautiful (and natural) *on their terms*. Nude art, unavoidably committed to Eros, accepts these terms.[12]

Clothing exercises as profoundly determining an influence upon living, breathing bodies as it does upon their literary and cinematic counterparts, affecting contour, weight, muscle development, posture, movement, and libidinal circulation. Dress is one of the most important cultural implements for articulating and territorializing human corporeality—for mapping its erotogenic zones and for affixing a sexual identity.

Proust's *Remembrance of Things Past* offers a brilliant account of corporeal transformations that took place as the consequence of one major change in fashionable female clothing—the demise of the bustle. The passage in question also dramatizes the semiotic shift that occurs during any such change, that is, the relegation of the now-superseded look to the wastebasket of artificiality and absurdity, and the enshrinement of the new look as natural and free. At the same time, through its emphasis upon the occasional unruliness and superfluity of Odette's flesh, it shows the current fashion to be as fully constructed as the outdated one. It is finally not Odette's body but her cambric and silk that are "liberated" by the passing of the bustle:

Odette's body seemed now to be cut out in a single silhouette wholly confined within a "line" which, following the contours of the woman, had abandoned the ups and downs, the ins and outs, the reticulations, the elaborate dispersions of the fashions of former days, but also, where it was her anatomy that went wrong by making unnecessary digressions within or without the ideal form traced by it, was able to rectify, by a bold stroke, the errors of nature, to make good, along a whole section of its course, the lapses of the flesh as well as of the material. The pads, the preposterous "bustle" had disappeared, as well as those tailed bodices which, overlapping the skirt and stiffened by rods of whalebone, had so long amplified Odette with an artificial stomach and had given her the appearance of being composed of several disparate pieces which there was no individuality to bind together. The vertical fall of the fringes, the curve of the ruches had made way for the inflexion of a body which made silk palpitate as a siren stirs the waves and gave to cambric a human expression, now that it had been liberated, like an organic and living form, from the long chaos and nebulous envelopment of fashions at last dethroned.[13]

In thus stressing the coerciveness and constraints of clothing, I do not mean to argue for the return to "prelapsarian nakedness," as Flügel ultimately does, or for a "rationalization" of dress that would permit more "natural" and "uninhibited" corporeal movement and development. Even if my sympathies were not fully on the side of extravagant sartorial display, I would feel impelled to stress as strongly as possible that clothing is a necessary condition of subjectivity—that in articulating the body, it simultaneously articulates the psyche. As Freud tells us, the ego is "a mental projection of the surface of the body," and that surface is largely defined through dress.[14] Laplanche makes a similar point when he insists upon the need for an "envelope" or "sack" to contain both body and ego, and to make possible even the most rudimentary distinctions between self and other, inside and outside.[15] In effect, clothing is that envelope.

Before commenting upon some of the different vestimentary envelopes currently available to us, I would like to make a few final remarks about normative male dress since the Great Masculine Renunciation, and about its implications for male sexuality. To begin with, class distinctions have "softened" and gender distinctions have "hardened" since the end of the eighteenth century. In other words, sexual difference has become the primary marker of power, privilege, and authority, closing the specular gap between men of different classes and placing men and women on opposite sides of the great visual divide.

Second, whereas in earlier centuries dominant male dress gave a certain play to fancy, it has subsequently settled into sobriety and rectitude. Since the sartorial revolution, male dress has also given a very small margin to variation, remaining largely unchanged for two centuries. These last two features define male sexuality as stable and constant, and so align it with the symbolic order. In other words, they help to conflate the penis with the phallus.

Last, but by no means least, conventional male dress since the end of the Great Masculine Renunciation has effaced everything about the male body but the genital zone, which is itself metaphorically rather than metonymically evoked (that is, represented more through a general effect of verticality than through anything in the style or cut of a garment that might articulate an organ beneath). This "sublimation" is another important mechanism for identifying the male subject with the phallus.

Female dress, on the other hand, has undergone frequent and often dramatic changes, accentuating the breasts at one moment, the waist at another, and the legs at another. These abrupt libidinal displacements, which constantly shift the center of erotic gravity, make the female body far less stable and localized than its male counterpart. I would also argue that fashion creates the free-floating quality of female sexuality, a quality that Flügel was one of the first to note:

> [A]mong the most important of [sexual] differences is the tendency for the sexual libido to be more diffuse in women than in men; in women the whole body is sexualized, in men the libido is more definitely concentrated upon the genital zone; and this is true . . . both for showing the female body and for looking at it. Hence exposure of *any* part of the female body works more erotically than exposure of the corresponding part of the male, save only in the case of the genitals themselves.[16]

The endless transformations within female clothing construct female sexuality and subjectivity in ways that are at least potentially disruptive, both of gender and of the symbolic order, which is predicated upon continuity and coherence. However, by freezing the male body into phallic rigidity, the uniform of orthodox male dress makes it a rock against which the waves of female fashion crash in vain.

In arguing that gender has replaced class as the primary distinguishing marker within clothing over the past two centuries, I do not mean to suggest that economic and social differences no longer figure centrally there. Although fashion constructs a "new" female body every year, and thereby challenges the assumption of a fixed identity, it does so at the behest of capital, and in the interests of surplus value (fashionable time "clocks over" long before any garment can be worn out or used up). Moreover, although the fashion industry operates through replication and mass production, making variants of the same garments available to every class, a temporal lag always separates the moment at which such a garment is available to a select few from the moment at which it is generally disseminated. This temporal lag guarantees that by the time most people have access to a given "look," it will no longer be "really" fashionable, and so asserts class difference even in the face of the most far-reaching sartorial homogenization.

I would also agree with Bell that "the history of fashionable dress is tied to the competition between classes, in the first case the emulation of the aristocracy by the bourgeoisie, and then the more extended competition that results from the ability of the proletariat to compete with the middle class."[17] However, this competition is not always a matter of the middle class aspiring to dress like the upper class, or of the proletariat trying to dress like the middle class. Fashionable change is often the result of creative pressure from "below"—from the middle class in the case of the

Great Masculine Renunciation, and from the working class in the case of skinheads and punks.

Increasingly, in the second half of the twentieth century, imaginative dress has become a form of contestation—a way of challenging not only dominant values, but traditional class and gender demarcations. Clothing may function as a subcultural flag, as the zoot-suit did for the Latinos; it may assert personal style in the face of sartorial hegemony, as it did for Baudelaire's dandy;[18] it may become the banner of a whole youth movement, as beads, jeans, and T-shirts did for the hippies; it may become the mechanism for forcing a culture to confront the negativity upon which it is based, as it is for punk; or it may grow out of the desire to reclaim spectacle for the male subject, as is manifestly the case with rock music and MTV.

These oppositional gestures are never absolute. As Dick Hebdige remarks, they "in part contest and in part agree with the dominant definitions of who and what [their wearers] are, and there is a substantial amount of shared ideological ground . . . between them and the fashion industry."[19] Deviant dress is also quickly absorbed by the fashion industry. However, I think it is too easily assumed that the absorption means recuperation, in the sense of completely neuralizing what is politically, socially, or sexually significant about a particular vestimentary mode. If a given "look" is appropriated by the fashion industry from a subculture or subordinate class, that is because its ideological force and formal bravura can no longer be ignored—because it has won not only a style war, but a pitched cultural battle. It is, moreover, no small thing to effect a change in mainstream fashion. If, as I suggested earlier, clothing not only draws the body so that it can be seen, but also maps out the shape of the ego, then every transformation within a society's vestimentary code implies some kind of shift within its ways of articulating subjectivity.

Feminism has not demonstrated the sartorial audacity and imaginativeness of some recent subcultures, nor has it evolved a single, identifying form of dress. This obviously has something to do with the heterogeneous nature of feminism itself—with its strategic refusal to toe any one party line, or to concentrate its energies on a single common front. However, I would argue that the sartorial reticence of North American feminism is also part of a larger reaction against everything that has been traditionally associated with female narcissism and exhibitionism, that it is the symptom of what might almost be called "The Great Feminine Renunciation." As I look about me in the mid-eighties, I am forcibly struck by the fact that every current vestimentary code that insists upon women's social and political equality also tends either toward the muted imitation of male dress (jeans and shirts, slacks and jackets, the "business suit"), or its bold parody (leather jackets and pants, the tuxedo "look," sequined ties). Feminism would seem to be in the process of repeating male vestimentary history.

I would like to conclude this essay with the defense of a rather different sartorial system, one that is not at present the uniform of any subcultural group (although it sprang out of the black and hippie subcultures of the 1960s), but one that, because of its capacity for including the past by reconceiving it, would seem able to provide the female subject with a more flexible and capacious "envelope"—that style of dress which is commonly known as "vintage clothing" or "retro."

In an essay published in the *New York Times* in 1975, Kennedy Fraser proposed that retro "represents the desire to find style, but obliquely, and splendor, but tackily, and so to put an ironic distance between the wearers and the fashionableness of their clothes."[20] The phrase "ironic distance" coincides theoretically with what others have called "masquerade,"[21] and it underscores several important features of thrift-shop dressing: its affection for objects that were once culturally cherished but have since been abandoned; its predilection for a tarnished and "stagey" elegance; and its desire to convert clothing into costume or "fancy dress." However, Fraser is oblivious to the ideological implications of what she notes; for her, retro is simply a way of "saying something quite intense but only in a footnote."[22] She is also much too quick to characterize it as another of fashion's wiles, rather than—as I would argue—as a sartorial strategy that works to denaturalize its wearer's specular identity, and one that is fundamentally irreconcilable with fashion.

In *Système de la Mode,* Roland Barthes describes fashion as a discourse that vehemently denies the possibility of any relation with its own recent past—as a discourse predicated upon the disavowal of its own historical construction: "As soon as the signified *Fashion* encounters a signifier (such and such a garment), the sign becomes the year's Fashion, but thereby this Fashion dogmatically rejects the Fashion which preceded it, its own past; every new Fashion is a refusal to inherit, a subversion against the oppression of the preceding Fashion; Fashion experiences itself as a Right, the natural right of the present over the past."[23] A critical aspect of this disavowal is the binary logic through which fashion distinguishes "this year's look" from "last year's look," a logic that turns upon the opposition between "the new" and "the old" and works to transform one season's treasures into the next season's trash.

Retro refuses this antithesis. Because its elements connote not only a generalized "oldness" but a specific moment both in the (social) history of clothing, and in that of a cluster of closely allied discourses (painting, photography, cinema, the theater, the novel), it inserts its wearer into a complex network of cultural and historical references. At the same time, it avoids the pitfalls of a naive referentiality; by putting quotation marks around the garments it revitalizes, it makes clear that the past is available to us only in a textual form, and through the mediation of the present.

By recontextualizing objects from earlier periods within the frame of the present, retro is able to "reread" them in ways that maximize their radical and transformative potential—to chart the affinities, for instance, between fashions of the forties and feminism in the eighties, or between fashions of the twenties and the "unisex look" of the late sixties. Vintage clothing is also a mechanism for crossing vestimentary, sexual, and historical boundaries. It can combine jeans with sawed-off flapper dresses or tuxedo jackets, art deco with "pop art" jewelry, silk underwear from the thirties with a tailored suit from the fifties and a body that has been "sculpted" into androgyny through eighties-style weight lifting.

Thrift-shop dressing recycles fashion's waste, exploiting the use value that remains in discarded but often scarcely worn clothing. Because it establishes a dialogue between the present-day wearers of that clothing and its original wearers, retro also provides a means of salvaging the images that have traditionally sustained female subjectivity, images that have been consigned to the wastebasket not only by fashion but by "orthodox" feminism. In other words, vintage clothing makes it possible for certain of those images to "live on" in a different form, much as postmodern architecture does with earlier architectural styles of even with the material fragments of extinct buildings. It is thus a highly visible way of acknowledging that its wearer's identity has been shaped by decades of representational activity, and that no cultural project can ever "start from zero."

Notes

1. The most influential feminist critique of female spectacle is Laura Mulvey's "Visual Pleasure and Narrative Cinema," *Screen* 16, no. 3 (1975): 6–18.
2. See René Konig, *The Restless Image,* trans. F. Bradley (London: Allen & Unwin, 1973), 11, 139; and Quentin Bell, *On Human Finery* (London: Hogarth, 1976), 23–24.
3. Bell, *On Human Finery,* 141.
4. Ibid., 126.
5. Ibid., 123f.
6. J. C. Flügel, *The Psychology of Clothes* (London: Hogarth, 1930), 117–119.
7. Vladimir Nabokov, *Lolita* (Greenwich, Conn.: Fawcett, 1955), 99.
8. Angela Carter, *Nothing Sacred* (London: Virago, 1982), 162–163.

9. Jacques Lacan, *The Four Fundamental Concepts of Psycho-Analysis,* trans. Alan Sheridan (New York: Norton, 1978), 106.

10. Ibid., 82.

11. Eugenie Lemoine-Luccioni, *La Robe* (Paris: Seuil, 1983), 147.

12. Anne Hollander, *Seeing Through Clothes* (New York: Viking, 1975), 91.

13. Marcel Proust, *Remembrance of Things Past,* trans. C. K. Scott Moncrieff and Terence Kilmartin (New York: Random House, 1982), 1:665.

14. This is the approved editorial gloss of the following line from *The Ego and the Id:* "The ego is first and foremost a body-ego; it is not merely a surface entity, but is itself the projection of a surface" (*The Standard Edition of the Complete Psychological Works of Sigmund Freud,* trans. James Strachey [London: Hogarth, 1953–1966], 9:26).

15. Jean Laplanche, *Life and Death in Psychoanalysis,* trans. Jeffrey Mehlman (Baltimore: Johns Hopkins University Press, 1976), 80–81.

16. Flügel, *Psychology of Clothes,* 107.

17. Bell, *On Human Finery,* 155.

18. Baudelaire describes dandyism as "the burning desire to create a personal form of originality," a "cult of the ego" that "can even survive what are called illusions" (*Selected Writings on Art and Artists,* trans. P. E. Chavet [Cambridge, England: Cambridge University Press, 1972], 420).

19. Dick Hebdige, *Subculture: The Meaning of Style* (London: Methuen, 1979), 86.

20. Reprinted in Kennedy Fraser, *The Fashionable Mind: Reflections on Fashion, 1970–1982* (Boston: David R. Godine, 1985), 125.

21. See, for instance, Mary Ann Doane, "Film and the Masquerade: Theorising the Female Spectator," *Screen* 23, nos. 3 and 4 (1982):74–87.

22. Fraser, *Fashionable Mind,* 125.

23. I quote from the English translation of this book, *The Fashion System,* trans. Matthew Ward and Richard Howard (New York: Hill and Wang, 1983), 273.

Iris Marion Young

Women Recovering Our Clothes

"See yourself in wool" (figure 1). Yes, I would like that. I see myself in that wool, heavy, thick, warm, swinging around my legs in rippling caresses. And who might I be? An artist, perhaps, somewhat well established, thinking of my next series. Or maybe I will be a lecturer coming off the airplane, greeted by my colleagues, who will host me at a five-star restaurant. Or perhaps I'm off to meet my new lover, who will greet me face to face and stroke my wool.

But who's this coming up behind me? Bringing me down to his size? Don't look back, I can't look back, his gaze is unidirectional, he sees me but I can't see him. But no—I am seeing myself in wool seeing him see me. Is it that I cannot see myself without seeing myself being seen? So I need him there to unite me and my image of myself? Who does he think I am?

So I am split. I see myself, and I see myself being seen. Might such a split express a woman's relation to clothes, to images of clothes, to images of herself in clothes, whomever she imagines herself to be? Can we separate the panels? I wonder if there's a way we can get him out of the picture.

MATTING: IS THIS A FRAME-UP?

In her monumental book *Seeing Through Clothes,* Anne Hollander argues that the meaning of clothes is conditioned by pictorial images. Through-

Figure 1. "See Yourself in Wool."

out the modern period, Western artists have depicted and sanctified clothing images, associating clothes with kinds of personages and situations. This representation of clothes freezes the conventional into the natural, and people measure women in their clothes in relation to the natural aesthetic created by clothing images.[1]

For most of the modern period, this thesis about the relation of the experience of clothing to images of clothing applied only to those classes able to buy artworks or invited to places where they are displayed. As Ewen and Ewen discuss, however, the mid-nineteenth century witnessed a revolutionary proletarianization of the image with the invention of cheap methods of color printing. By the early twentieth century it would seem that the experience of clothing, especially women's experience of clothing, is saturated with the experience of images of women in clothing—in advertising drawings and photographs, catalogs, and film.[2]

Hollander cites the historical specificity of twentieth-century women's clothing standards and images conditioned by cinema. The nineteenth century held an image of women's demeanor as statuesque, immobile, hiding or hobbling the limbs. The twentieth century, by contrast, emphasizes the mobility of women in clothes—the exhibition of legs, skirts and pants that do not so much inhibit movement. Images of clothes show women on the move—striding down the street, leaping with excitement, running on the sands, leaning over a desk. If she is standing still, her hair or skirt or scarf flies with the wind. Contemporary images of women's clothes capture a single movement in a narrative whose beginning and end lie outside the frame.[3]

In wearing our clothes, Hollander suggests, we seek to fashion ourselves in the mode of the dominant pictorial aesthetic. In this project the mirror provides us a means of representation. In the mirror we see not the "bare facts" but a clothed image reverberating the dominant magazine and film images of us in our clothes. Contemporary urban life provides countless opportunities for us to see ourselves—in hotel and theater lobbies, in restaurants and powder rooms, in train stations and store windows.[4] I love to walk down a city street when I feel well dressed and to catch sight of my moving image in a store window, trying not to see myself seeing myself. I imagine myself in a movie, freely swinging down the street in happy clothes, on my way. The mirror gives me pictures, and the pictures in magazines and catalogs give me reflections of identities in untold but signified stories. The feminist question is: *Whose* imagination conjures up the pictures and their meanings?

PANEL I: REFLECTIONS ON SNOW WHITE'S MIRROR

Our experience of clothes derives from film in more than a merely asso-
ciative way, Maureen Turim suggests, but also through producing the implicit narrative imagination of our clothes.

> Films not only expose new fashions to a mass audience, they not only
> provide the fashion industry with a glittering showcase; because we see
> those fashions within a narrative context, films also invest fashions with
> unconscious attachments, connotations. This process, the narration of
> fashion, means more than the association of a style with a given story or
> fiction. It is a process that fuses the unconscious effects of film experience
> with the very lines and colors of clothing designs.[5]

My question is: How shall I describe a woman's pleasure in clothes? If I
live my identification with the clothing images through my experience of
film narrative, it may not be too wild to explore our pleasure in clothes
through feminist film theory. Following a Lacanian framework, feminist
film theorists have developed an account of a female experience of pleasure
in the objectified female body within a patriarchal order. The story goes
something like this.[6]

Subjectivity is crucially constituted by relations of looking. Through
active looking at an image of himself in the mirror, the subject gains a
sense of narcissistic identification with a totalized motor being misrepre-
sented as a unity. In the phallocratic order, however, this subject who takes
pleasure in looking at objects other than himself and who takes pleasure
in looking at totalized images of himself is a male subject. The phallocratic
order splits looking into active and passive moments. The gaze is masculine, and that upon which it gazes is feminine. Women are only lack, the
other that shores up the phallic subject, the object that gives power and
unified identity to men's looking. If women are to achieve any subjectivity
it can only be through adopting this position of the male subject who takes
pleasure in the objectification of women.

In film the activity of looking has two aspects—a voyeuristic and a fetishistic—and film positions women's bodies in relation to both sorts of
looking. Voyeuristic looking takes a distance from the object of its gaze,
from which it is absent and elsewhere. From this distance the object of the
gaze cannot return or reciprocate the gaze; the voyeur's look is judgmental,
holding power over the guilty object of the gaze by offering punishment
or forgiveness. In fetishistic looking, on the other hand, the subject finds
his likeness in the object, represented as the unity of the phallus. In film

both voyeuristic and fetishistic looking deny the threatening difference of the female, either judging her lacking and guilty or turning her body or parts of her body into an icon in which the subject finds himself, his phallus.

Women also watch films and enjoy them. What, in this account, makes women's pleasure in films possible? Only identification with the male subject. I quote Ann Kaplan:

> Why do we find our objectification and surrender pleasurable? . . . Such pleasure is not surprising if we consider the shape of the girl's Oedipal crisis. . . . The girl is forced to turn away from the illusory unity with the Mother in the prelinguistic realm and has to enter the symbolic world which involves subject and object. Assigned the place of object (lack), she is the recipient of male desire, passively appearing rather than acting. Her sexual pleasure in this position can thus be constructed only around her own objectification. Furthermore, given the male structuring around sadism, the girl may adopt a corresponding masochism. . . . We could say that in locating herself in fantasy in the erotic, the woman places herself as either passive recipient of male desire or, at one remove, as *watching* a woman who is passive recipient of male desires and sexual actions.[7]

I cannot deny that these analyses apply to our experience of clothes, to our experience of images of women in clothes. The voyeuristic gaze is often implicit or explicit in magazine advertising for clothes, and it is easy to find the language of guilt and imperfection attached to the clothed woman. Sandra Bartky describes how women internalize the objectifying gaze of what she calls the "fashion-beauty complex," a gaze that deprecates and evaluates a woman's body.

> I must exist perpetually at a distance from my physical self, fixed at this distance in a permanent posture of disapproval. Thus, insofar as the fashion-beauty complex shapes one of the introjected subjects for whom I exist as object, I sense myself as deficient. Nor am I able to control in any way those images which give rise to the criteria by which those deficiencies appear. . . . All the projections of the fashion-beauty complex have this in common: they are images of *what I am not*.[8]

Good clothes, new clothes, this year's clothes will cover up my flaws, straighten me out, measure me up to the approving eye.

Maureen Turim discusses how within the matrix of film imagery women's clothing fashions fetishize the female body. Through what she calls the "slit aesthetic," clothing cuts play fabric off against bare skin, turning the body or body parts into fetishes. Sweater cut low in front or back, bathing suits and lingerie cut high on the hip, cutoffs in midriff at the waist, skirt slits or short skirts, cutoff pants—all pattern the clothing cut to focus on bare flesh, and frequently the cuts also direct attention to the fetishized neck, breasts, stomach, genitals, thighs, calves, ankles.[9] The slit aesthetic creates the image of the sexy clothed body, an image of phallic female power. We women sometimes respond to this image with desire, the desire to be that sexy woman.

It's all true, I guess; at least I cannot deny it: in clothes I seek to find the approval of the transcending male gaze; in clothing I seek to transform myself into a bewitching object that will capture his desire and identity. When I leaf through magazines and catalogs I take my pleasure from imagining myself perfected and beautiful and sexual for the absent or mirrored male gaze. I take pleasure in these images of female bodies in their clothes because my own gaze occupies the position of the male gaze insofar as I am a subject at all. I will not deny it, but it leaves a hollowness in me. If I simply affirm this, I must admit that for me there is no subjectivity that is not his, that there is no specifically female pleasure I take in clothes.[10]

But I remember the hours that Suzanne and I played with paper dolls, cutting, drawing, coloring, trading their clothes, stacks of their clothes in shoe boxes. Suzanne and I talked about the clothes, and we dressed up the dolls for their activities—going to work or on vacation, visiting each other or going on shopping trips; yes, they went on dates, too, though I don't remember any men paper dolls. I remember playing paper dolls with Suzanne, and I want to be loyal to her.

Panel II: through the looking glass

Luce Irigaray's book *Speculum of the Other Woman*[11] concerns how Western culture expresses a masculine desire and has silenced and repressed a specifically female desire. The masculine discourse that receives expression in Western ontology conceives being in solid objects, self-identical, one and the same thing, to be observed, measured, passed around from hand to hand in the relations of commodity exchange that bind the male social contract. In patriarchal society woman is the supreme object, the possession that complements his subjectivity. In the patriarchal discourse of Western culture, Irigaray suggests, woman serves as the mirror for masculine subjectivity and desire. She reflects back to him his self, as the mother who engendered him or the wife who serves him and gives him his image in a child. The male-gaze theory I have summarized illustrates this function of femininity as the mirror in which man sees himself reflected. The institutions of patriarchy contribute to enhancing male subjectivity by organizing women's desire and action to be identified with his, desiring to make herself into a beautiful object for his gaze, finding her pleasure in his satisfaction.

The subversion of patriarchy, then, according to Irigaray, requires that women speak our desire, not as it has been formed in the interests of men but from and for ourselves. Speaking for ourselves to one another from our own female flesh and imagination, our creation of a different voice can pierce the smug universality of transcendental subjectivity. I am not sure what Irigaray means by our lips speaking together, but for me it means a discovery, recovery, and invention of women's culture. We can mine traditionally female social practices and experiences and find in them specific ways that we as women relate to one another and to ourselves, female-specific intrinsic values. There is no question that there are race, class, and sexuality differences in women's relations to one another, and in this women's culture women most often relate to women of the same race or class identification as themselves. Still, I have often found it easiest to bridge such differences between myself and another woman by talking about elements of women's culture—often clothes.

The project of speaking such women's culture does not deny women's oppression and that structures of femininity support that oppression. But if we have always been agents, we have also expressed our desire and energy in positive symbols and practices. Irigaray suggests that whereas patriarchal masculine desire is obsessed with identifiable objects that can be seen, women's desire is plural, fluid, and interested more in touch than in sight. She links a phallocentric logic of identity with property, the propensity to draw borders, count and measure, and keep hold of one's own; when the goods (women) get together, she suggests, they might speak different relationships. As I recover our clothes, or perhaps cut them out of whole cloth, I shall follow these lines.

Patriarchal fashion folds create a meticulous paradigm of the woman well dressed for the male gaze, then endows with guilt the pleasure we might derive for ourselves in these clothes. Misogynist mythology gloats in its portrayal of women as frivolous body decorators. Well trained to meet the gaze that evaluates us for our finery, for how well we show him off, we then are condemned as sentimental, superficial, duplicitous, because we attend to and sometimes learn to love the glamorous arts.[12] The male gazers paint us gazing at ourselves at our toilet, before the table they call a vanity. In their own image, the male mythmakers can only imagine narcissistic pleasures. Outside this orbit of self-reference, I find three pleasures we take in clothes: touch, bonding, and fantasy.

But for whom do I speak in this "we"? For women. But how can I speak for women? This question expresses a dilemma. Patriarchal domination requires the subversion of its authority by the speaking of a specifically female desire beyond its power to know. But there cannot be a woman's desire; the very project of feminist subversion leads us to the dissolution of such universals. When I speak, then, for whom do I speak? For myself, of course. But this is politics, not autobiography, and I speak from my own experience, which I claim resonates with that of other women. My own experience is particular and limited, and it is possible that it most resonates among white, middle-class, heterosexual professional women in late capitalist society. At least I can claim to speak only for the experience of women like me. I believe that some of the experience I express resonates with that of other women, but that is for them to say. The differences among women do not circumscribe us within exclusive categories, but the only way we can know our similarities and differences is by each of us expressing our particular experience. I offer, then, this expression of women's pleasure in clothes.

Touch

Irigaray suggests that masculine desire expresses itself through visual metaphors, that the experience of seeing, gazing, is primary in a masculine aesthetic. Sight is the most distancing of the senses, in which the subject stands separate and against the object, which is other, there. A patriarchal seeing, however, according to Irigaray, separates only in order to know the objects, to master them with the mind's eye and thereby find in the objects the reflection of the subject's brilliance.

Feminine desire, Irigaray suggests, moves through the medium of touch more than sight. Less concerned with identifying things, comparing them, measuring them in their relations to one another, touch immerses the subject in fluid continuity with the object, and for the touching subject the object touched reciprocates the touching, blurring the border between self and other. By touch I do mean that specific sense of skin on matter, fingers on texture. By I also mean an orientation to sensuality as such that includes all senses. Thus we might conceive a mode of vision, for example, that is less a gaze, distanced from and mastering its object, than an immersion in light and color. Sensing as touching is within, experiencing what touches it as ambiguous, continuous, but nevertheless differentiated.

When I "see" myself in wool it's partly the wool itself that attracts me, its heavy warmth and textured depth. Some of the pleasure of the clothes is the pleasure of fabric and the way the fabric hangs and falls around the body. Straight skirts with slits may give thigh for the eye, but the skirt in all its glory drapes in flowing folds that billow when you twirl. History documents the measurement of nobility and grace through fabric. Women have been imprisoned by this history, have been used as mannequins to display the trappings of wealth.

But feminine experience also affords many of us a tactile imagination, the simple pleasure of losing ourselves in cloth. We wander through yard-goods stores, stroke the fabrics hanging off the bolts, pull them out to appraise the patterns, imagine how they might be best formed around the body or the chair or on the windows.

Some of our clothes we love for their own sake, because their fabric and cut and color charm us and relate to our bodies in specific ways—because, I almost want to say, they love us back. Those wool-blend pin-striped elephant-bottom pants that held a crease so well and flopped so happily around my ankles. The green herringbone wool blazer I made with my own hands and after the lining fell apart sadly gave to my sister because the new lining was too small. The wine-red-print full-sleeved smooth rayon blouse, gathered at the shoulders to drape lightly over my chest. Many of our clothes never attain this privileged status of the beloved, perhaps because our motives for having most of them are so extrinsic: to be in style or to give our face the most flattering color, to be cost-effective, or to please others. Some we love with passion or tenderness, though, and we are sad or angry when they become damaged or go out of fashion.

Bonding

The dedication of Diane Kurys' marvelous movie *Peppermint Soda,* about two teenage sisters in a Paris lycée, reads: "To my sister, who still hasn't given me back my orange sweater."

Clothes often serve for women in this society as threads in the bonds of sisterhood. Women often establish rapport with one another by remarking on their clothes, and doing so often introduces a touch of intimacy or lightness into serious or impersonal situations. When we are relaxing with one another, letting down our guard or just chatting, we often talk about clothes: what we like and what we can't stand, how difficult it is to get this size or that fabric, how we feel when we wear certain kinds of clothes or why we don't wear others. We often feel that women will understand the way clothes are important to us and that men will not. Other women will understand the anxieties, and they will understand the subtle clothing aesthetic. We take pleasure in discussing the arts of scarf tying and draping, the rules and choices of mix and match. Women often have stories to tell about their clothes—and even more often about their jewelry—that connect these items they wear to other women who once wore them, and we often bond with one another by sharing these stories.

Often we share the clothes themselves. Girls often establish relations of intimacy by exchanging clothes; sisters and roommates raid each other's closets, sometimes unpermitted; daughters' feet clomp around in their mothers' shoes. I love my sweater, and in letting you wear it you wear an aspect of me, but I do not possess it, since you can wear it. Or I go into a fit of rage upon discovering that you have gone out in my favorite blouse, for in doing so you have presumed to take my place. As the clothes flow among us, so do our identities; we do not keep hold of ourselves, but share.

In these relations my clothes are not my *property,* separate things with identifiable value that I might bring to market and thus establish with others relations of commodity exchange that would keep a strict accounting of our transactions. I do not possess my clothes; I live with them. And in relating to other women though our clothes we do not just exchange; we let or do not let each other into our lives.

Women often bond with each other by shopping for clothes. Many a lunch hour is spent with women in twos and threes circulating through Filene's Basement, picking hangers off the racks and together entering the mirror-walled common dressing room. There they chat to one another about their lives and self-images as they try on outfits—the events coming up for which they might want new clothes, their worry about getting a cut that will not emphasize the tummy. Women take care of one another in the dressing room, often knowing when to be critical and discouraging and when to encourage a risky choice or an added expense. Women buy often enough on these expeditions, but often they walk out of the store after an hour of dressing up with no parcels at all; the pleasure was in the choosing, trying, and talking, a mundane shared fantasy.

Fantasy

Women take pleasure in clothes, not just in wearing clothes, but also in looking at clothes and looking at images of women in clothes, because they encourage fantasies of transport and transformation. We experience our clothes, if Hollander is right, in the context of the images of clothes from magazines, film, TV that draw us into situations and personalities that we can play at.

Implicitly feminist critics of media images of women have tended to assimilate all images of women in advertising into the pornographic: that such images position women as the object of a male gaze. Clothing ads are split, however (occasionally visually, as we have seen, which creates a complex and oppressive irony), between positioning women as object and women as subject. Clothing images are not always the authoritative mirror that tells who's the fairest of them all, but the entrance to a wonderland of characters and situations.

Roland Barthes analyzes the rhetoric of fashion magazines to show how they evoke such fantasy. In using Barthes's ideas to describe women's experience of clothes, I no doubt will tear them from their systematic fabric. Only a man, I think, would have presumed to present *The Fashion System* between two covers.[13] Barthes is a self-conscious theoretician of ideology, aware that no theoretician transcends the ideology he analyzes. At the close of *The Fashion System* he writes, "There remains a word to be said about the situation of the analyst confronted with, or rather, *within* the systematic universe he has just dealt with; not only because it would be akin to bad faith to consider the analyst as alien to this universe, but also because the semiological project provides the analyst with the formal means to incorporate himself into the system he reconstitutes."[14]

Here is the sensitive theoretician, withdrawing from the authority of the transhistorical gaze precisely in relation to a universe from which he *is* alien, one that speaks a rhetoric not addressed to him. For all his reflexive attention to history and social context, Barthes never remarks on the position of the Fashion analyst as a man.

I don't know that this surprising silence makes his analysis unsatisfactory, or more unsatisfactory than it would otherwise be. Barthes offers wonderfully evocative discussions of the meaning of the rhetoric of fashion magazines that I think express the pleasure of fantasy that clothes can give women. Fashion, he says, offers women a double dream of identity and play—indeed, the invitation to play with identities.[15] The fantasies I have as I leaf through the magazine or click the hangers on the rack, or put on the outfit in the dressing room, may be fleeting and multiple possibilities of who I might be, character types I try on, situations in which I place myself imaginatively. I see myself in wool, but in the mode of another (or several others) in transforming possibilities, all without the real-life anxiety of having to decide who I am. "Yet, in the vision of Fashion, the ludic motif does not involve what might be called the vertigo effect: it multiplies the person without any risk of her losing herself, insofar as, for Fashion, clothing is not play but the *sign* of play."[16]

This fantasy of multiple and changing identities without the anxiety of losing oneself is possible because Fashion creates unreal identities in utopian places. In our clothing fantasies we are not the voyeuristic gaze before whom the narrative reel unfolds, because the pictures come to us only with the feeling of a narrative, not with narrative itself. Clothing ads, catalogs, music videos, and so on present images of situations, clips of possible narratives, but without any thread and temporality. "The doing involved in Fashion is, as it were, abortive: its subject is torn by a representation of essences at the moment of acting: to display the being of doing, without assuming its reality."[17] Fashion images are vague, open—a woman walking on a street, sitting on a patio, leaning on a bed, climbing up a rock. The variables in the formulae can be filled in with any number of concrete narrative values, and our pleasure in the fantasy of clothes is partly imagining ourselves in those possible stories, entering unreality. The very multiplicity and ambiguity of the fantasy settings evoked by clothes and by fashion imagery of these clothes contributes to such pleasure.[18]

There is a certain freedom involved in our relation to clothes, an active subjectivity not represented in the male gaze theory. Here I draw on Sartre but not his gaze theory. In *The Psychology of Imagination,* Sartre proposes imaginary consciousness as a modality of freedom.[19] An image is consciousness of an unreal object. In imagining, I am aware of an unreal object and aware that the object is unreal. The pleasure of imagining derives from just this unreality, for the unreal object has no facticity, no givenness that constrains us, no brute physicality that freedom must deal with or face the consequences. The unreal object has no aspects not presented to me in the image, no "other side" that transcends my apprehension, as does the perceived object. The image gives the affective dimensions of a person or situation, what it feels like to be or to see them, without their material context and consequences. The freedom of the imaginary object lies in the fact that there is nothing in the object that has not been put there by imaginary consciousness.

Part of the pleasure of clothes for many of us consists of allowing ourselves to fantasize with images of women in clothes, and in desiring to become an image, unreal, to enter an intransitive, playful utopia. There are ways of looking at oneself in the mirror that do not appraise oneself before the objectifying gaze, but rather desubstantialize oneself, turn oneself into a picture, an image, an unreal identity. In such fantasy we do not seek to be somebody else. Fantasizing is not wishing, hoping, or planning; it has no future. The clothing image provides the image of situations without any situatedness; there is an infinite before and after; thus the images are open at both ends to an indefinite multitude of possible transformations.

One of the privileges of femininity in rationalized instrumental culture is an aesthetic freedom, the freedom to play with shape and color on the body, to don various styles and looks, and through them exhibit and imagine unreal possibilities. Women often actively indulge in such theatrical imagining, which is largely closed to the everyday lives of men or which they live vicariously through the clothes of women. Such female imagination has liberating possibilities because it subverts, unsettles the order of respectable, functional rationality in a world where that rationality supports domination. The unreal that wells up through imagination always creates the space for a negation of what is, and thus the possibility of alternatives.[20]

In the context of patriarchal consumer capitalism, however, such liberating aspects of clothing fantasy are intertwined with oppressing moments. Perhaps such ambiguity characterizes all mass culture that succeeds in tapping desire. To the degree that feminine fashion fantasy serves as an escape from and complement to bureaucratic scientific rationality for everyone, women's bodies and imaginations are the instruments of a cultural need.

The fantasy of fashion, moreover, often has specifically exploitative and imperialist aspects. Fashion imagery may be drawn indiscriminately from many places and times, and the clothes themselves come from all over the world, usually sewn by very poorly paid women. The fashion fantasies level and dehistoricize these times and places, often contributing to the commodification of an exotic Third World at the same time that they obscure the real imperialism and exploitation that both the fantasies and realities of clothes enact.[21]

It may not be possible to extricate the liberating and valuable in women's experience of clothes from the exploitative and oppressive, but there is reason to try. We can speak of the touch and bonding that move in the shadows, hidden from the light of the phallocentric gaze, and criticize the capitalist imperialist fantasies even as we make up our own.

NOTES

1. Anne Hollander, *Seeing Through Clothes* (New York: Viking Press, 1978).

2. Stuart Ewen and Elizabeth Ewen, *Channels of Desire: Mass Images and the Shaping of American Consciousness* (New York: McGraw-Hill, 1982).

3. Hollander, *Seeing Through Clothes,* 345–352.

4. Ibid., 391–416.

5. Maureen Turim, "Fashion Shapes: Film, the Fashion Industry and the Image of Women," *Socialist Review* 71 (September–October 1983): 86.

6. I derive my account of the male gaze and film from the following authors: Turim, "Fashion Shapes"; Laura Mulvey, "Visual Pleasure and Narrative Cinema," *Screen* 16, no. 3 (Autumn 1975); Annette Kuhn, *Women's Pictures: Feminism and Cinema* (London: Routledge and Kegan Paul, 1982), 47–65; and E. Ann Kaplan, *Women and Film: Both Sides of the Camera* (New York: Methuen, 1983), 23–35.

7. Kaplan, *Women and Film,* 26.

8. Sandra Bartky, "Narcissism, Femininity and Alienation," *Social Theory and Practice* 8, no. 2 (Summer 1982): 136.

9. Turim, "Fashion Shapes," 86–89.

10. Kim Sawchuck, for one, agrees that feminist literature criticizing Fashion is a primary commodifier of women, a major source of the reproduction of women's oppression in patriarchal capitalism; she argues, however, that such accounts are usually too monolothic and one-sided, tending "to fall within the trap of decoding all social relations within patriarchy and capitalism as essentially repressive and homogeneous in its effects" (56). See "A Tale of Inscription/Fashion Statements," *Canadian Journal of Political and Social Theory* 9, no. 1–2 (1987): 51–67.

11. Luce Irigaray, *Speculum of the Other Woman,* trans. Gillian C. Gill (Ithaca, N.Y.: Cornell University Press, 1985).

12. Sawchuck, "Tale of Inscription," 58.

13. Roland Barthes, *The Fashion System,* trans. Matthew Ward and Richard Howard (New York: Hill and Wang, 1983).

14. Ibid., 292.

15. Ibid., 255–256.

16. Ibid., 256–257; cf. 260–261.

17. Ibid., 249; cf. 253, 262, 266.

18. See Steve Neal, "Sexual Difference in Cinema—Issues of Fantasy, Narrative and the Look," in Robert Young, ed., special issues of *Oxford Literary Review* on "Sexual Difference," vol. 8, nos. 1–2 (1986): 123–132.

19. Jean Paul Sartre, *The Psychology of the Imagination* (New York: Philosophical Library, 1948).

20. Herbert Marcuse, *The Aesthetic Dimension* (Boston: Beacon Press, 1978).

21. Julia Emberly, "The Fashion Apparatus and the Deconstruction of Post-modern Subjectivity," *Canadian Journal of Political and Social Theory* 9, no. 1–2 (1987): 38–50.

Diana Fuss

*f*ashion and the

Homospectatorial Look

Women's fashion photography and the industries of mass clothing production and commercial advertising it supports all presume and indeed
participate in the construction of a heterosexual viewing subject. This
"photographic contract," like the "cinematic contract," appears to operate
as a cultural mechanism for producing and securing a female subject who
desires to be desired by men—the ideal, fully oedipalized heterosexual
woman.[1] Playing on the considerable social significance attributed to a
woman's value on the heterosexual marketplace, women's fashion photography scopophilically poses its models as sexually irresistible subjects, inviting its female viewers to consume the product by (over)identifying with
the image. But this "concealed" ideological project—to fashion female
viewers into properly heterosexualized women—stands in direct tension
with (and appears to work against) its own surface formalist structure and
mode of address, which together present eroticized images of the female
body for the explicit appreciation and consumption by a female audience.
In fact, the entire fashion industry operates as one of the few institutionalized spaces where women can look at other women with cultural impunity. It provides a socially sanctioned structure in which women are
encouraged to *consume,* in voyeuristic if not vampiristic fashion, the images
of other women, frequently represented in classically exhibitionist and
sexually provocative poses. To look straight *at* women, it appears, straight
women must look *as* lesbians.

Sometimes the exhibitionism is coy, as in the ad for "knockout knits"

Got the knit knack?
What it takes: a svelte bod.

Figure 1. Advertisement, Cosmopolitan, *August 1989. Photo: Barry Hollywood; reproduced through the courtesy of Cosmopolitan.*

Figure 2. Cover, Cosmopolitan, *September 1989. Photo: Francesco Scavullo; reproduced through the courtesy of Cosmopolitan.*

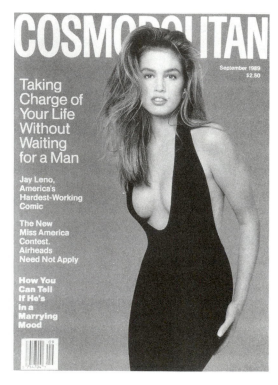

(figure 1) in which the model playfully clutches the bottom hem of her knitted dress, ostensibly concealing and protecting the triangular zone of the genital area from the viewer's intrusive gaze, but, in so doing, drawing our attention more irresistibly to it. The genital zone (for Freud, of course, the infamous biologistic site of women's talent for "plaiting and weaving") is not occluded so much as framed, given shape, and magnified by the inverted triangle of the model's arms, the V-shape of her cleavage, and the curve of her own body. Other typical shots in women's fashion photography are even more explicitly erotic, presenting to the female spectator an image typically found in straight male pornography: the image of an all too receptive, quite nearly orgasmic woman waiting to be taken by more than a camera (figure 2). Even the covers of magazines like *Vogue, Elle, Glamour,* or in this case *Cosmopolitan,* could be mistaken for the covers of some skin magazines commercially produced and marketed for consumption by heterosexual men were it not for the teasers running down the side that tell us that the image of this woman is intended to function for its female audience not as an object of desire but rather a point of identification.[2] Presumably, the readers of these magazines are to desire to *be* the woman, not to *have* her.

The purpose of this essay is to begin to decode the complicated operations of identification and desire, of being and having, that are at work in the social production of female spectatorial subjectivity. In an attempt to account psychoanalytically for the enduring fascination that commercial fashion photography holds for its female viewers, I will draw on Freud's theories of primary and secondary identification, Lacan's readings of specularity and subjectivity in relation to the preoedipal mirror stage, and Kristeva's notions of abjection and the "homosexual-maternal fact." Throughout I will be attempting to demonstrate, through a narrowly delimited reading of contemporary signifying codes of fashion photography, that "identities" can never be isolated from or adequately understood outside the institutions of identification that work to produce them in the first place.[3] Identity, because it is never in a moment of critical repose, because it resists the forces of suspension or negation, and because it neither begins nor ends at a point of total immobility, draws its very lifeblood from the restless operations of identification, one of the most powerful but least understood mechanisms of cultural self-fashioning.

FASHION FETISHISM

The Lacanian subject is a subject fashioned in and by identifications, a subject that comes-into-being (*devenir*) through the agency of a complex network of identificatory processes—narcissism, aggressivity, misrecognition, and objectification—all working variously with and against each other at different moments in the child's psychical development and continuing on into adulthood. The importance Lacanian psychoanalysis attributes to specularity and identification in the formation of the sexed subject suggests several points of entry to the psychical geography traversed and bounded by the arena of women's commercial fashion photography. I will argue that these photographs work as post–mirror phase images that create fascination precisely through a cultural staging of pre–mirror phase fantasies; they, in effect, mirror the pre–mirror stage, directing our gaze solipsistically back to our own specular and fictive origins. Through *secondary* identification(s) with the sequence of images fashion photography serially displays, the female subject is positioned by the photographic codes of framing, color, lighting, focus, and pose to rehearse repetitiously the introjection of the (m)other's imago, which is itself a complex rehearsal of the infant's primary identification or absorption with the (m)other.[4] These images of the female body reenact, obsessively, the moment of the female subject's earliest self-awareness, as if to suggest the subject's profound uncertainty over whether her own subjectivity "took." This subject is compelled to verify herself endlessly, to identify all her bodily parts, and to fashion continually from this corporeal and psychical jigsaw puzzle a total picture, an imago of her own body.

The specular image of the body women's fashion photography constructs is a reimaging of the body in pieces (*le corps morcelé*), the fragmented and dispersed body image that Lacan posits as the infant's pre-mirror experience of its amorphous self. These photographs recall Lacan's identification in "Aggressivity in Psychoanalysis" of a group of images categorized as *"imagos of the fragmented body"*: "images of castration, mutilation, dismemberment, dislocation, evisceration, devouring, bursting open of the body."[5] Some of the most common and prevalent shots of female bodies in women's fashion photography are those of decapitation and dismemberment—in particular headless torsos and severed heads. In a L'Oréal ad for waterproof makeup (figure 3), a woman's head floats above the water, her face, framed in medium close-up, detached from any visible body, supported only by her reflection in the water below. This very reflection is an extension of the body: woman as mirror is all face. But more terrifying than an economy of looking that overinvests the woman's face as the primary site of subjectivity is the flip side of this same scopic economy that divests the woman of subjectivity altogether. A Chanel ad, for example, phantasmically constructs an unthinkable body—a body without identity, a body without face or surface to convey any distinctive

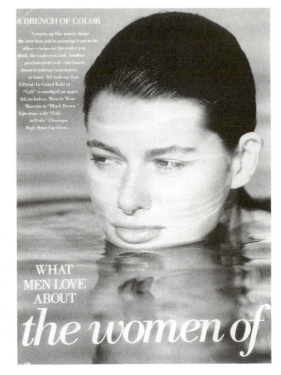

Figure 3. Advertisement, Glamour, July 1989. Photo: Ken Browar; reproduced through the courtesy of Glamour. Copyright © 1989 by Condé Nast Publications, Inc.

identifying features beyond the class- and gender-inflected signifiers of the clothes themselves. By "amputating" the model's head and legs, and by rendering invisible any flesh or skin tones, the camera presents to the viewer the fantasy not of a body without organs but a body without a subject. The terror and fascination evoked by the Chanel ad is that of the complete erasure of subjectivity. But then, the floating head and the headless torso offer only apparently different "takes" on the female subject, for overpresence figures a kind of absence, and to be the mirror is simultaneously to be without a self-image of one's own.

This representational body in pieces also functions for the female spectator as a cultural reminder of her fetishization, of the "part" she plays in the disavowal of the mother's castration. A fetish (typically a woman's legs, breasts, face, or other body part) is a substitute for the missing maternal phallus, a prop or accessory fashioned to veil its terrifying absence. In a patriarchal Symbolic a fetishist is one who continually strives to deny the "truth" of the mother's castration by registering the phallus elsewhere, seeking to resecure and to hold in suspense the early imaginary attachment to the phallic mother that was lost with the subject's entry into the

Symbolic and its subjugation to the law of the father.[6] Photography, which similarly seeks to fix an image in an eternal moment of suspense, comes to function not merely as a technological analog for the psychical workings of fetishism but as one of its internal properties—that is, the fetish itself has "the frozen, arrested quality of a photograph."[7] This intimate co-dependency of fashion, fetishism, photography, and femininity suggests that in the dominant regime of fashion photography, femininity is itself an accessory: it operates as a repository for culture's representational waste. Images of waste and refuse make visible the Symbolic representations of femininity, which Luce Irigaray identifies as the "shards," the "scraps," the "uncollected debris," the "scattered remnants of a violated sexuality."[8] While it is the incorporation *and expurgation* of the feminine that constitutes the founding order of subjectivity for both boy and girl, only the girl attains subjectivity by becoming "the negative image of the subject," the photographic inversion, the materials of the mirror itself, its scattered shards.[9] Juliet MacCannell's metaphor of the "trash can" to describe female subjectivity is thus entirely relevant to this discussion of fashion and fetishism. "'Woman' as generality," she writes, "is only seen in pieces (in part-objects, in the 'trash can' of overvalued zones of her body—breast, eyebrow, ankle, smile): any part that can be 'phallicised' or made, as a single part, into a metaphor for a wholeness that the woman lacks."[10] All of this is simply to suggest that it is possible to read fashion fetishism in photography in the same way that film theorist Kaja Silverman has read commodity fetishism in Orson Welles's *Citizen Kane:* as "a vain attempt to compensate for the divisions and separations upon which subjectivity is based."[11]

THE HOMOSEXUAL MATERNAL FACE(T)

So far, this reading of fashion photography has only suggested the *discomfort* these images may be assumed to provoke for their female viewers—specifically, the fear and anxiety generated by (over)exposed fragmented body parts, remnants of an abjected existence prior to the mirror stage formulation of an economy of subjects and objects. It may be helpful here to turn directly to the work of Julia Kristeva, the writer perhaps most often associated with the difficult enterprise of theorizing the mechanisms of primary identification, primary narcissism, and abjection. Buried within a theory of sexuality noted for its persistent heterocentrism and its tendency toward maternalism is a concept nonetheless particularly suggestive for understanding the endless fascination fashion photography holds for its female spectators—suggestive precisely *because* of its insights into the Symbolic privileging of the maternal in the cultural production of feminine subjectivity.[12] Kristeva's notion of the "homosexual-maternal facet" posits a fundamental female homosexuality in the daughter's pre-oedipal identification with the mother, thus posing the larger question of the role that homosexuality plays (its repression and/or its mobilization) in the psychosocial constitution of *any* female subject.[13] This homosexual-maternal facet is for Kristeva a particular modality of the semiotic *chora,* that period and place of indistinction prior to the various splittings (subject/object, self/other, mother/child) initiated by the mirror stage. In the pre-mirror stage, the still-to-be-gendered presubject is "face to face with primary narcissism" (*D,* 265), caught in a primary identification with the mother that, for the girl, positions her along with the mother on a homosexual continuum. Importantly, it is the mother's face that functions as a screen providing the child with its first mirror image and facilitating the process of the *child's* identity formation by *effacing* itself: the mother's face becomes a lost object. At the very point the mother's face reflects the child's image back to him/her, this screen is itself "lost," eclipsed by its own reflective properties. For the girl, such a loss is a double deprivation since the mother's image is, simultaneously, her own.

The prevalence of close-ups of the woman's face in fashion photography would seem to suggest that one possible explanation for the fascination these images hold for women involves the pleasures evoked by the potential restitution of the lost object—specifically the reconstitution of the mother's face. A Revlon advertisement (figure 4) for an antiageing moisturizer is surprisingly self-conscious about the psychical processes it so powerfully puts into play; it works its appeal by way of an imperative, commanding the spectator to "recover" the lost object in order to "discover" eternal youth. In its soft-focus lighting and languid radiance, the black-and-white image is strikingly reminiscent of a cinematic close-up of Greta Garbo or Claudette Colbert. The advertisement's spectatorial appeal is much the same as that of a film close-up, perhaps even heightened by the immobility of the photographic image—its unrelenting overexposure to the viewer.

Mary Ann Doane's comments on the cinematic close-up may help explain its analogous appeal in fashion photography: "At moments it almost seems as though all the fetishism of the cinema were condensed onto the image of the face, the female face in particular. . . . The face is that bodily part not accessible to the subject's own gaze (or accessible only as a virtual image in a mirror)—hence its overrepresentation as *the* instance of subjectivity."[14] The image object, whose hold on subjectivity is always a precarious one, may derive a special pleasure from this "face-to-face"

Figure 4. Advertisement, Cosmopolitan, *August 1989*. Reproduced through the courtesy of Revlon, Inc. Copyright © 1989.

RECOVER.

encounter with a shimmering, luminous, reconstituted image of the mythic "Mother";[15] the photograph's structure of visualization stages a homosexual-maternal encounter by symbolically imagining for the spectator a fantasized preoedipal relation with the face of the maternal. As one of the earliest planes of psychical organization, the mother's face is refigured by the photographic apparatus as eternally present—fashioned, fetishized, and fixed by the gaze of the desiring subject. These images instill pleasure in the viewer by at once constructing and evoking the memory of a choric union; they bear "the imprint of an archaic moment" (*D*, p. 283) achieved through the technological simulation of a past event.[16] Often in these shots of a severed woman's head we see the face from the distance and perspective that an infant might see it. For example, in figure 5 the face wells up in front of us, its charged presence almost too large for the frame to hold, while in figure 6 the face is more indistinct, shadowy, blurred, remote. The lighting in both cases (orange-yellow, pink-black) is never quite "natural," as if these images were always either under- or overexposed. The closeness of the faces to the viewer and the awkward play of

Aapri gentle cleansing lotion leaves no oily or greasy feeling, just perfectly fresh, clean skin.

Aapri. A refreshing way to wipe away the day.

Figure 5. Advertisement, Elle, July 1989.

ALFEX
of
SWITZERLAND

MACY'S
BULLOCK'S

$175⁰⁰

Figure 6. Advertisement, Elle, October 1989. Reproduced through the courtesy of the Swiss Watch Corporation.

light and shadow in both shots further suggest that no camera produced these particular images, and indeed they belong to a second-order genre in advertising based on the *simulated photograph:* drawings that mimic the immediacy and referentiality of a photographic copy and, in so doing, draw attention to the status of the photograph itself as a product of representation, a cultural simulation.

The reproduction of photographic codes in these imitative drawings functions as a reminder of the phantasmic intensity of their subject (the mother's frozen face), as if the machinery of photographic representation cannot bear such close proximity to the object of desire whose reflective properties it so jealously seeks to capture and to refine. Clearly, we are operating fully within the realm of fantasy here, for the choric reunion evoked by these images can only ever have the status of a fantasized memory and can only be purchased, paradoxically, at the price of disabling the very identity this fantasy purportedly seeks to secure in the first place. Any return to the semiotic *chora* and the homosexual-maternal continuum involves a regression to primary narcissism and thus to the moment before the formation of the subject's identity as subject. Kristeva's "ravishing maternal jouissance"—which constitutes the powerful lure of the "choric fantasy"—is balanced and set against the equally powerful repulsion of its "terrorizing aggressivity" (*D*, 263).[17] One of Kristeva's most important contributions to psychoanalytic theories of subject formation may well be her insistence that the "idyllic" dual relationship Freud identified between mother and child—the "soothing" symbiosis of the imaginary relation—represents in fact Freud's own defensive negation of the knowledge that the mother-child relation is anything but utopic. The primary narcissism implied by the homosexual-maternal facet is weighted with hostility and laden with uncertainty: "the archaic relation to the mother, narcissistic though it may be, is . . . of no solace to the protagonists and even less so to Narcissus." Primary narcissism, by erasing the borders between subject and object and immersing both mother and child in abjection, "threatens" the ego and "menaces" subjective identity.[18] In opposition then to a psychoanalytic understanding of female film spectatorship, which reads the woman's fascination with her image as a symptom of her "predisposition" to (primary) narcissism, I am suggesting that the female spectator's fascination with her etherealized image in fashion photography operates not as an Imaginary *effect of* primary narcissism but as a Symbolic *defense against* it—against all the terrors primary identification with the mother holds for the always imperfectly oedipalized woman. What these angelic images of the mother's face provide for the female spectator is a *negation* of the uncertainty that disturbs her psychic borders and a *disavowal* of the pain born out of her primary identification with the (m)other—a negation and a disavowal made visible through a representational excess (which is always a kind of waste): namely, the cosmetic beautification and beautification of the mother's face.

One thinks here of Georges Bataille, perhaps the preeminent theorist of waste, refuse, and the violence of refusal, which he sees as the very precondition of desire. To possess the object of desire—to "take" it, like a photograph—would be simultaneously to *take away* the motivation for the desire and thus desire itself. For Bataille, however, woman's cultural utility as repository of beauty operates to disguise the animal nature of heterosexual intercourse and further to mask what he terms the "ugliness" and crudity of the sexual organs. In Bataille's "vision of excess," it is specifically the woman's face—heavily adorned and meticulously masqueraded—that attracts the male subject's gaze away from the sex organs and toward a more luminous surface.[19] Bataille's theoretical figuration of the female face as "beautiful" enacts a slight shift in registers from *re*flection to *de*flection: the fashionable face (the female face on display) has the power to send the look through a circuitous route, from the vertical lips to the horizontal lips, not to effect an eclipse of the genital by the facial but rather to collapse one bodily site onto the other.[20] This is not a new or perhaps even very interesting story: Freud's reading of the terrifying decapitated head of Medusa as a representation of the female genitals (specifically, the mother's genitals) similarly insists on the symbolic connection between female face and female genitalia.[21] These two cultural readings (Bataille's and Freud's) of the iconic power of a woman's face tell us less about a woman's complex relation to her private body parts than about the parts her privates have been made to play in the history of Western representations of *male* subjectivity. To understand the fear and fascination the mother's face holds for a *female* subject, one needs to turn away from Medusa.

VAMPIRIC IDENTIFICATION

Disavowal, as is its wont, simultaneously involves for the subject in discord both a denial *and* a recognition of the source of its pain. It is, after all, the very immobility of the photographic image of the mother's face that threatens to capture and overwhelm the subject in the archaic confusion of its own libidinous drives. If the high cost of regression to the preSymbolic is psychosis, which Kristeva defines in an eloquent turn of phrase as "the panicking at the loss of all reference" (D, 139), then the photographic apparatus itself comes to function as a paradigm for the workings of psychosis, a loss of reference triggered by the face-to-face encounter with primary narcissism and the possibility of both plenitude and loss reflected in and by the mother's magnified, beatific face. On the one hand, photography, unlike other systems of representation, can never deny the existence of the referent—the "that-has-been" status, as Roland Barthes puts it, of the lost object.[22] On the other hand, photography never ceases in its attempt to restore the lost object, the referent that has been but is no longer.[23] Like the mother's face, the photographic image is the place of both a constitution and a fading of subjectivity: both are "screens" that operate for the subject as sites where identity emerges *and* recedes. Photography simulates and mechanizes the reflective properties of the mother's look, suggesting that if the mother's face operates as the primary "plane" of abjection, photography may represent its most perfect science. Abjection, defined by Kristeva as that boundary where "'subject' and 'object' push each other away, confront each other, collapse, and start again," is the psychical equivalent of photography's mechanical transformation of subjects into objects.[24] Barthes writes that "the Photograph . . . represents that very subtle moment when . . . I am neither subject nor object but a subject who feels he is becoming an object: I then experience a microversion of death (of paranthesis): I am truly becoming a specter."[25] Photography, the very technology of abjection, functions as a mass producer of corpses, embalming each subject by captivating and fixing its image. Along with vampirism and psychoanalysis, photography can be seen as yet another of the "rival sciences of the undead."[26]

This idea of the "undead," when combined with the spectacle of women "feeding off" the images of other women, points toward a vampiric structure of the look in women's fashion photography. The vampirism of the gaze is directly thematized through the prevalence of neck shots: images of women with their heads thrown back, their eyes closed, their lips slightly parted, their necks extended and exposed (figures 7 and 8). This is, of course, the classic pose of sexual ecstasy for the woman, a pose that virtually demonstrates how a woman's very vulnerability and passivity are culturally eroticized. Only this time it is women themselves who are invited to actively consume the image—female spectators who are constrained to assume the position of lesbian vampires. Laura Mulvey, in her well-known reading of the narrative codes of classical Hollywood cinema, theorizes two possible spectatorial relations to the image on the screen: scopophilia, which implies "a separation of the erotic identity of the subject from the object on the screen," and narcissism, which demands "identification of the ego with and recognition of his like."[27] Vampirism, I would like to suggest, marks a third possible mode of looking, a position that demands both separation and identification, both a having and a be-

Figure 7. Advertisement, Vogue, October 1989. Photo: Skrebneski; reproduced through the courtesy of Flemington Furs, Flemington, N.J.

Exclusively at **flemington furs**

Flemington, New Jersey
One of the World's Largest Specialists in Fine Furs

Figure 8. Advertisement, Elle, September 1989. Photo: Gideon Lewin for Martha International.

Jeanette for St. Martin

Martha

Park Avenue   Palm Beach   Bal Harbour   Trump Tower

coming—indeed, a having *through* becoming. The spectatorial relation of the woman to her image serially displayed across the pages of the fashion magazine is structurally vampiric, involving neither immediate identification nor unmediated desire but rather a complicated and unstable exchange between already mediated forms.

Becoming the other by feeding off the other presents a tropological way of understanding identification that is not without precedent in psychoanalysis. In Freud's understanding of the process of secondary identification, introjection of the imago works specifically through "the oral, cannibalistic incorporation of the other person," an act of consumption that seeks to satisfy the ego's insatiable desire to become the other by devouring it whole.[28] But as a cultural figure for the psychical process of identification, vampirism differs from cannibalism in that the vampire does more than incorporate the alterity of the other in her erotic feedings; she also creates a shadow or reflection of herself by transforming her "victims" into fellow vampires. Vampirism works more like an inverted form of identification—identification pulled inside out—where the subject, in the act of interiorizing the other, simultaneously reproduces itself externally to that other. Vampirism is both other-incorporating and self-reproducing; it delimits a more ambiguous space where desire and identification appear less opposed than coterminous, where the desire to be the other (identification) draws its very sustenance from the desire to have the other. Vampiric identification operates in the fashion system in the way that the photographic apparatus positions the spectator to identify with the woman precisely so as not to desire her, or, to put it another way, to desire to be the woman so as to preclude having her. But in order to eradicate or evacuate the homoerotic desire, the visual field must first *produce* it, thereby permitting, in socially regulated form, the articulation of lesbian desire within the identificatory move itself.

The vampire—and, I would propose, the lesbian vampire specifically—represents the perfect trope for allegorizing the activity of fashion photography's voracious female spectators. A rare, explicit acknowledgment of how the fashion system works through vampiric identification is presented by a striking advertisement for Italian clothing designer Moschino (figure 9). Assuming the form of a rough sketch rather than a glossy photograph, this antifashion fashion statement crosses out not simply any woman's face but a vampire's face. Red splotches connote both the red paint of the *X* and the red blood dripping from the vampire's fangs. Eyes, nose, and mouth are all blocked out: this woman sees red, but, as a vampire, she also smells it and tastes it. The violence of the image lies in its refusal of what I have argued is the spectatorial position that the fashion

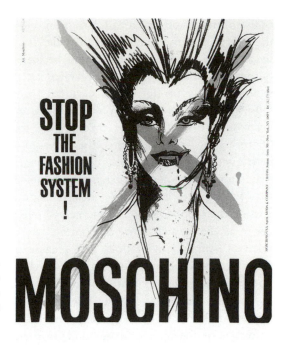

Figure 9. Advertisement, Elle, March 1990. Reproduced through the courtesy of Moda and Company.

system constructs for its female viewers, namely, lesbian vampirism. Female spectatorial subjectivity is precisely what is denied by the injunction to "**STOP** THE FASHION SYSTEM!" Yet the subtle play with spacing and typography in the visual presentation of "**STOP** THE FASHION SYSTEM!" suggests a possible counter-reading: if we place the emphasis on the imperative—**STOP**—as the word's size and placement on the page encourage us to do, we can then gloss the line as a different kind of command: a bid for our attention, an alert to **STOP** and to take notice of THE FASHION SYSTEM. The connotative ambiguity encoded by the text permits a second order of meaning that significantly complicates the first, suggesting perhaps that the point we really should register here is the fashion system's ability to renew and to perpetuate itself by continually invoking the specter of its death or obsolescence—in much the same way, it could be argued, that heterosexuality secures its identity by at once disavowing and perpetually calling attention to its abject, interiorized, and ghostly other, homosexuality.[29]

A psychoanalytic reading of heterosexuality needs to look beyond the standard repression hypothesis of sexuality in order to fully account for the way in which heterosexuality, far from constituting itself through the simple sublimation of homosexuality, works through and by the dialectic of its continual activation and disavowal. Homosexuality is "repressed" to the degree that the structure it provides for the formation of the hetero-sexual subject is so apparent that it becomes transparent; the very obvi-ousness of the lesbian eroticism evoked by women's fashion photography simultaneously produces and occludes the homoerotic structure of the look.[30] Fashion photography works to ensure the formation of a subject's heterosexual object-choices through the stimulation and control of its "homopathic" identifications; the same-sex desire one might imagine to be triggered by the erotically charged images of women's bodies is subli-mated into the camera's insistence on same-sex identification (being rather than having the woman). Yet these structural identifications, while har-nessing the tabooed desire, nonetheless give it a certain play, licensing the desire as that which must be routinely managed and contained. Desire operates *within* identification, destabilizing the grounds of a heterosexual identity formation and undermining its defensive claims to a "pure" or "uncontaminated" sexuality. This play of homosexual desire within a homophilic identification may explain the fashion photograph's greatest lure: the pull of a forbidden desire, there (if only) for the taking.

Images of the female form—and, in particular, the woman's face—in contemporary fashion photography inspire in the viewing subject a certain "preoedipal nostalgia." That is not to suggest, however, that the power and attraction of these images derive from any simple evocation of early childhood memories. Rather, the "memory" these ads seem to "tap into" are contemporary fictional constructs projected back into the subject's preconscious to function as screens to protect against an all too present pain: the cultural repression of same-sex desire. In this regard, each photo-graph achieves the status of Freud's earliest understanding of a "screen memory"—a memory (for example, of maternal plenitude, the beatific face) manufactured and mapped onto the past in order to disguise a present anxiety (the subject's painfully distant relation to that face and the dis-avowal of homosexual desire). Actually, Freud offers us two ways to theo-rize a screen memory: first, as an early impression utilized as a screen for a much later event, and second, as a later impression used to disguise an early childhood event.[31] The images offered by fashion photography op-erate both ways: as defenses (or screens) against the early interruption of the homosexual-maternal continuum, but also and more importantly as defenses against the pain that this psychical rupture continues to inflict on the adult subject. In other words, these images function as counter-memories that tell us as much about the subject's current history as they do about her already shadowy prehistory, perhaps even more. What they tell us is that heterosexuality is profoundly unstable, tenuous, and precarious, and therefore must be continually reinforced and resecured. Nostalgia for the preoedipal, *itself a construction of the oedipal,* works as a psychical mechanism for strengthening the homopathic identification so that the socially sanctioned heterosexual object–choice can be perpetually sustained. In constant threat of dissolution, female heterosexuality must be critically maintained through the cultural institutionalization of the homosexual look. This strategic deployment of a homospectatorial look may partially account for what has long been a puzzling contradiction: how is it that, in the dominant sexual Symbolic, there can be homosexual looks but no homosexuals?

Even Freud eventually came to recognize that a daughter's unconscious preoedipal homosexual desire for the mother continually impacts upon her conscious adult life; it is precisely this same-sex desire that is evoked, which is to say *provoked,* by photographic images of the female body— powerfully activated, mobilized, and channeled (or *Chanel*led, as it were). The problem, of course, is that any female subject *as subject* is already situated in the Symbolic, and no matter how uncertain this symbolization is for the woman, the mother's face as lost object is fundamentally irrecuperable. Still, the fantasy of repossessing the lost object, the *promise* these photographic images hold of reconnecting (re-fusing?) the homosexual-maternal relation, goes a long way toward explaining the enduring fascination that fashion photography holds for its female viewers, the pleasures it seeks to provide, as well as the discomforts it may inadvertently summon.

CONCLUSION

The lesbian looks coded by fashion photography radically deessentialize conventional notions of the identity of the viewing subject that posit desire in the viewer, prior to any operations of spectatorial identification. We need to theorize "homoerotic looks" not in terms of anything inherent to the viewing subject but in terms of a visual structuring and identification that participates in organizing the sexual identity of *any* social subject. One question I have not addressed is how lesbian viewers might consume these images.[32] What is at issue in this reading, however, is not "homosexual" versus "heterosexual" spectatorship but the homosexualization of the viewing position itself as created by the contemporary codes of women's fashion photography. This is not to deny that more work needs to be done on how spectators from different gendered, racial, ethnic, economic, national, and historical backgrounds might appropriate or resist these images, but only to insist that if subjects look different, it is the enculturating mechanisms of the look that instantiate and regulate these differences in the first place.[33]

A second implication of a study like this one, which draws heavily on recent film theory, is a recognition nonetheless of the limited uses to which this theory can be put in the critical analyses of photography. Photography differs from film in its organization of both spacial and temporal orders and in its relation to referentiality and alterity.[34] In its frozen time and circumscribed space, the photograph constitutes another frame of reference, a different structure of visualization, an alternative field of vision. And, especially important for this particular investigation of photography, the photograph constructs an entirely other identificatory structure from that described by Mulvey, for whom the spectatorial look produced by the classical film apparatus is masculine, heterosexual, and oedipal. I have suggested in this essay that the spectatorial position mapped by contemporary commercial fashion photography can be read, by contrast, as feminine, homosexual, and preoedipal.

Finally, we need to rethink the always complicated relation between desire and identification in the formation of the subject's identity. For Freud, Lacan, and Kristeva, desire and identification are mutually interdependent but counterdirectional trajectories in which identifying with one sex is the necessary condition for desiring the other. To identify with *and* to desire a person of the same sex is, in this logic, a structural impossibility. But such a symmetrical, rigid, chiasmatic relation between terms may disguise the ways in which any identification *with* an other is secured through a simultaneous and continuing desire *for* that other. In Freud's only case study of a female paranoiac, he insists that the analysand can "free" herself of her homosexual "dependence" on her mother only by becoming her mother through renewed secondary identifications.[35] This becoming is presumed to erase all desire, or rather to reroute the desire toward a wholly different love object. But the desire to be *like* can itself be motivated and sustained by the desire to *possess:* being can be the most radical form of having. Identification may well operate in the end not as a foreclosure of desire but as its most perfect, and most ruthless, fulfillment.

NOTES

1. The contractual metaphor is Teresa de Lauretis's; see her *Technologies of Gender: Essays on Theory, Film, and Fiction* (Bloomington: Indiana University Press, 1987), 105.

2. Since desire and the structures of fantasy, not to mention the very formations of subjectivity, change and transmogrify under the weight of historical pres-

sures, I will further limit the focus of this essay to the fashion codes of late twentieth-century postindustrial capitalism. The photographs that form the basis of the present reading are all culled from recent issues (1989–1990) of the currently most widely marketed women's fashion magazines in the United States: *Vogue, Elle, Glamour,* and *Cosmopolitan.* Readers interested in analyses of the fashion system based on the history of Western fashion, its role in a consumer culture oriented toward women, or its privileged if problematic status in the debates on postmodernism might wish to consult the following: J. C. Flügel, *The Psychology of Clothes* (London: The Hogarth Press, 1930); Anne Hollander, *Seeing Through Clothes* (New York: The Viking Press, 1978); Alison Lurie, *The Language of Clothes* (London: Heinemann, 1981); David Kunzle, *Fashion and Fetishism: A Social History of the Corset, Tight-Lacing, and Other Forms of Body-Sculpture in the West* (Totowa, N.J.: Rowman and Littlefield, 1982); Rosalind Coward, *Female Desires: How They Are Sought, Bought and Packaged* (New York: Grove Press, 1985); Valerie Steele, *Fashion and Eroticism: Ideals of Feminine Beauty from the Victorian Era to the Jazz Age* (New York and London: Oxford University Press, 1985); Kaja Silverman, "Fragments of a Fashionable Discourse," in *Studies in Entertainment: Critical Approaches to Mass Culture,* ed. Tania Modleski (Bloomington: Indiana University Press, 1986), 139–152; *Fabrications: Costume and the Female Body,* ed. Jane Gaines and Charlotte Herzog (New York and London: Routledge, 1990); and Cathy Griggers, "A Certain Tension in the Visual/Cultural Field: Helmut Newton, Deborah Turbeville, and the *VOGUE* Fashion Layout," *Differences* 2, no. 2 (Summer 1990): 76–104. My own investigation seeks to redress a symptomatic aporia in all of these important studies, namely, the fashion system's institutionalization of a homospectatorial look.

3. The study with which any reading of fashion photography may immediately invite comparison is Roland Barthes, *The Fashion System,* trans. Matthew Ward and Richard Howard (New York: Hill and Wang, 1983). Whereas Barthes's structuralist analysis is limited to the decoding of articles about fashion in commercial magazines, my own poststructuralist analysis is largely based on a reading of the photographic images. Both are at best partial and severely circumscribed investigations into the "fashion system."

4. *Imago* is a term Lacan borrows from Freud's famous distinction between two different kinds of identifications: primary identification, which signifies the child's preoedipal state of nondifferentiation with the mother, and secondary identification, which signifies the child's oedipal introjection of the imago of the same-sex parent. Freud's primary and secondary identifications correspond roughly to Lacan's pre-mirror and mirror phases, thus predating the subject's oedipal drama and situating the roots of identification and desire firmly in the presubject's imaginary relation to the mother.

5. Jacques Lacan, *Écrits: A Selection,* trans. Alan Sheridan (New York: W. W. Norton and Company, 1977), 11.

6. For a particularly precise and detailed reading of fetishism, as contrasted with psychosis, to which my own understanding of these psychical mechanisms is partially indebted, see Elizabeth Grosz, *Sexual Subversions: Three French Feminists* (Sydney, Australia: Allen & Unwin, 1989), 56–69.

7. Parveen Adams, "Of Female Bondage," in *Between Feminism & Psychoanalysis,* ed. Teresa Brennan (London and New York: Routledge, 1989), 252.

8. Luce Irigaray, *This Sex Which Is Not One,* trans. Catherine Porter with Carolyn Burke (Ithaca: Cornell University Press, 1985), 30.

9. Ibid., 78.

10. Juliet Flower MacCannell, *Figuring Lacan: Criticism and the Cultural Unconscious* (Lincoln: University of Nebraska Press, 1986), 108.

11. Kaja Silverman, *The Acoustic Mirror: The Female Voice in Psychoanalysis and Cinema* (Bloomington: Indiana University Press, 1988), 86.

12. See for example, Judith Butler, *Gender Trouble: Feminism and the Subversion of Identity* (New York and London: Routledge, 1990), chap. 3; Silverman, *The Acoustic Mirror,* chap. 4; and Jennifer Stone, "The Horrors of Power: A Critique of 'Kristeva,'" in *The Politics of Theory,* ed. Francis Barker et al. (Colchester: University of Essex Press, 1983), 38–48.

13. Julia Kristeva, *Desire in Language: A Semiotic Approach to Literature and Art,* trans. Thomas Gora, Alice Jardine, and Leon S. Roudiez, ed. Roudiez (New York: Columbia University Press, 1980), 239; hereafter abbreviated *D.*

14. Mary Ann Doane, "Veiling over Desire: Close-ups of the Woman," in *Feminism and Psychoanalysis,* ed. Richard Feldstein and Judith Roof (Ithaca: Cornell University Press, 1989), 108. Peter Matthews, in his absorbing reading of Greta Garbo as gay male icon, also reads the face as fetish, arguing that the feminine face is the site where spectators immerse themselves and momentarily relinquish their subjectivity. See Peter Matthews, "Garbo and Phallic Motherhood: A 'Homosexual' Visual Economy," *Screen* 29, no. 3 (Summer 1988):27.

15. In figure 4 we are presented with an image of "the Great White Mother," a radically marked iconography of feminine beauty that betrays a Western nostalgia for the "recovery" of racial "purity." Commercial fashion photography persistently plays out such fantasies of racial purification through its calculated matching of products with models; after surveying thousands of images, I was struck by the overwhelming predominance of *white* women's faces in those advertisements selling specifically skin creams, makeup, facial cleansers, and other skin care products.

16. It should be clear by now that this reading of the woman's face as maternal icon relies heavily upon that body of work in feminist art history that insists that "the body to which representation refers is always, however specific the representation, the maternal body" (Griselda Pollock, "Missing Women: Rethinking Early Thoughts on Images of Women," in *The Critical Image: Essays on Contemporary Photography,* ed. Carol Squiers [Seattle: Bay Press, 1990], 211).

17. I take the especially useful term "choric fantasy" from Silverman, *The Acoustic Mirror,* 101.

18. Kristeva, *Powers of Horror: An Essay on Abjection,* trans. Roudiez (New York: Columbia University Press, 1982), 63. For an interesting and suggestive discussion of the *mother's* abjection, and a theory of subject formation based on identification with the desire *of* the mother rather than with a desire *for* her, see Cynthia Chase, "Desire and Identification in Lacan and Kristeva," in *Feminism and Psychoanalysis,* 65–83, and "Primary Narcissism and the Giving of Figure: Kristeva with Hertz and de Man," in *Abjection, Melancholia, and Love: The Work of Julia Kristeva,* ed. John Fletcher and Andrew Benjamin (London and New York: Routledge, 1990), 124–136.

19. Georges Bataille, *Eroticism: Death and Sensuality,* trans. Mary Dalwood (San

Francisco: City Lights Books, 1986), 129–146. In Bataille's erotics of waste and refuse, "beauty is desired in order that it may be befouled" (144). See also Bataille's *Visions of Excess: Selected Writings, 1927–1939,* trans. and ed. Allan Stoekl (Minneapolis: University of Minnesota Press, 1985).

20. For an alternative use of Bataille's erotics of waste that is read through the discourse of fashion, see Peter Wollen, "Fashion/Orientalism/The Body," *New Formations,* no. 1 (Spring 1987):5–33. Wollen accurately points out that for Bataille the general economy of waste, of excess spent without return, is the very domain of the erotic. It is also, I would add, the domain of Irigaray's "feminine."

21. See Sigmund Freud, "Medusa's Head" (1922), *The Standard Edition of the Complete Psychological Works of Sigmund Freud,* trans. and ed. James Strachey, 24 vols. (London: The Hogarth Press, 1953–74), 18:273–274.

22. Barthes has this to say about the specificity of photography: "Photography's referent is not the same as the referent of other systems of representation. I call 'photographic referent' not the *optionally* real thing to which an image or a sign refers but the *necessarily* real thing which has been placed before the lens, without which there would be no photograph. Painting can feign reality without having seen it. Discourse combines signs which have referents, of course, but these referents can be and are most often 'chimeras.' Contrary to these imitations, in Photography I can never deny that *the thing has been there*" (*Camera Lucida: Reflections on Photography,* trans. Richard Howard [New York: Hill and Wang, 1981], 76).

23. A reminder of the precise psychoanalytic definition of psychosis might help clarify the relation I am positing here between this psychical mechanism and photographic technology. Psychosis is "a primary disturbance of the libidinal relation to reality" in which its manifest symptoms "are accordingly treated as secondary attempts to restore the link with objects." See J. Laplanche and J.-B. Pontalis, *The Language of Psychoanalysis,* trans. Donald Nicholson-Smith (New York: W. W. Norton & Company, 1973), 370.

24. Kristeva, *Powers,* 18.

25. Barthes, *Camera Lucida,* 14.

26. Laurence Rickels, *Aberrations of Mourning* (Detroit: Wayne State University Press, 1988), 318.

27. See "Visual Pleasure and Narrative Cinema," in *Feminism and Film Theory,* ed. Constance Penley (New York and London: Routledge, 1988), 61.

28. Sigmund Freud, "New Introductory Lectures," in *Standard Edition,* vol. 22:63. See Freud's discussion of the primal father's murder and cannibalism by the sons in *Totem and Taboo* (*Standard Edition,* vol. 23), and Freud's association of identification with the earliest phase of infantile sexuality, the libidinal oral phase, in which the ego incorporates the object by devouring it, a process described both in *Group Psychology and the Analysis of the Ego* (*Standard Edition,* vol. 18) and in "Mourning and Melancholia" (*Standard Edition,* vol. 14). On eating as a figure for the interiorization of the other, see also Jacques Derrida, "Subverting the Signature: A Theory of the Parasite," *Blast* (Blast unLtd, 1990), 16–21, and Jean-Luc Nancy's interview with Derrida entitled "'Eating Well,' or the Calculation of the Subject," in *Who Came After the Subject?,* ed. Eduardo Cadava, Peter Connor, and Jean-Luc Nancy (New York and London: Routledge, 1990), 96–119.

29. Another aspect of the vampire trope that seems relevant here is the absence

of the vampire's reflection in the mirror. The vacant mirror names the subjectless subject discussed earlier in this essay, specifically in regard to the eclipsing of the mother's face.

30. Or, in Judith Butler's incisive phrasing of the problem, "homosexuality emerges as a desire which must be produced in order to remain repressed" (*Gender Trouble,* 77).

31. Freud develops the first of these theories in "Screen Memories" (1899), *Standard Edition,* vol. 3:301–322, and the second, more common understanding in *The Psychopathology of Everyday Life* (1901), *Standard Edition,* vol. 6. In "Screen Memories," Freud provides a further reason for casting suspicion on the efficacy of reading representational images simply as evocations of early childhood memories: "It may indeed be questioned whether we have any memories at all *from* our childhood: memories relating *to* our childhood may be all that we possess" (322).

32. One recent attempt to do just this is Danae Clark's "Commodity Lesbianism," in *Camera Obscura* 25–26 (January/May 1991):181–201.

33. I have in mind the kind of work showcased by a recent issue of *Camera Obscura* on "The Spectatrix," edited by Janet Bergstrom and Mary Ann Doane. See no. 20–21 (Summer 1990). See also "The Last 'Special Issue' on Race?" edited by Isaac Julien and Kobena Mercer in *Screen* 29, no. 4 (Autumn 1988), and a special issue on "(Un)Naming Cultures," edited by Trinh T. Minh-ha, in *Discourse* 11, no. 2 (Spring–Summer 1989).

34. For a lengthier discussion of the differences between cinema and photography, see Jacques Derrida's essay on Marie-Françoise Plissart's photographs in *Droit de Regards* (Paris: Editions de Minuit, 1985).

35. See Freud, "A Case of Paranoia Running Counter to the Psychoanalytic Theory of the Disease" (1915), *Standard Edition,* vol. 14:263–272.

Cheryl Herr

*t*errorist Chic:
Style and Domination in
Contemporary Ireland

Much has been written, especially in the past few years, about costume and period clothing in Ireland; largely descriptive, this material does little to enhance an outside viewer's understanding of the complex meanings and social contradictions negotiated in the Irish fashion industry itself and in the clothing adopted by various subcultures within Ireland. In this essay, I explore the meanings attached to certain politicized aspects of contemporary Irish women's clothing, and I consider these meanings in relation to some striking structural features of Irish life both in the Republic and in Northern Ireland. In recent years Ireland has been marked by a complex mixture of gynophobia, Europeanization, class rivalry, lingering capitalist colonialism, and hi-tech surveillance.[1] These are large-scale abstractions, often difficult to hold in focus. In this piece I invoke these general issues and then look at quite localized forms of resistance to abstract structuring social forces. In particular, I turn from antifeminist aspects of Ireland's constitutional apparatus to some specific, economy-driven changes in social attitudes, and from the status of the fashion in Ireland, past and present, to the question of what represents politically meaningful clothing for some young women in the republican areas of west Belfast. Both the disappointing legal status of women in the Republic and the crossfire situation that many in the north encounter resonate in the discourse about what people in Ireland wear and why they wear it.

To understand these issues, I bring into focus the challenging situation facing fashion designers in Ireland, north and south; explore the significance and evolution of paramilitary clothing within the decentered and surveillance-saturated world of the north, and concentrate attention on one woman whose uniform at a counterimperialism march in 1989 brings to the surface some of the mixed messages and contradictory demands made of working-class people in Northern Ireland. Each of these inquiries provides a necessary though not sufficient material context for interpreting the politically provocative clothing worn by this marching woman and her colleagues.

CLASS, NATIONALITY, AND THE STATUS OF WOMEN IN THE EUROYEAR OF 1992

In Ireland, clothing has always signaled the disciplinary conflation, exercised by imperialism, of class and nationality. The gradations of style from haute couture to streetwear, now as in the eighteenth century, designate a woman's ethnicity and her place in the indigenous order as well as the degree of her access to wealth and other hegemonic class prerogatives. These stylistic differences express a set of relationships between Irish women and patriarchal imperialism. And these relations register in what people are able to afford to wear as well as in the political allegiances that they signify through their choice of clothing. The relation of class and nationality maps an ongoing dialectic; Ireland is changing ever more quickly from traditional culture to European society and toward a highly commodified self-image that attempts to meet the demands of the EC market economy.

Traditionally, of course, under the gaze of the Irish male—that is, under the eye of the subject sanctioned by dominant institutions throughout most of Irish history—women have been objectified and their persons have been less significant to the state than, say, the fetuses that they carry when pregnant. Consider the 1992 constitution-challenging case of a child known jurisdictionally as "Miss X," the allegedly raped, pregnant, fourteen-year-old Irish girl whose parents took her to England to obtain an abortion and who was required by the Irish government to return to Ireland while the Supreme Court decided her fate. It is promising that, in the midst of considerable public demonstration pro and con, the justices ruled in favor of her right to travel outside Ireland for this medical procedure; that she was not allowed to rectify her situation according to her conscience (as well as that of her parents) in her own country suggests her almost absolute control by the state and by the men who run it (all of the Supreme Court justices who ruled on her case are men).

The Miss X controversy, which drew censure from all over Europe and the United States, took place in a season marked by extraordinary paramilitary violence, both UDA and IRA, in Belfast and other northern cities and towns.[2] That same month of March 1992 saw not only some of the highest levels of violence in Ireland since the mid-1980s but also a heated debate between the editors of the *Field Day* anthology of Irish literature and those who spoke for the many women writers who had been excluded from that aggressively marketed, canon-building collection. High levels of debate over the sad results of Irish political conflict, the objectification of Irish women, and the exclusion of Irish women identify a society in the midst of enormous changes. Caught up in dynamic and destructive social processes, the often mutually exclusive worlds of class, ideology, and gender that mark Irish life may nonetheless be studied to indicate an underlying cultural paradigm. In this essay, which attends to only one dialectically drawn thread in the larger cultural fabric, I argue that in Ireland, fashion and other forms of commodification, the objectification of women's bodies, and the dialectic between censorship and political defiance all register in the stylized clothing worn by women in IRA-promoting marching bands.

Hence, I am less concerned with "fashion" in Ireland than with clothing and its semiotic deployment in the midst of political upheaval and social change. The category of fashion remains, however, an important countervalence to Irish clothing, whether subcultural or traditional. And the categories of both "fashion" and "clothing" insist that we attend not only to social status but also to the relationship between antifeminist attitudes on the island and the ideological attitudes of the rest of the European Community (EC). Ireland's gynophobic society has been described especially well by Nell McCafferty, one of Ireland's leading journalists, and I believe that her conclusions point toward an important contemporary shaping of the old colonial and postcolonial model of economic relations so strongly registered over the centuries in the clothing of Irish women. An ardent feminist, McCafferty is also one of the few commentators on the plight of the pregnant Miss X to bring forward the relationship between the abortion controversy and the signing of the Maastricht agreement by the key European nations, "France, Germany, Portugal, Greece, Italy, Belgium, Holland, Spain, Luxembourg, Denmark and the United Kingdom." Bringing to mind the ongoing discussions in the EC on agricultural policy and trade, McCafferty envisioned all of Europe waiting for the decision of the Supreme Court:

> These countries, with Ireland, had designed an agreement at Maastricht that would bind them together, one for all, all for one, and that agreement contained a protocol which endorsed Irish ways and Irish laws on abortion.

Were the Supreme Court to uphold the child's constitutional internment,[3] and force her to give birth, the subsequent signing of the Maastricht protocol on behalf of other European people would mean that they,
too, endorsed her crucifixion. Were the Supreme Court to set the child
free, the Maastricht protocol, having international superiority, would
over-rule that decision, and oblige all of Europe to support further Irish
efforts to chase and detail other raped, pregnant girls.

The other countries of Europe have indicated their aversion to such
cruelty. They are poised to expel Ireland, to put it beyond the pale. Ultimately, then, no matter what the Supreme Court decides, it will come
down to a vulgar discussion of which matters more: the headage payment
for pregnant ewes, or the preservation of a human female's forcibly fer-
tilised ovum. Signs are that the sheep will be deemed of greater value.
Signs are that abortion, in some restricted form, will be legalised in Ireland and interim freedom to travel abroad for abortion will be welcomed
by the Irish people.

Not the church, not the state, the animal farm will dictate our fate. The
gadarene rush began when the government pleaded with the family of
the raped girl to take the money and run back to court.[4]

As it happens, McCafferty's prediction turned out to be correct. For whatever reasons, but certainly with an eye toward not rocking the Maastricht
economy, the Court decided swiftly to allow the child to go to England
for an abortion. The economics of Europeanization—currently fashionable and expected to be highly profitable—won the day.

The connections among global economics, gender, and Ireland's status
in the European eye came to an explicit focus in the Irish press in February
1992, when the *Irish Times* published on page one an eloquent cartoon by
Martyn Turner (figure 1). It showed a child holding a teddy bear, standing
on a tiny map of Ireland that was surrounded by barbed wire. The caption read, "17th February 1992 . . . the introduction of internment in
Ireland . . . for 14 year old girls . . . ." That the body of Miss X was being
treated in the Republic no differently from the body of an alleged paramilitary terrorist in the northern statelet was a thesis that did not require
explanation. Not the most radical of Irish papers by a long way, the *Irish
Times* overtly challenged the authority of the state in the matter of this
child's control over her already violated body. Ironically, to identify her
body with that of a "terrorist" is no great stretch of imagination for many
Irish readers, of whatever political and religious persuasion, even for those
readers who oppose abortion in all circumstances, who are ardently anti-
militarist, or who are unabashedly antifeminist. Turner's cartoon, I would
argue, taps into a level of collective consciousness that renders the drawing
forceful even for those who fiercely disagree with any or all of its implications. The cartoon thus underwrites my decision in the latter half of this

Figure 1. Cartoon from The Irish Times, February 22, 1992, 1. By permission, Martyn Turner, The Irish Times / C&W Syndicate.

essay to look closely at paramilitary clothing in Northern Ireland. The style of paramilitary dress that I have witnessed in that portion of the island is obviously part of a system of meaning, one that assumes relations and polarities (rich/poor, British/Irish, south/north, Empire/Third World, Euroculture/regional culture, chic/drab) that are not uniquely but are certainly distinctively Irish and that operate freely across the contested border. Before turning to a consideration of paramilitary garb, however, it is useful to map the history of high fashion in Ireland and its ambiguous status there.

DECENTERED FASHION AND FANON

During the week in which Miss X was on trial, Ireland's first woman president, Mary Robinson, was added to the global best-dressed list (which was compiled by polling 2,500 fashion editors and observers worldwide). She is thus the first Irish person ever to be included in such an elite grouping because of the excellence of her clothing (although it bears noting that Sinead O'Connor was "tenth in a list [as compiled by Richard Sylvan Selzer] of the worst dressed women of the past 30 years."[5] In honor of her accomplishment, President Robinson was pictured in the *Irish Independent* (22 February 1992) on the front page along with a picture of the Princess of Wales (already, of course, "an established high fashion leader") (figure 2). The article noted that when they went to her home to cover the story, "journalists, including a German television crew who . . . hope[d] that Mrs Robinson would comment further on the abortion crisis[,] were disappointed." Although she did call on the nation in a televised speech at Trinity College to come to terms with the issue of the Miss X abortion and of women's rights, she did not address the matter of fashion and the matter of rights in the same context; rather she commented only that her award was "welcome recognition for the Irish fashion industry and for Irish designers."[6] Paul Costelloe, most likely current candidate for Dublin's "fashion god,"[7] and not coincidentally a favorite of both the Princess of Wales and President Robinson, was delighted by President Robinson's selection for the best-dressed list.

Notably, the Irish Costelloe always designs for the international market. Only one week before the award, Costelloe's spring/summer '92 opening, held at his home in Dublin, received highly favorable coverage in the Irish press. The *Independent* cited his "slender tailored suits . . . in soft sherbert colours—mint greens, ice pop pinks and canary yellows," composed of jackets with "scooped, loveheart, or cowled necklines," and slightly above the knee skirts. In addition, he showed "relaxed linen jackets teamed up with ankle-length, floaty silk skirts"—referred to as "the looser safari styles" (figure 3).[8] These clothes are both colorful and aggressively generic. So it is of interest that, in a recent interview with Costelloe, a writer for *Northern Woman* (the north's women's glossy) draws out his 1992-on-the-verge-of-Europe reflections about the clothing of Irish women. After only a bit of thoughtful hesitation, he expressed a preference for southern style, with its links to the Europe of Lagerfeld, Versace, and Armani, over what he called the "'golf club' look" favored by the well-to-do of the north. But neither north nor south strikes Costelloe as a sufficient base for a designer; as he told the interviewer, "I really should be living in Paris as it is the only true fashion centre in the world."[9]

To be sure, "Ireland" and "fashion" are not intimately connected words in the international lexicon. A case in point is that although the world of magazine fashion boasts an American *Vogue,* a British *Vogue,* an Australian *Vogue,* and a dozen other national versions—each with a discernible style and markedly different month-to-month features—there is no Irish *Vogue.* Both the Republic of Ireland and Northern Ireland publish their own women's magazines, reasonably glossy, reasonably middle-class, bearing names such as *Image* and *Northern Woman,* but fashion is a category that

The First Lady of elegance . . .

● Princess Di . . . an
established high fashion
leader.

That's style — at the Aras

By DON LAVERY

PRESIDENT Mary Robinson was as gracious as usual yesterday when she learned she was now being described as one of the best dressed women in the world.

Every year, for the past 52 years, a list of the world's best dressed personalities is published in February and this year President Robinson is cited as a fashion leader with, among others, Princess Diana, Madonna, Ivana Trump, Audrey Hepburn, Paul Newman and others.

This year's list was compiled by Eleanor Lambert, who co-ordinated a written poll of 2,500 fashion editors and other qualified observers, world-wide.

Ms Lambert talks of the President as someone who only came to an understanding of the importance of fashion when she came to office.

She said the reason for Robinson's transformation into an "outstanding lady of elegance" is her discovery that fashion is not frivolous but a functional necessity when dealing with the public.

"Like others in public office, she has learned that it makes life easier to have an appropriate and co-ordinated wardrobe."

The accolade, the President said in Aras an Uachtarain, was a recogni-

● Leading in style . . . President Robinson at the reception for the judiciary last night   *picture by Tom Burke*

● **Presidential trend setter — Page 13**

tion for the Irish fashion industry and its designers as all of her clothes are Irish-made and designed.

One Dublin fashion expert said the award was well deserved as the President had a very distinctive style which was "chic but not overly dressy".

With husband Nick she met in the Aras yesterday with more than 30 members of the judiciary and their spouses. She was, of course, suitably dressed in an elegant Robert Jacob black Fortuna pleated suit and white pleated blouse which she wore at her inaugural State banquet.

As the judges and their wives arrived to be greeted by a battery of press photographers in the ornate

Aras drawing room, she urged them: "Don't be intimidated — run the gauntlet."

As a leading senior counsel, Ms Robinson personally knew many of the judges of the Supreme Court and High Courts who attended the drinks reception.

But journalists, including a German television crew, who went to the Aras in the hope that Mrs Robinson would comment further on the abortion crisis were disappointed.

"Ireland is always making headlines for the wrong reasons," one German journalist remarked.

Mrs Robinson had a warm welcome for Mr Justice Declan Costello and Attorney General Harry Whelehan, who was nonplussed by the media attention.

Figure 2. Irish Independent, *February 22, 1992, 1. By courtesy of* Irish Independent.

Figure 3. This photograph accompanied an article by Claire Shiells, "Interview: Paul Costelloe," in Northern Woman, *March 1992, 64. By courtesy of Claire Shiells.*

most outsiders and even the majority of Irish do not associate with the island. A writer from Clare, hearing that I was putting together an essay on "Irish fashion," told me comically but unequivocally that it's "like Irish cuisine: there ain't no such thing." And *Vogue*-world, however questionable, comical, or retrograde as a source of value, almost seamlessly constitutes the Emerald Isle as Other. Fashion as personified and marketed by Condé Nast decidedly turns her elegantly made-up face away from pre-EC modern Ireland, as from many other regions with problematic Third World populations.

Whatever the success of Costelloe and his fellow Irish designers, in place of the en vogue, Ireland itself overwhelmingly markets to the world at large the kitsch come-on of native costume. More often than not, *Trachtenmoden* (national costume) stands in for internationally viable style. So it is that images of Irish clothing come to most of us outside Ireland only in catalogues advertising fisherman-knit sweaters, linen blouses with lace trim, and tweed cloaks and jackets. The items are of high quality, the woolens boasting good seams and proving excellent at keeping out the weather. This short list of marketable traditional garments curiously merges class codes: the nineteenth-century Aran Islander wearing his handmade sweater of elaborate design (the better to identify him if he washed overboard and was recovered from the sea only in fragments) would have had little in common with the landed lady of the same period whose lace and linen translucently echoed her marble skin. Perhaps neither could have fraternized for long with the urban entrepreneur in his Donegal tweeds. At the risk of sounding comically pompous, one might argue that in order to sell clothing at all outside its borders, the Irish have had to participate in a ruthless rewriting of their history, have had to obfuscate, fragment, pretty-up—operations in which their most immediate colonizers, the British, have tutored them for centuries. Outside this model of Irishness, indigenous designers like John Rocha, Richard Lewis, Robert Jacob, Lainey Keogh, and Michael Barrie remain mostly unknown in the world at large, even to, say, the American consumer who is familiar with their British counterparts from Laura Ashley to Katherine Hamnett and Vivienne Westwood. Like most Irish artists who achieve international recognition, designers must relocate to Britain, the United States, Italy, or France; they must Americanize or Eurostyle themselves. If they insist on being Irish designers, limited distribution, uneven economic backing, low visibility, and rigid consumer expectations all conspire against them, while the ersatz folk clothing of the catalogues succumbs ever more fully to a counterhistorical and improbable yuppification in the service of the export market.

As in so many other matters involving the colonial and postcolonial world, Frantz Fanon provides an invaluable guide to the analyst seeking to reinvoke something like unmediated Irish "history" and to account for the continued marginalization of Ireland in the imagination of international design. Judging from his positioning of the Third World in relationship to the powers that be, I believe that Fanon would find the European concept of fashion highly dependent on the illusion of a fixed center. The wearer approaches cynosure status by signifying proximity to material and political power points—London, Paris, New York, Milan. Peripheral to Europe, Ireland today is as far removed from being synonymous with power as any country in the EC, a fact that Costelloe acknowledges along with his success in partially overcoming that difficulty.

This marginalization was not always the case. During the eighteenth century, Dublin was the second city in Great Britain, a great capital in its own right, a mecca for fashionable aristocrats, and the home of the Irish Parliament. Lord Edward Fitzgerald and his French wife, Pamela, were at the head of the anti-British insurgency and at the forefront of Dublin's fashion world. Indeed, part of Lord Edward's preparation for the 1798 Rising was ordering a one-of-a-kind military uniform in shades of green; it was delivered to him shortly before his untimely capture.

But when 1798 brought about a violent although unsuccessful uprising in Ireland, the British responded by imposing the Act of Union; from 1801 on, the Irish parliament was disbanded, and Dublin witnessed the flights of the aristocrats along with its own catastrophic economic decline. The architectural historian Kevin Kearns reports that after 1801,

> Dublin experienced profound socio-economic metamorphosis. Few Dubliners could have anticipated or prepared for their new historical fortunes—or misfortunes. In a real sense, the Act of Union committed the city to sleep, plunging it into a prolonged period of social and economic dormancy. The most immediate and conspicuous consequence of political change, directly following the dissolution of the Irish Parliament, was the mass exodus of wealthy and prominent citizens.

He quotes Froude on this matter: "With the sudden departure of people of wealth, fashion and power, Dublin's former brilliance was noticeably dimmed. . . . Indeed, so swift was the change that Lord Cloncurry, writing in his Personal Recollections, notes with dismay that the Dublin to which he returned in 1805 was 'in many respects, so different' from the city he had left in 1797 that he was compelled to digress from his personal narratives just to reflect upon the nature of these changes." "Property values plummeted to unimaginable levels. Georgian houses which had been

purchased for £8,000 in 1791 sold for only £2,500 a mere decade later."
And Dublin became a city not of the francophile and the fashionable but
of the professional person and tradesman.[10] An historian of Irish clothing,
Mairead Dunleavy, while maintaining that Dublin's 1801 decline has been
overstated, nonetheless admits that there was a loss of prestige; rather than
draw the aristocracy, Dublin Castle was a magnet for the newly rich,
whose attention to being up on the latest styles was substantially less authoritative than had been the case when Parliament cut the social fabric to
its own fashions.[11]

That profound political decentering was compounded by the 1921 par-
tition of the country, which contributed largely to making the history of
modern Ireland a narrative of decentering. And yet, Ireland's underground
resistance network has maintained, through successes and failures, a consistent presence in Irish political life over the past two centuries. As Roy
Foster reminds us, after the Act of Union all that remained of the recent past was "an organized peasant underground" opposing Anglo and
Protestant rule.[12] From that submerged zone important effects, including
distinct styles of dressing, have entered public (as distinguished from marketing) space. The past two decades and more of extravagant turmoil in
the north have evolved a local resistance style that has little to do with
fisherman knits, laces, linens, or tweeds, little to do with the commodification of clothing, but everything to do with the coherence and expression
of a distinct subculture in Northern Ireland.

PARAMILITARY CULTURE: INVISIBILITY AND SURVEILLANCE

Although Paul Costelloe finds little to admire in the country club attire of
the northern middle and upper classes, to my knowledge no one has interviewed him about his response to indigenous working-class street style,
either in Dublin, where he lives, or in Dungannon, the northern town
where his clothes are manufactured. Within the registers of Irish society
that remain uninterrogated by women's magazines, the uniforms worn by
paramilitaries of every sect—and the outfits worn at parades by marching
bands supporting one political group or another—constitute a style that is
deeply inscribed with value. Given its local prominence, it is surprising
that the clothing side of Northern Irish visual and material culture has not
received attention by semioticians or cultural critics within Ireland.

Sadly, the most pertinent exploration of paramilitary and paraparamili-
tary style occurs only indirectly in Michael Selzer's dated and simplistic

1979 study of violence in advertising.[13] Selzer's distinctly American argument, in which he coopted Tom Wolfe's term "terrorist chic," suggests a reversibility between advertising and terrorism. His analysis takes place entirely within a commodified worldview, and thus his thesis is profoundly inadequate to the "underdeveloped" Northern Irish situation. But how can outsiders read Irish paramilitary clothing? With what kind of information is the eye encoded that is educated in this form of terrorist chic? What system of meanings comes to the fore in Ireland when clothing and politics traverse each other? And do the meanings embodied in this clothing justify the semi-invisibility allocated by the media to a significant portion of the north's working-class world? Moving between my own observations and points in Selzer's analysis, I seek some answers to these questions.

To begin with personal observation, it was in 1989, during the summer that marked twenty years of the "Troubles," that I visited the north on an extensive research trip. Part of my larger agenda was to observe what people of various political orientations wear in what is sometimes styled a war zone, in a place that has been repeatedly decentered and progressively catapulted into Third World poverty and disfranchisement.[14] But on this occasion I wanted particularly to find out what an "underground" peasant style might have transformed itself into over the centuries, and so I concentrated my own attention on nationalist ghettos in the north—places like Crossmaglen, the Bogside in Derry, Strabane, West Belfast—places in which technologies of surveillance and countersurveillance dominate. Looking from the point of view of dispossessed but politically engaged women in Northern Ireland, I would say that a counterfashion uniform has been constructed not from the privileging of an external center but rather from the assumption that any site, any *body* is always utterly visible within a three-dimensional techno-media network in which power passes among various crown forces and indigenous forces, in which the center is literally in constant motion. What any given inhabitant of Northern Ireland (of whatever political persuasion) might consider to be a hostile or "terrorist" gaze is replicated in so many ways by this network that everyone may be said to be scrutinizing everyone else. The frequent attempts by outsiders and insiders to assign rightness and wrongness, to praise or blame any single political entity in the north, take place within a framework that automatically renders such attempts inadequate, noncomprehensive. The effect is a bit like the 1960s British television series *The Prisoner:* surveillance and countersurveillance radically undermine fundamental social concepts—good and bad, ours and theirs, private and public. And clothing, which is often used to mark those concepts in "normal" society, becomes a peculiarly versatile and socially charged form of signification.

TERRORIST CHIC

I now return for a moment to an American viewpoint. Michael Selzer sought a way of accounting for the violence that he found infecting advertising, popular culture, and various "lifestyle" issues in the seventies. Terrorism provides a template for understanding these phenomena, he believes, because although terrorism is not a significant material condition of "our lives," it is "a spectacle to which we are compulsively drawn."[15] What the terrorist wants is to get our attention, to make an impact on us. In that sense, terrorism shares much with the fashion industry, which seeks a definitive response of some kind in the viewer. If the style in question is hard-core punk, the viewer is generally construed to be conformist and therefore insulted, offended, or reduced to outraged gawking at the aesthetic governing punk style. Sometimes that same effect is taken over by the world of high fashion, as when major designers launch their shows with costumes that, although often drawn from street style, could "never" be worn on the streets by the audience in attendance or the perusers of *Vogue* and *Elle*.

According to Selzer's analysis, for which he claims support in the work of psychiatrists and social scientists, the terrorist suffers from extreme boredom or other lack of affect, and therefore has a tremendous need to create havoc. The appropriation of terrorist behavior by advertising Selzer finds sinister: "Terrorist Chic shows that we are attracted and excited by the fantasies which motivate the terrorists themselves. . . . Terrorist Chic is thus the outer limit society is able to allow itself in expressing the fantasies which terrorists themselves make explicit through their behavior."[16] It has to be allowed Selzer that the overt connection between fashion and warfare is far-ranging and important to the shape of women's culture everywhere. Fashion designers mount their marketing endeavors as generals would a military campaign. Anything from color to cut may be described as dangerous, a visual assault. And even in the midst of wars, people have craved the latest fashions. In *Gone With the Wind,* Scarlett O'Hara glows when Rhett Butler brings her the newest hat from Paris, an event drawn from Eliza Frances Andrews's *Wartime Journal of a Georgia Girl*. Similarly, during the Gulf War of early 1991, a report in *Mirabella* noted: "There we were in Paris, during a war centered around the very countries—Kuwait,

DRESSED TO KILL?

The most widely distributed media images of the IRA
uniform. Republican newspapers, British tabloids, and
magazines render up a weary visual litany of balaclavaed n
dressed in American-style fatigues and carrying Armalite rif
of us who attend to changes in the style of formal IRA gear w
these depictions, whether of female or male revolutionary unit
present commemorative events, of the funeral of Provo Micha
or that of Volunteer Gerry Casey—all leave a retinal residue of t
entiated occlusion, a somber display of solidarity coded into black
and drab clothing. The Irish analyst John Darby addresses this unifo
in his fine study of political cartoons called *Dressed to Kill*. He remind
that IRA wearables have altered over the years, most markedly since t
1920s. When, in 1969, political events began to recreate vigorous paramilitary activity in Northern Ireland, some immediate adjustment in international cartoon depictions—from old-style IRA to the newer Provisional
IRA had to be made:

> Somewhere in the recesses of the media's folk memory of Irish violence
> lay the image of the Irish Republican Army. So closely linked were the
> two in the popular imagination that the IRA began to invade cartoons
> even before the Provisionals were formed in 1970. . . . To fix the image
> of the newcomers, cartoonists simply picked it up where it had been left
> at the time of partition in 1921. Trench coats, slouch hats and Tommy
> guns were dusted off and called into service again, at least until new cues
> could be established. . . . The transformation of this outmoded stereotype
> was gradual and somewhat confusing. Black berets and dark glasses ap-
> peared, and even the trench coats eventually gave way to combat jackets.
> The confused image was turned to advantage by Mahood, who con-
> trasted ancient and modern paramilitary modes [Darby refers to a *Punch*
> cartoon in which a man in a striped suit is greeted by a trenchcoated
> volunteer: "Jasus Sean! You can't go out to murder people dressed like
> that!"], and by Martyn Turner, who pointed out that paramilitary pris-
> oners in fact conformed to a disturbingly normal and alarmingly young
> pattern [a *Fortnight* cartoon showing a child wearing too-large shoes, a
> beret, fatigue jacket, and short pants].
>
> The dark glasses adopted primarily by loyalist groups became a fa-
> vourite subject. . . . [m]ost cartoonists were inclined to lump together
> not only all the different loyalist groups, and all the republican groups,
> but all paramilitaries.[21]

Certainly, the look has changed over time. In Tom Collins's excellent
The Centre Cannot Hold: Britain's Failure in Northern Ireland, there is a

rabia and, to a lesser extent, the United States—that have provided
stomers for haute couture. Though we were far from the Persian
Paris haute couture, itself ever a war zone, was engaged in a mother
attle. It was hard to recognize friend from foe. . . . Halfway through
collections we heard the news that Arab princesses, stuck in their na-
lands, were clamoring for the fashion videos, notably those of Louis
aud and Jean-Louis Scherrer. The shows must go on."[17]

More than that, the eye must go on, seeking images that fortify its sense
hat the female body courts aggressive control in any and every social
cene, and that fashion has an inherently violent as well as obviously fetishistic quality. This argument is part of what *The Panic Encyclopedia* implies in its entry for "Panic Fashion." Arthur Kroker tells us that the
French guru of postmodernism, Jean Baudrillard, has it wrong when he
emphasizes the reduction of every aspect of culture to mediatized events
and images. Rather, Kroker says that fashion is "itself the spectacular sign
of a parasitical culture which, always excessive, disaccumulative, and sacrificial, is drawn inexorably towards the ecstasy of catastrophe."[18] Kroker
thus reinforces the 1984 argument of Paul Virilio that perception and warfare have, in our culture, become complexly intertwined.[19] The "surface
aesthetics of deep sign-continuity" helps us to draw together terrorism and
chic, to reinforce aspects of Seltzer's intuitive but insufficiently interrogated connection of advertising with horror.[20]

Now, contemporary Irish self-assessments often bring forward the cultivated ability of the individual in Ireland to live in more than one world,
even when the various spaces so designated might be construed by an
outsider as contradictory or mutually exclusive, even when one of those
spaces is a war zone. Whatever the need for examination of such national
self-stereotyping, the fact remains that clothing in Ireland often presup-
poses one or more undergrounds, one or more kinds of war zone, the
necessity of managing irreconcilable contradictions, and the imminence of
an "ecstatic" social catastrophe. In relationship to women, of course,
James Joyce famously sums up some of these splintering pressures when
he invites us to enter the world of Stephen Dedalus, whose schematizing
of women into virgins and whores poses tremendous problems for the
character's piece of mind and ability to get along with the females of th
species. It is under the sign of this traditional dichotomizing of wome
that Ireland's continued objectification of the female body resides. And
is in contradistinction to the surrounding material Euro-world of desigi
fashion that I would position the clothing worn by IRA supporters ;
volunteers.

photograph of a 1978 republican march along Belfast's famous Falls Road, a demonstration in which dress gear was worn: an insigniaed beret, a black turtleneck, wide-bottom dark pants, and either wool or leather sports jacket, all combined with over-the-ear hair, all worn by men. No doubt in an effort to solidify their public image, from time to time the Provos have also allowed specific photo opportunities for journalists. Hence, Collins also shows a Provo in paint-spotted, shapeless beige jacket, full-face balaclava, and black cotton gloves, holding an "accessorizing" weapon. Collins's caption reads, "Member of the Provisional IRA exhibiting sub-machine gun during a kind of military fashion show at Casement Park, Belfast, at end of Provisional parade on 12 August 1979" (figure 4). A draped cloth provides the photographic backdrop.[22] Alternatively, in the catalogue of Ireland's first photographic exhibit in the early eighties, we

Figure 4. Member of the Provisional IRA. By permission, Pacemaker Publications.

Figure 5. "Belfast 1980." Another angle on figure 4. By permission, Ea-monn O'Dwyer.

are treated to the same incident as captured by a more critical photographer (figure 5), the angle of vision this time above the Provo to display the purposely draped cloth, the eerily posing paramilitary, and a cluster of press photographers clicking away. There is considerable irony in this open display of an organization that most Americans, at least, would assume to be always hidden, secretive. World media keeps most of us largely unaware of the immensely public profile of the IRA in its communities. In nationalist territory, such paramilitary fashion shows educate viewers, especially young viewers, about the existence of indigenous, if illegal, power, and they hold a place for what is missing in their sectors of society—political autonomy and cultural centeredness.

A few more examples of IRA style will provide a sense of the current "looks" in paramilitary wear and indicate the developing attention in marxist and nationalist publications to successful marketing of that style. For instance, on the cover of *Living Marxism,* August 1989, is a picture of now-dead Charles English, a Bogside Derry resident who was an IRA volunteer (figure 6). In the photo he stands in uniform, surrounded by smiling, probably admiring crowds who are moving past him, presumably at or toward a rally. He wears a fitted army jacket and a wide, light belt. He carries a machine gun in black-gloved hands and wears a black

Figure 6. Charles English on the cover of Living Marxism, *August 1989.* By permission, Jim Collins, Camerawork Derry.

ski-mask topped by a beret. This is the full-dress look, and the appreciation of his viewers appears as sincere as that extended by socialites to the latest by Ungaro or Calvin Klein.

Another instance: on the cover of the 1988 Sinn Féin calendar for County Derry and Southwest Antrim (figure 7), we see obviously posed field maneuvers, in the foreground a woman, her midlength red hair emerging from her beret, wearing a dark drab hooded army jacket and a wool scarf over the bottom of her face (the preferred masking technique, apparently, for IRA women); to my eyes, the touching part of this photo is not her femaleness, although foregrounding her gender seems to be the intention, but the condition of her gun, which is old, chipped, and rusty. That this photograph is a posed bit of propaganda finds emphasis in the Republican Resistance Calendar for 1990, on the cover of which we find two men helping each other with what looks like a mini-missile launcher, a machine gun, and a two-way radio. Looking stalwartly toward the viewer is the same red-haired model, now holding a more impressive machine gun. All three wear half-masks, and the hole on the side of one man's facial covering suggests that the short mask is produced by folding down the full balaclava. The look takes on a curious comedy when combined, as on the Sinn Féin calendar for 1987, with sunglasses. A whole unit in drab,

Figure 7. Cover photo, Sinn Féin calendar for 1988. By permission, Republican Sinn Féin, Dublin.

Figure 8. Wall mural, 1989. Photograph by Cheryl Herr.

one woman wearing a skirt instead of pants (a style registered in the wall mural from 1989 shown in figure 8), stands at attention in a cemetery, while above them pikeheaded flagstaffs pierce the air and around them press photographers with huge lenses angle in for the best view of the proceedings.[23]

The supersign that I am calling Irish terrorist chic brings together violence and clothing, but also explores and challenges both the association of fashion with wealth and the world media's commitment to censorship of IRA subculture. Dedicated to insuring that working-class life remains relatively invisible and the defiance of terrorist activity available only in its horrifying dimensions, the media has an uneasy kinship with the systems of surveillance dominating whole subregions of Irish life. Refusing to allow the outside world to inspect the north at all levels of experience and design, the powers that be also collude to render nationalist ghettos hypervisible, marketing and using the latest surveillance technology to do so. So it is that wearers of resistance style are caught in a complex visual logic; they seek high visibility within the world at large but can achieve it only within a circumscribed space in which being seen amounts to being incautious, betrayed, co-opted, or otherwise discovered. While Selzer argues an insidious connection between the violence of advertising and the psychology of terrorism—a sort of corruption of consciousness across the grain of western civilization—it is also necessary to notice that many layers of meaning intersect in the case of those styled "nationalist." In addition to the overarching objectification of women's bodies in Ireland, there is also the official scrutiny of the body for subversive information and the rendering up of the body to such scrutiny in the service of communal defiance. In conditions of hypersurveillance, the attention of a community has to be focused, enhanced, generalized, and packaged as though there were international recognition of a discrete, gendered, political identity.

SATURATION SURVEILLANCE

There is an ironic relationship among the media censorship of paramilitary conflict, the eerie openness of paramilitary support on the streets of Northern Ireland, and the intense surveillance to which republican communities in particular are subjected. What I must emphasize is that enormously contradictory experiences—of being visible and invisible, of being commercially hidden and politically defiant, of expressing one's partisan beliefs and of being optically interrogated against one's will, of being willfully not seen when one most desires attention—inform the visual culture of the particular class formation that I am addressing in this essay. In Northern Ireland, I realized that I wanted to unpack the issue of surveillance in the north and to consider its relevance to the behavior of women in the resistance community.

Nationalist people in Northern Ireland often observe that they live in an open prison, under persistent personal and electronic reconnaissance. Consider, for example, the town of Crossmaglen in the "bandito country" of South Armagh. In that borderland of unapproved roads, smuggled petrol and appliances, listening towers, armed forts, helicopter oversight, and justified paranoia on all sides, surveillance is a way of life. The nationalist occupants of that area accept as part of the environmental conditions that the British army, using listening posts staked onto the hillsides, can eavesdrop on what goes on in anyone's living room, can see into any space. It is assumed that surveillance devices are so sophisticated now that they can be anywhere at any time, overhearing, seeing, and recording every movement, word, and intention. As they say on the border, the IRA lads don't hold their conversations just anywhere, and people have normalized the fact that they are the objects of a massive viewing machinery, an institutionalized look perfected by the military. Similarly, in the strangely beautiful cities of Derry and Belfast, there is saturation surveillance of the ghettos—helicopters crisscrossing overhead, parked cars with cameras hidden in the headlights, closed-circuit TVs, Land Rovers throwing searchlight beams into private homes, video cameras where you might least expect them. Regardless of the legitimacy or illegitimacy of their efforts for political self-determination, the IRA-identified people of the north have existed for twenty years in a situation of high-level scrutiny, and their collective subjectivity has been deeply marked by this climate of espionage. Again, this is not to say that all of Northern Ireland suffers from constant watching. But it has been estimated that the British government pays £8,000 per hour to maintain this level of visual penetration, and those areas—self-conscious, clannish, isolated from the context-society by the machinery of government—that are strongly nationalist bear witness to the particular effects of saturation surveillance.

In Northern Ireland, the surveillance equivalents of the cinematic apparatus distribute the gaze into the entire fabric of the nationalist subculture. In that zone, everyone constantly suffers what Beckett called "perceivedness" and, through the agency of the IRA, just as persistently returns the look in a projected violence that endlessly rebounds on both penetrated victim and the immanently invading beholder, the terms intersecting in endless transit.[24] Given that the sine qua non of international fashion is the caressingly voyeuristic camera, how does clothing style respond to these conditions of hyperviewing? The answer appears to be twofold: the subject often withdraws behind a mask and abandons individuality in favor of a selectively public uniformity, and the resulting collective body transforms the necessity for fear and masking into a visibility so high that it alters the terms of visual exchange. This alteration may be read both as mere reversal of the power relations and as a more complex refiguring of asymmetry as diffusion, as decentering. For my purposes, this reformulation of terms reinvokes the gendered and erotic dimensions of the gaze in order to insist that the economic and material conditions of women in the north be acknowledged. Seeking one kind of information, the counterrevolutionary gaze discovers ever more complexly constructed scenarios and produces effects at the level of group identity that resist the institutional work of stilling, installing, inspecting, discovering.

POWER FASHION SHOWS

By far the most moving moment of my trip occurred one evening in the town of Strabane, and I want to attend closely to this place—and to the town's collective gaze—in the context of nationalist activities. It was in this town that I watched a memorial band practicing for a demonstration to be held in Belfast on August 12. After dinner, sounds of drums and flutes floated over the community, drawing people to a scene that was, to my eyes, surrealistic. Watched over by neighbors and surrounded by buildings on which revolutionary murals had been painted, the band played its repertoire of perhaps seven numbers over and over again. The band, or rather their situation of performance, constituted a visual and aural center for the town; rather than linger over tea or stout, the parents and friends of these teenagers came to hear their music and watch their solemn parading around a macadam lot. Against the pressure to watch TV, they responded to a live event that supplied a material although impermanent focal point for their community's political position, economic plight, and cultural heritage. In fact, as Strabane's nationalist young people paraded around and around the square lot, all of the community seemed to be drawn there to watch them. Teenagers with bleached postpunk hair or "straight" permed hair; kids in jeans or tight skirts and heels; an old man with his pet goat on a rope; housewives in the process of losing their slim figures; unemployed males; a prisoner recently back from thirteen years in an English prison; a softspoken liberationist priest; a mother of four who had been reared in the Free State but moved to Strabane eighteen years earlier and who told me she would never consider leaving her friends now. Interestingly, the punk-clad kids did not jeer their performing neighbors; the band's uniforms are apparently consistent with the resistance strategies of British-inspired punk and postpunk style. Everyone present seemed to be an enthusiastic supporter of the band and its assumption of subcultural centrality.

It is necessary to emphasize the material conditions surrounding and traversing the band's garments. Strabane is a town with a population of about 12,000 (and falling—emigration is a large problem here). The town is mostly nationalist, the outlying areas loyalist: both Protestant and Catholic communities throughout the north of Ireland suffer terrifying rates of emigration, unemployment, and underdevelopment. Strabane is said to have the highest unemployment rate (40 percent) in Europe. The band, only four years old in 1989, had already lost at least fifteen members to prison. To my surprise, the band wore the Provo uniform—black beret, black shirt and pants, wide white belt, black boots. On the beret is a little red crest. The costume finds depiction repeatedly on the famous murals of Strabane, Derry, Belfast, and other republican neighborhoods; in the murals, uniformed people pay homage to fallen comrades, engage in combat with the loyalist paramilitary, or heroically posture with gun in hand and slogans to the fore. The costume assimilates the wearer to existing material culture—to the gable walls of tenement houses, the rippled sunlit field, the mourning draperies at nationalist funerals. And when the Provo costume is isolated from those conventional settings and poses, it carries them with it, along with the essence of the Irish slogan most visible here—*Tiochfaidh ar La*—"Our day will come."

As the band began performing in earnest, I watched these teenagers with their flutes, drums, and flags, and realized that soon many would be joining neighbors in prison or possibly dying in a Provo maneuver. What impressed me was not only the energy and clarity of their music but also the fact that certain numbers included a refrain that I was surprised to hear chanted in public. As the drums took over the burden of performance, the fluteplayers stood with legs apart and instruments at waist level. I—Thump—Thump—R—A: shouting the letters defiantly, the band members looked alternately stalwart, passionate, proud. They did not look pathetic, despite the seeming hopelessness of their community's political efforts. As the band played through their repertoire once, twice, and a third time, the little community did not tire of gazing gladly at its offspring. No one told the children that another course in life might be wiser. The priest wants peace and justice in Ireland, but he did not dissuade the band from its display of bravado, its challenge to British law and rule. As the music rounded over the lower hills and penetrated every home in Strabane, I took pictures of the band against, on the one side, a terrific sunset that pushed through clouds to throw golden light on the flags being paraded in front of them, on the other, a huge gable wall mural of an unmasked, black-clad Provo with the caption "THEY CAN KILL THE REVOLUTIONARY BUT NEVER THE REVOLUTION."

In the midst of such extravagant staging, we might yet ask, what is the situation of women in the band? How, precisely, are they objectified or freed by their participation in this community-sanctioned activity? The response of women was certainly enthusiastic. Indeed, in Strabane, community attention, somber but highly valued uniforms, and shiny instruments win even children to the IRA cause. The fact that they watch the parade and join it, then veer off to push baby carriages, inculcates the notion that taking part in political action is no different from any other female and family function that the children observe (see figures 9 and 10). There is a seamless blending of Provo ideology, the "open imprisonment" of the nationalist community, and baby care or other signs of domesticity. Although the women in the band are absorbed into patriarchal military costume, the setting does not suggest anything even remotely terrorist or terrifying except perhaps in the overt presence of helicopters and surveillance towers.

So the effect within the community is to absorb frightening signs, to domesticate them, to make them both a bit sexy and a bit homely, to accept them. On one level, the technology of surveillance renders these people frighteningly open to inspection. On another plane, media black-

*Figures 9 and 10.
Women and children
at IRA parade in
Strabane.
Photographs by
Cheryl Herr.*

outs render their defiance illegitimate and hidden. And in a third register, the community's self-approbation finds expression via the sign of the fashionably exposed, stylized, objectified women's body (perhaps the only vehicle that can speak to all parties at once in a language that can be understood in any way at all).

On the other hand, it is well known that despite the recent election of Mary Robinson to the position of president of the Irish Republic, women have rarely occupied central, controlling positions in Irish life. On this evening in Strabane, however, at the precise center of the band's formation was a young woman, a flute player. She was about sixteen years old, had long dark hair, healthy good looks, and a stereotypical fierce expression in her eye. When she shouted "I—R—A," for the moment I could entertain a belief that armed struggle and its somewhat hollow triumphalism could prevail here in the way that she apparently imagined it. She assumed a position of power as she stood motionless and spoke her illegal political affiliation in a spot where the Royal Ulster Constabulary often patrolled. I felt that her clothing drew my gaze, held it, and insisted that she be recognized as a female potential Provo, a nonauxiliary revolutionary.

What must be emphasized, too, is that there was nothing simulacral in her slight distantiation from the real thing of IRA active service. That is, she did not exist primarily in the media spacetime of video replay and commodified images. Perhaps only time separated her from political activity; the media care nothing about her, refuse to grant her even a provisional status in a technologized register of images.[25] Again, there is immense effort to keep her and her cohorts off camera, to render them invisible to the eye even of the Irish public. When I returned to Dublin after my visit to the north, I watched a Radio Telefis Eireann account of the Belfast march and discovered that the more potent images of protest had been effaced. Strabane's marching band was too small and insignificant ever to make it to the TV screen in any event, and yet what I witnessed in the community's square was, among other things, a power fashion show, a sophisticatedly presented event complete with theatrical mural backdrop. Obviously, this kind of collective local staging has been perpetuated to offset the media wipeout and distortion of ecstatic semiotic catastrophe, the making of a world that cannot experience its own capacity for violence without panic, its own necessity for being seen without objectifying others.

That evening, a little girl I will call Bridget, who was seven years old and had shiny brown hair tendriling over her shoulders, told me that she was going to be in the band someday and that she wanted to play the drums. Given that all of the people I met simply assumed that they and their children would continue to struggle against the British presence for an indefinite period of time, Bridget's prospects of being in the band seem pretty good. These children—little girls tottering in their mothers' discarded heels, three-year-olds holding the hands of siblings and friends, boys pretending to beat drums and play flutes—all clustered and marched behind the band, lacking formation but clearly patterning after their older neighbors, brothers, and sisters. Talking with Bridget, I vividly recalled a few years earlier when I saw other children marching in Ireland. That was June, during Wexford's annual Strawberry Festival, when marching bands gather to parade the streets before everyone engages in celebratory consumption of local strawberry dishes and Guinness. Many of the children wore colorful tunics and caps, the colors not signifying any political affiliation; their activity was a child's activity, not one overtly patterned after adult behavior and politics, certainly not one likely to eventuate in anyone's dying. Both in Strabane and in Wexford, Irish children enter the public eye on parade, to the sound of marching music. The southern children I saw were not subjected both *to* and *by* the double gaze of community and political surveillance. And yet as the case of Miss X suggests, children in the Republic can readily assimilate to the same "northern" logic of colonial occupation at the somatic, as well as sartorial, level.

I would argue that in Strabane, during band practice, the British gaze—an intensified and politicized version of the ordinary male optical logic—is replaced or folded over and recoded by the temporarily invoked collective look of the community. The privileged Provo uniform exists in the visual circuit by which the community knows itself. Rather than allowing itself to be constituted as the "other"—the gazed-upon and penetrated—Strabane overturns or recirculates the gaze by peering inward while allowing its collective ego defiantly to look back. The desire of Britocratic convention to discover criminal activity is renegotiated in the circuit of surveillance by which the IRA—a surrogate for the community—appropriates the right to be the watcher of itself and of its oppressors. The very act of looking back finds substance in the nationalist murals that are everywhere in this country. And the production of selfhood, of superidentity, comes about under multiple gazes, or more accurately, under the eye of the community, as a process of returning the look. However desperate the struggle and saturated the surveillance, there is a periodic reinscribing of collective agency in the highly visible event of uniformed performance. So insistent is this visual program that it would be ludicrous to assume that when I, as an outsider, watched the band, I was placed in the subject position of oppressor. At that moment, the occupying forces were held at bay and abstracted into a tenuous machinery. Rather than being constituted as a function of the phallocratic Britocracy, the band existed under a variety of gazes, including one that is communal and Gestaltic and that reflexively installs in the space of self-scrutiny a superidentity composed of rhetoric and display. Through media-censored fashion power shows, there is a periodic reinscribing of a highly adaptable collective agency. Isolated in Strabane, the band of some twenty members seemed cut off from the real world in so many ways that I was unprepared to see their like replicated by a score or more in the parade of bands to commemorate the 1969 deployment of troops in Northern Ireland. When I arrived in Belfast to view this protest, I discovered Basques, South Africans, Scots—contingents that came to Belfast annually in order to express the unity of their causes and a working-class solidarity of limited scope but intense conviction. The urban space of Belfast provided a richer and more international context for Provo subculture, however limited its numbers. Here, the surveillance society juggled all of its anomalies. The parade was under heavy coverage by choppers, gunners on roofs, Land Rovers, RUC, UDR, and binoculared SAS waiting on buildings.[26] While the British penetrated every space with monitoring devices, the Provo community was as visible as possible, marching past two-story murals celebrating their mythology, playing music in the streets and chanting "I-R-A." This parade, like the one in Wexford, included children as sweetly costumed participants, wearing white and green. The one who caught my eye was the littlest, perhaps eight years old, marching with a cluster of children being socialized not only into polarization, contradiction, surveillance, defiance, and self-destruction but also into community, collectivity, and solidarity (figure 11). But by far the majority of marchers were adults. Band after band came out clad in basic black (figure 12).

It was in Belfast that I saw a countertext to the grown-up version of Bridget that I had seen at the center of the marchers in Strabane. Again there was the dark hair and determined expression. But this marcher was part of an all-female accordion band. Their members wore the de rigeur black beret, the black shirt, the black shoes; they also wore short black skirts, black hose, and black sunglasses. The woman who appeared to be their orchestrator (figure 13) wore a feather in her beret, long earrings, and two-inch heels. She reminded me of Mauricio Lasansky's "The Disappeared Son," a painting that shows a woman holding a picture of a child, a boy's face. Her own face we see only as prominent nose, gritted teeth, and yellowish veil covering the eyes. One hand looks wrinkled, the other frail and strained. Her dress is nondescript and knee-length. She exudes the pain of catastrophic loss. Startlingly, she wears black hose and fetishistic black two-inch heels.

Figure 11. IRA parade in Wexford. Photograph by Cheryl Herr.

Figure 12. IRA parade in Wexford. Photograph by Cheryl Herr.

Figure 13. Leader of an all-female accordian band in Belfast. Photograph by Cheryl Herr.

Never mind that this accordionist was going to walk for blocks and blocks down the Falls Road. Never mind that it was threatening to rain and that the UDR had moved tanks and troops into position all along the route of the parade, which might at any moment dissolve into turmoil. An urban version of Strabane's young marchers, she upscaled her look into something fun, a sexy version of Provo garb. In that field of ideological black, there remained a measure of difference, which women claimed as theirs. Clearly, this difference is not the same as that purchased by the wearer of couture—a fashionable and fashioned individuality—but rather a ripple occurring within and as part of the fabric of subcultural and continuously rewoven collectivity. Her self-identification was rendered piquant for me by her insistence on a stylish and even sexual presence in this public space claimed for political resistance and uniformed collectivity, on a desire to be transgressive while remaining politically in the fold that turns back the reconnaissance gaze.

The Belfast woman and her band appropriated some of the energy of that encircling scrutiny, created a provisional center, and playfully interrogated that center's putative patriarchy. Does "the organization" itself accommodate women as easily as the band costumes that are the traces of its presence in public? By all reports, no. The IRA remains a largely patriarchal organization in which women still have to fight for equal status. In the best of circumstances, the IRA woman marks a site of innumerable contradictions. She is constantly divested of power on several fronts while she constantly accrues meaning in the effort to find expressive possibilities within a masculinist mode, to inhabit conflicting subworlds of religion, family, tradition, and politics.

Momentarily positing the uniform as fashion, as a style that allows for privilege and playfulness, the accordionist seemed to me an emblem for the extraordinarily complicated ideological maneuvers engendered in and by Northern Ireland's nationalist community. Her shiny black heels, in this instance the essence of style, took on the significance of liberatory praxis, of looking back. It would be easy enough for an observer with an American viewpoint to turn from this erstwhile Provo Madonna to the kinds of destabilizing and controversial gestures enacted by the "real" Madonna of MTV fame as well as to the terrain of Irish Catholic female subjectivity marked by the virgin/whore dichotomy. In fact, one reader of an early version of this essay remarked to me that the virgin/whore polarity might unfold into a reading of visual resistance strategies that posit both the terrorist and the nun—the political and the religious—as participants in a "holy war" that characterizes Northern Ireland today and for the past twenty years. That easy slide into the greased grooves of Joycean cultural interpretation and of an imposed media misinterpretation of the Troubles as essentially religious, does enable a certain kind of access to this young woman's "look" but not, I think, as much to her material situation as we outside might like to think. Among other things, her self-styling pushes against Madonna's highly commodified mixed messages to insist that we recognize the intolerable—rather than marketably manageable—contradictions in which her subjectivity has been engendered.

This woman lives with real violence (rather than staged video violence) and has no choice but to live with it; she does choose to represent it and to confront it. Her clothing and demeanor, like the subculture that she represents, put a spin on the dichotomy of simulacral versus real and virgin versus whore: she emphasizes the signifying status of ordinary clothing that pointedly follows its own history in implied resistance or even indifference to that of haute couture. In larger terms, she helps us to grasp that history acts as an expressive force that drapes all of us in its contentious garments.

Notes

1. The term *capitalist colonized* "refers to a situation where during the past five hundred years one or other of the following European countries—Spain, Portugal, The Netherlands, Britain, France, Denmark, Belgium, Germany, or Italy—established sovereignty over another territory and ruled the food producing peoples of those other territories for the profit of capitalists in the metropoles" (Raymond Crotty, *A Radical's Response* [Dublin: Poolbeg, 1988], 51).

2. The IRA is, of course, the Irish Republican Army, a radical republican organization seeking the socialist unification of the island. The IRA is divided into the Official IRA and the militant Provisional IRA or "Provos." Their adversaries, the Ulster Defence Association (UDA), support a militant loyalism to the British state. The UDA often operate under the name of the Ulster Freedom Fighters (UFF).

3. McCafferty chose the word *internment* with care. At the time, some quarters were calling for a reinstatement of internment in the north of Ireland because of the widespread bombings and killings there. Always controversial, the policy of internment specifically allows the British government to arrest people suspected of being terrorists but against whom no explicit evidence has been gathered.

4. Nell McCafferty, "14, Irish, Raped, Pregnant, and a Prisoner," *Hot Press,* March 12, 1992, 6–7.

5. "Clothes Horses," *Irish Times,* October 26, 1991, Weekend 2.

6. "World Beater," *Irish Independent,* February 22, 1992, 13.

7. "I'm Too Sexy For My Shirts," *Dublin Tribune,* February 13, 1992: 18.

8. Kathleen O'Callaghan, "Man Who Loves To Dress Women," *Irish Independent,* February 17, 1992, 6.

9. Claire Shiells, "Interview: Paul Costelloe," *Northern Woman,* March 1992, 65.

10. Kevin C. Kearns, *Georgian Dublin: Ireland's Imperilled Architectural Heritage* (North Pomfret, Vt.: David & Charles, 1983), 42.

11. Mairead Dunleavy, *Dress in Ireland* (London: B. T. Batsford Ltd., 1989).

12. R. F. Foster, *Modern Ireland: 1600–1972* (New York and London: Viking Penguin, 1989), 284–285.

13. Michael Selzer, *Terrorist Chic: An Exploration of Violence in the Seventies* (New York: Hawthorn Books, 1979).

14. Of course, like any other country, Northern Ireland has its wealthy citizens as well as its less advantaged masses, and the relationship between the fashionable set in the north and the instability of the design industry in the Republic is a topic that deserves considered attention but is beyond the scope of this essay.

15. Selzer, *Terrorist Chic,* 180.

16. Ibid., 185–186.

17. Gladys Perint Palmer, "Showtime: A View from the Front Row," *Mirabella,* May 1991, 156.

18. Arthur Kroker, Marilouise Kroker, and David Cook, *Panic Encyclopedia: The Definitive Guide to the Postmodern Scene* (New York: St. Martin's Press, 1989), 97–98.

19. Paul Virilio, *War and Cinema: The Logistic of Perception,* trans. Patrick Camiller (London: Verso, 1989).

20. Kroker et al., *Panic Encyclopedia,* 98.

21. John Darby, *Dressed to Kill: Cartoonists and the Northern Ireland Conflict* (Belfast: Appletree Press, 1983), 85–86.

22. Tom Collins, *The Centre Cannot Hold: Britain's Failure in Northern Ireland* (Dublin, Belfast: Bookworks Ireland, 1983).

23. It is likely that the scene is from one of the Wolfe Tone annual commemorations held in Bodenstown, in the Republic, every June 21.

24. In her controversial work on the cinematic apparatus and its role in relation to the patriarchal unconscious, Laura Mulvey described a system with fixed, determining, and violently unequal subject positions. Other theorists, such as Kaja Silverman and Mary Ann Doane, have reformulated her interrogation of the camera to account for perceived flexibilities in the equipment, for role changes that perhaps enable the gazed-upon women of classic film to exploit the machinery for their own erotic and political ends, for the symmetries between Mulvey's project and others involving the visual inscription of subjectivity. See Laura Mulvey, *Visual and Other Pleasures* (Bloomington: Indiana University Press, 1989).

25. Again to quote Kroker, *Panic Encyclopedia,* fashion is "itself the spectacular sign of a parasitical culture which, always excessive, disaccumulative, and sacrificial, is drawn inexorably towards the ecstasy of catastrophe" (97–98).

26. The Royal Ulster Constabulary and the Ulster Defence Regiment police the streets of Northern Ireland. The SAS (Special Air Service) are highly trained special troops used in emergency antiterrorist situations.

Barbara Brodman

*P*aris or perish:

The Plight of the Latin American Indian

in a Westernized World

> I crossed the border carrying
> dignity . . .
> I carry the huipil of colors for the
> fiesta when I return . . .
> I will return tomorrow . . .
> **Rigoberta Menchú,**
> *Patria Abnegada*

Like Mother Fashion, Paris delivers her haute couture designs to the world at large. From fashion hub to fashion hub, city to city around the world, disciples of Western fashion bow to their Parisian mecca. Yet, not all have accepted the hegemony of Paris and the West in matters of style and dress. In the Americas, for example, indigenous peoples continue to wear with pride the tribal designs that mark them as Indian. Their dress is an expression of culture as rich in history and symbolism as oral literature or other indigenous art forms. It is part of the glue that holds Indian cultures together and that safeguards them against extinction. Sadly, the price Indians pay for preserving their native fashion is social degradation, persecution, and, often, death. Adoption of Western dress is part of an ongoing process of Western colonialism that began almost five centuries ago, and it may signify the demise of cultures that have existed and thrived for millennia.

In the two areas of the Americas where indigenous populations are most concentrated, the Andean region of South America and Middle America (Mexico and Central America), Indians face economic and legal discrimination, and have even become victims of blatant, sustained genocidal campaigns. Often, the Indians' choice of whether to adopt Western dress or continue to wear native designs determines whether they will live or die. In 1932, for example, after troops of the dictator Maximiliano Hernández Martínez slaughtered 30,000 Indian peasants, indigenous peoples in El Salvador stopped wearing traditional Maya garb, and Indian identity all but disappeared. In Guatemala, however, a particularly brutal conquest led to the creation of a tradition of revolt and the retention of culture. Of today's Guatemalan Indians, some 40 percent speak one of over 120 dialects of 22 Maya languages as their primary tongue and wear with pride one of hundreds of distinct costumes that not only mark them as Indian but also proclaim their village or town of origin.[1]

Considered one of the worst violators of human rights in the Western Hemisphere, Guatemala focuses its pogroms on the elimination of its indigenous people, who are considered naturally susceptible to "communist subversion." With the largest percentage of Indians in Mesoamerica—some 60 percent of the total population—Guatemala provides a fine killing field for death squads and civil patrols for whom the Guatemalan Indian wears his or her native garb like a red flag. It should come as no surprise that Indians make up a large percentage of the estimated 45,000 "disappeared" and 100,000 persons murdered in Guatemala since the mid-1960s.[2]

In Guatemala, as elsewhere in Indo-America, to dress like an Indian is to be an Indian. And to be an Indian is to be socially and economically deprived, at best, and persecuted to death, at worst. Yet, many Guatemalan Indians choose to perish rather than accept the cultural dictates—including fashion—of a world in which indigenous peoples and their cultures have become increasingly expendible.

CULTURAL SIGNIFICANCE OF DRESS

Worldwide, fashion is a clear and definitive expression of the culture from which it derives. Western fashion, for example, reflects the dynamism of modern industrial societies characterized by rapid change and innovation, by individualism coupled with an increasingly global perspective, and by a superficiality that, to some, represents a threatening uniformity. Western fashions change with the seasons and at the whim of the fashion industry.[3] By direct contrast, consistency of style and design characterizes native American dress.

Among indigenous Latin American peoples, like the Maya of Guatemala, dress reflects little of the capriciousness and superficiality of Western fashion because it is linked to cultural survival. It symbolizes a time when ancient American civilizations were among the most advanced in the world, when being Mexican or Maya, Chibcha or Inca, was a source of pride and power, not degradation. In contemporary Middle America, as elsewhere in Indo-America, patterns of native dress reflect not only the rich symbolism that lies at the heart of Indian ritual life but the basic institutional framework of the culture. Within this context, native dress helps perpetuate divisions of labor, family systems, and hierarchical orders that have stood the test of millennia and that today are threatened.

Once the Maya were the greatest cultural force in the Americas. They left copious records of their history, cosmology, and achievements, but most of them were destroyed before or during the Spanish Conquest. Today, the splendor of those times is perpetuated mainly in an oral tradition and in the style and design of traditional Maya clothing. So linked to cultural identity and survival are the sacred symbols and colors that characterize Maya dress and textiles that their mythical origin is recounted in the *Popol Vuh, The Sacred Book of the Ancient Quiché Maya.* It explains that the great god Tohil presented the ancient Maya with the symbols and colors of their being painted on three cloths.[4] Their contemporary descendants use the same designs and colors in memory of that event. They employ the figures of the jaguar, the eagle, wasps, and bees, and the colors of the Maya cosmology: green, the royal color, signifying eternity and fertility; red, the color of the sun and of blood, signifying life; yellow, the color of death and of maize, the staple food of life and the substance of which man was made by the gods; black, the color of obsidian, symbol of war; and blue, the color of sacrifice. All remind the Maya of a time when they communed directly with the gods and produced a high culture unsurpassed in the hemisphere. Indigenous designs thus form a text of Maya origins, religions, and history and, as such, help keep alive a culture that is increasingly threatened. All the colors of the Maya cosmology can typically be seen in contemporary Guatemalan marketplaces, including the flower market in Chichicastenango (see figure 1). The traditionally woven fabrics worn by the flower women are elaborately brocaded and embroidered with designs and colors that reflect both ancient and modern influences. Note, however, that the flowerwoman's sweater of synthetic fabric, symbol of the encroachment of Western dress into Maya culture, mars the splendor of this display of Maya textile art.

It may be that when the Maya cease to use the ancient symbols on their clothing and textiles, their culture will have died; and they will indeed have been westernized. In the face of genocidal campaigns, planned dislocations, and forced assimilation into a hostile culture and environment, preserving these overt and material vestiges of culture becomes all important. The imposition of Western fashion, within this context, is no less than a subtle form of genocide.

But it is not just the mythical/religious symbolism reflected in Middle

Figure 1. All the colors of the Maya cosmology brighten a typical scene of the flower market in Chichicastenango. Photo by Barbara Brodman.

American textile and clothing design that renders its preservation essential if Indian cultures are to survive. The "text" of a weaving more often incorporates a broader theme: the worldview and basic institutions founded on that worldview that serve as the framework of Maya culture. Incorporated in native dress is the blueprint of an entire social system: agriculturally based, community oriented, and decidedly non-Western. Within this broader context, dress helps perpetuate divisions of labor that harken back to earlier periods of cultural development and achievement, when the Indian community offered its members—females included—a level of prosperity, security, and safety that no longer exists, except in the most remote areas.

From ancient times, a woman's life revolved around weaving. The technology and skills used in this all-important female activity were, like the designs and colors they incorporated, gifts of the gods. In ancient codices, Ix Chel, the Mother Goddess, is depicted sitting at her backstrap loom, one end tied to a tree, the other around her waist, her shuttle in hand. According to legend, Ix Chel first attracted the attentions of the sun god by her weaving, and from their union was produced a daughter, Ixchebel Yax, patroness of embroidery. Young Maya girls still pray to Ix Chel, patroness of weaving, for skill with the loom sufficient to attract them good husbands, and some continue to use the bone needle of Ixchebel Yax to create elaborately embroidered huipiles. To the Westerner, this link between industry and myth signifies a level of inefficiency and ignorance that rightfully, in accordance with the Judeo-Christian and capitalist world view, targets a people for exploitation. To the Maya, however, it represents a continued bond between the people and their tribal gods that is perceived by many as their only hope and protection in an otherwise totally hostile environment. "Children, wherever you may be, do not abandon the crafts taught to you by Ixpiyacoc," the *Popol Vuh* exhorts them, "because they are crafts passed down to you from your forefathers. If you forget them, you will be betraying your lineage."[5] To sever such bonds would not only shatter the cosmic reality of the Maya but would upset the very institutions that have helped preserve them as a culture. Although the affluence of others might be enhanced by the destruction of traditional Maya ways, what hope of affluence and harmony remains for the Maya people today and in the future may well rest on their preserving certain divisions of labor and economies upon which their ancient affluent culture rested.

In ancient times, as today, women were responsible for clothing themselves and their families and for producing the exquisitely made textiles that adorned priests and temples. As mothers, they were responsible for passing their skills on to their daughters, whose status in the community rested largely on their skill as weavers. On the basis of their skill, they could, regardless of class, gain prestige and fame. The material from which they wove their cloth and the dye plants they used to color it varied from region to region, but the weaving tools and techniques they used and the style of garments they wore were fairly standardized. Thus it was the individual skill of the weaver that served to distinguish one garment from another, not innovations in style. Weaving, then, provided not only an essential economic commodity (textiles having been valuable trade items long before the Conquest) but provided as well for a degree of egalitarianism and female mobility that is impressive even by modern standards. In contrast with the extreme "machismo" and socioeconomic disequilibrium that characterize mainstream Latin American culture, such a system seems far less inefficient and born of ignorance.

The construction and tailoring of native garb has always been of the simplest kind; but the textiles of which that garb is made are the product of a complex technology, by which are woven into each piece the threads of a harmonious and affluent village economy. Through weaving and textile design the ancient American was able to perpetuate symbols and designs that reflected the Indian view of the cosmos and that clearly proclaimed the status and role of the wearer and the weaver. Although Indian dress has changed somewhat over the past half-millennium, it remains an essential expression of cultural continuity.[6]

CONTEMPORARY PATTERNS OF DRESS

Rarely, however, do modern indigenous people completely preserve the ancient style of dress. Even the primitive Lacandon of the Usumacinta River region that separates Mexico and Guatemala have eschewed their traditional bark fiber garments for tunics of cotton—which they wear with high plastic boots for trips to town. When Europeans invaded and conquered the New World, they imposed their manner of dress and customs upon the native peoples of the region. In Mesoamerica, as elsewhere in Spanish America, Spaniards replaced the native elite classes and assumed all power and access to wealth. The Indian assumed the lowest position in society, although always with the option of rising above his humble status merely by assuming the look of the Spaniard. Those who chose to retain their Indian identity paid a heavy price.

Despite this, important vestiges of ancient dress remain, particularly in the Maya heartland. These are most evident in women's dress, which more clearly reflects a pre-Columbian tradition. But they are not lost in the typical male garb. True, in all but the most conservative villages and among older Maya males, the ancient turbanlike head covering (the "tzut") has been replaced by the ubiquitous cowboy hat; and the traditional sandal, often quite elaborate if the wearer were a nobleman, has in most of the region been replaced by shoes and boots of Western design and construction (including, alas, plastic). Nonetheless, in the southern Mexican state of Chiapas, Maya males continue to wear ribbon-strewn straw hats that serve as the post-Columbian equivalent of ancient plumed headdresses, and brightly colored textiles of assorted design continue to distinguish members of one village from another. In Guatemala, it is not unusual to see village men wearing long pants, a Western-inspired garment, made of handwoven Maya fabric and topped with an overpant that resembles the peculiar, short, "eared" trousers of ancient times, the symbols on which identify the male's age group and status in the community.

A visit to any major marketplace in the Guatemalan highlands will reveal the degree to which traditional male garb has been preserved, on the

Figure 2. In this typical Chichicastenango market scene are reflected both Western and traditional Maya influences. Photo by Barbara Brodman.

one hand, and has given way to Western influences on the other (see figure 2). In this scene the women wear the traditional dress of their village, while the men in the foreground display a mixture of Western and Maya dress. Their woven short pants and skirt reflect their village and cultural ties, but to this traditional garb they have added Western shirts and the ubiquitous cowboy hat. The young man in the background has clearly adopted Western dress to the exclusion of any traditional items. For him, as for many, the pressures of modern commercial relations have led to the complete abandonment of traditional dress. For others, the transition has been less complete. Despite some significant additions and modifications, most men preserve key elements of their indigenous heritage through their dress and distinguish themselves from their more Western-influenced compatriots. They are Maya first and Guatemalan second. However, since, traditionally, it has been the indigenous male who has interacted most with Spaniards and "ladinos," often against his will, it is not surprising that male dress should reflect a strong Western influence.[7]

Women's costume has changed little since ancient times. The costume of a conservative Maya woman still consists of a traditional upper garment, the huipil; a wraparound skirt, or "corte"; a woven belt; and a head covering or braid wrap (see figure 3). In the more conservative villages of

Figure 3. Two young girls display the typical female costume of Santiago Atitlan: cortes of geometrical design; striped, embroidered huipiles; woven belts and the rolled headdress unique to that region. Photo by Barbara Brodman.

Mexico and Guatemala, Indian women continue to produce the textiles for these garments on backstrap looms identical to those employed by their earliest ancestors. These looms are light and portable enough to allow a woman to use them while attending to other chores, like tending sheep or caring for home and family. They are also versatile. On a backstrap loom, a woman can produce intricate designs using complicated techniques impossible to replicate on commercial looms. Even a woman of the simplest means can produce a fabric of great intricacy (see figure 4). A textile technique known as brocade allows the Indian woman to weave designs and symbols of ancient origin into the cloth itself. From the textile emerge images of gods and animals who give fertility to the earth, protect the growth of corn, and symbolize the Maya cosmology. Women who devote their lives to brocade and become skillful in the complicated techniques and symbolism it incorporates are venerated. It is through them that ancient myths, symbols, and visions of the cosmos are preserved. To her weaving skills a woman may also add her skill in embroidery, as she embellishes the seams and borders of her simply constructed garments with traditional designs of great complexity and beauty.[8]

Figure 4. A girl sits at her backstrap loom in the doorway of her family's shop in San Antonio Aguas Calientes. Above her hang a variety of cloths, sashes, and huipiles woven by local women. Note the apron that is a required part of her traditional costume and the discarded, Western-inspired footwear. Photo by Barbara Brodman.

Although dress and class are no longer as indistinguishable as they were in ancient times, traditional village costumes still reflect slight differences in status and wealth. Officeholders generally wear elaborate costumes for ceremonial occasions, and often put themselves in debt to do so. In general, though, costume reflects not rank but village affiliation. In less conservative villages and towns, men and women alike have borrowed freely from Western fashion. In addition to garments of Western origin, one sees costumes of machine-made textiles, sometimes machine-embroidered, and incorporating designs of nonindigenous origin. In these places Indian identity is threatened.

In the more traditional villages, this is not the case. Each village has its distinctly colored and patterned costume, in which it takes great pride. Although once a means of distinguishing combatants in war, this custom serves today not only to foster pride and solidarity within villages but also to promote pride and solidarity among Indian peoples who are fighting for cultural survival. In Guatemala, where almost 300 distinctive village costumes have been identified, Maya Indian culture remains strong even under the impress of Western religion. A woman in native dress standing

Figure 5. A Maya woman swings an incense burner before the entrance to the Church of Santo Tomas in Chichicastenango. Photo by Barbara Brodman.

before a church thus serves as a symbol of religious syncretism in the Maya heartland, where the distinction between Catholicism and indigenous ritual and religion is blurred (see figure 5). Note that in her role of "chuchkajau" (independent native religious practitioner) she displays more of the Indian than Western influence. Her dress, with the exception of the shoes, is traditional Maya.

But Maya culture is severely threatened. In much of Middle America, the Indian has been forced to assimilate into mixed-blood, Western-based society. Those who have chosen to preserve their ancient customs and way of life have been relegated to the lowest levels of the socioeconomic scale. Increasingly, that position alone singles them out for physical destruction.

DRESS AND CULTURAL SURVIVAL

There is no more obvious expression of Indian identity than costume. Perhaps for that reason, so many groups intent on influencing or controlling Indian peoples have attempted to alter their patterns of dress. First the missionary, intent on imposing his religion on the peoples of the New

World, forced the Indian to dress like a Christian (who, by some strange coincidence, dressed like a European). Since then, land barons, armies, churches, and guerrilla rebels have attempted to do the same as part of a larger plan to change or adjust the Indians' relationship to their land.

At the heart of genocidal campaigns in Guatemala and elsewhere in this hemisphere is the threat of land reform inspired by the existence of culturally unified peoples who are tied to the land but increasingly landless. In Guatemala, some 80 percent of cultivated land is owned by 2 percent of landowners, who, aided by centuries of institutionalized racism and the ever-increasing rapaciousness of the agro-export sector, continue to rob Indians of land that they need to survive. Agro-exports have made Guatemala one of the strongest economies in Central America. Yet 74 percent of the rural population, most of whom are Maya Indians, live below the level of absolute poverty, while 85 percent of rural households are landless or possess insufficient land to satisfy the basic food needs of their families.[9] Consequently, families routinely watch their children die of malnutrition and find themselves forced to labor on the *fincas* (plantations) of the wealthy Ladinos, separated from their communities and stripped of their dignity as members of a once great and still multitudinous race. On the fincas, Indians endure an appalling deficiency of food and health care, the cruelty of overseers, and backbreaking labor for wages that are criminally inadequate. They often return to communities that are systematically ravaged by the Guatemalan military, whose fear of Maya insurgency, born of deteriorating living standards and an increasingly threatened way of life, inspires them to commit unconscionable acts of brutality. In the last decade alone, the Guatemalan army has razed hundreds of Indian villages, forced tens of thousands of Indians into "model villages" that are little better than concentration camps, and subjected thousands of rural Maya, young and old, male and female, to rape, torture, and murder, often as public spectacle. Nominally, these atrocities are aimed at deterring the growth of "communism"; in reality, they are aimed at discouraging highly justified and growing calls for reform. It is a hope of the privileged class that by "ladinizing" the Indians they can better control them and assimilate them into systems that favor the interests of the few over the many.

For Ladinos it is enough to glorify ancient Maya culture, as a means of proclaiming ethnic pride and individuality in the face of foreign domination, while denigrating modern indigenous peoples whom they revile and treat as slaves. No better evidence of this Ladino paradox exists than the national Folklore Festival held every August in Cobán. The festival culminates in the selection of an Indian beauty queen. Contestants, selected earlier by the ladino authorities of towns throughout Guatemala, parade their distinct regional costumes before a largely foreign and non–Indian audience that flocks to Cobán to participate in this widely advertised celebration of national identity. For the contestants themselves, who are required by law to travel from their villages to the festival at their own expense, the spectacle is often a source of humiliation and impoverishment. But for the Ladinos it is an opportunity to bask in the splendor of Maya textile art—among the best in the world—and a Maya heritage that they rarely associate with modern indigenous peoples about whom they prefer to remain ignorant.

Among those who are regularly drawn to this display of exquisite indigenous fashion are buyers and representatives of designers and clothing manufacturers from around the globe. For them, the festival provides a unique opportunity to view a living catalog of masterfully woven fabrics that can be purchased at astoundingly low prices and fashioned into some of the world's most expensive designer creations. That the weavers and wearers of these incomparable textiles are being exploited, perhaps to the point where their craft will eventually disappear, seems not to occur to these entrepreneurs, for whom the people and culture that produced such beauty are of little interest. Increasingly, Indians realize that as long as they remain unable to communicate with Ladinos in their own language or understand and work within the Ladino system they will be exploited and robbed of their land, their dignity, and their lives. Although the more conservative Maya still prefer isolation from Ladino society, they cannot escape the degradation of folk festivals in which they are reluctant participants nor the brutality of military and civil forces bent on eliminating the call for reformed systems by exterminating the people who would most benefit from reforms.

Growing political activism among the Maya reflects their awareness that to learn about and work within the Ladino system does not require that the Indian *become* a Ladino. Indeed, it may only be through some emergence from cultural isolation and greater dialogue with the outside world that traditional Maya culture can be preserved in the future. It is a lesson of the Conquest that the Indian cannot defeat what he or she does not understand. In the last few years, rural Maya have become active in a burgeoning network of organizations established to deal with issues of labor and land reform, human rights abuses at the hands of the government and military, and the retrieval of bodies of "disappeared" family and community members.

Many of those involved in these organizations have been forced into exile. For them to leave the communities and land in which their Maya identity is rooted is a personal tragedy. But it has allowed them to bring their struggle to the attention of international organizations without whose support they will probably be unable to counter the genocidal campaigns of the government or accomplish reforms that will improve conditions for the Indian majority. These reluctant refugees proudly continue to wear their native Maya garb in the capitals of Europe and the Americas as proof that political activism need not threaten indigenous culture but may indeed be a means of preserving it.

There are those who believe that survival of traditional societies in the twenty-first century is impossible. The better-intentioned of these individuals believe that improving the lives of indigenous peoples is more important that preserving their cultures. Others believe that cultural survival is essential at any price. It is often said that the Maya spirit was never conquered, although the Indian was subjugated to Ladino rule. It is this undaunted spirit, kept alive and venerated in oral tradition and dress, that suggests a less radical solution to the problems that confront the Maya today. Survival of Indian culture in Guatemala and elsewhere in Latin America may depend, in the future, upon the ability of indigenous peoples to balance change with tradition. In Guatemala, this balance may be achieved by focusing both on radical, long-term political and social reforms (including land reform) and on increased integration of Indians into the commercial infrastructure of the nation.

Within this context, and assuming an ever increasing role in the battle for cultural survival through commercial integration, are the Maya women who produce the native garb that helps perpetuate their culture. Perhaps because of the male-centered nature of Spanish society, Maya women have escaped some of the exigencies imposed on Maya males. Being invisible, except when it benefits ladino culture to put them on display for tourists and entrepreneurs, Maya women have been able to retain their ancient crafts and costumes, even when in fairly regular contact with Westerners. The complex and central role of women in the village life and economy of the Maya has gone largely unnoticed by members of the mainstream culture; and, thus, it is only recently that they have begun to take notice of the growing number of weavers' cooperatives and female-run commercial enterprises through which Maya women may improve their own and their families' standard of living without sacrificing their culture in the process.

Decades of civil war and state-sanctioned genocide have catapulted women into realms of political and economic activism that were formerly closed to them (and largely unnecessary within the traditional balance of power structure of the village). Sheltered (or trapped) under the umbrella of a patriarchal ideology, Maya women have traditionally, and unobtrusively, shouldered a disproportionate burden of labor within the household, serving not only as household managers and agricultural laborers but as weavers and clothers of their people as well. They are, therefore, well positioned for assuming a dominant role in preserving Maya culture while at the same time working to achieve greater integration into the national economy, for, next to agriculture, the most important economic activity of the Maya is textile production. The growing demand for Maya textiles, so popular today in the fashion industry, has led to increased use of the foot loom, a method of textile production introduced by the Spanish and, until recently, used only by men. However, the best and most valuable cloth is still that produced (only by women) on the backstrap loom. The work of producing such pieces is slow and painstaking, but thanks to the creation of weaving cooperatives, women can, for the first time, receive a fair price for their efforts.

On the other hand, cooperatives are generally viewed as politically subversive. Although eliminating ladino middlemen is often enough to increase a weaver's earnings several times over, the reaction of those disaffected may be severe. After centuries, conditions established by the Spaniards have not ameliorated. Indians who wish to prosper or, indeed, subsist in the ladino economy are forced to adapt to the mainstream culture in ways that threaten their indigenous lifestyles, while those who wish to retain key elements of their culture find it increasingly perilous to do so. Today, the Western fashion industry collaborates in a process of oppression and exploitation that goes back centuries. Perhaps it does so unwittingly: first by sanctioning the encroachment of Western dress into non-Western cultures; and next through the co-optation of native textile arts into Western fashion. Co-optation need not signify exploitation, however. If, indeed, imitation is the purest form of compliment, then isn't it also a means of preserving cultures in danger of extinction?[10]

The fashion industry is a powerful special interest. Although it may not recognize itself as actively involved in international affairs, its involvement is considerable. Take the recent case of Liz Claiborne and the "model village" of Acul, in the Guatemalan highlands. In 1983, Acul became Guatemala's first "model village," an army-controlled enclave, inspired by U.S. counterinsurgency in Vietnam, and reviled by Indian and human rights advocates for whom it and others like it are little more than concentration camps. A year ago, Guatemalan officials discovered that the residents of this particular village were skilled at crocheting. They contacted executives of Liz Claiborne in New York, with whom they developed a project that would give the Maya of Acul "a chance at a brighter future."[11] Using seed money from the Guatemalan government, Claiborne and the government-sponsored National Fund for Peace developed a project to teach Acul villagers to redirect their skills toward hand-knitting sweaters for sale in the United States, where they would sell, with Claiborne labels, for up to $200 each. The villagers were to earn up to $40 per sweater, a great deal by regional standards. After two months of knitting, however, villagers were yet to receive any pay for their work, whereas their crocheting had brought them instant earnings. In addition, the sweaters they made, but did not design, did little to perpetuate Maya culture. While Guatemalan officials optimistically billed this project as one that could produce "as many as 20,000 jobs over five years," the people of Acul remained skeptical.[12] All in all, the project promised to do little for the Maya villagers; and Liz Claiborne, however unwittingly, had helped perpetuate the traditionally exploitive relationship between Native Americans and the fashion industry.

Projects like this one can, however, benefit Indians and the fashion industry alike. They can be designed to direct profits to Indians and not to middlemen. And they can be designed to promote the preservation of traditional designs and textile-making skills on which cultural survival in part rests. In the long run, the fashion industry will benefit from preserving important sources of quality textiles and artistic inspiration. To do so, though, will require a greater and more responsible involvement of the industry in the preservation of indigenous cultures. It will, above all, require a commitment on the part of the fashion industry to turn its international lobbying powers in a new direction. First, it must sensitize itself to the practices within the industry that may contribute to the exploitation, oppression, and even extermination of indigenous peoples. It should work hand in hand with organizations already committed to the cause of human rights and cultural survival for indigenous peoples. And, certainly, it should assist directly in the protection and proliferation of weavers' cooperatives, through which women can produce and market their textiles while, at the same time, preserving and perpetuating the ancient designs and techniques that periodically "revitalize" haute couture.

The future of indigenous cultures in the Americas is by no means assured. Already, in many nations of Latin America, Indian identity has disappeared. In other nations of the region, it is severely threatened. The survival of indigenous culture depends, in great part, on the Indians' ability to preserve its essential elements, like dress, while at the same time adapting more and more to the political and economic exigencies of the times. Nothing proclaims the tenacity of Indian cultures more than their refusal to succumb to the hegemony of the West in matters of style and dress. And nowhere is that tenacity more evident than in Guatemala.

In her internationally acclaimed autobiography, Maya political activist

Rigoberta Menchú states that "what hurts Indians most is that our costumes are considered beautiful, but it's as if the person wearing it didn't exist."[13] Rigoberta expresses the desire of all Indians in Latin America that they be accorded the respect and opportunity that is their right as human beings and as descendants of once-great civilizations.

After five hundred years, voices like Rigoberta's are being heard. For over a decade, Rigoberta has championed Indian rights from exile. During that time she has continued to wear the traditional dress of her Guatemalan Highlands village. Her style has been a vital part of her message. Rigoberta Menchú's receipt of the 1992 Nobel Peace Prize attests not only to her own tenacity and devotion to culture but to that of all Native Americans. Tradition tells us that when Indians stop wearing their native garb they will have lost their culture. Then they will truly not exist. But as long as they preserve the fashions of their ancestors, their culture survives— until better times.

NOTES

1. For excellent historical analyses of the role and plight of Indians in Latin America generally and Middle America specifically, see E. Bradford Burns, *Latin America: A Concise Interpretive History,* 5th ed. (Englewood Cliffs, N.J.: Prentice Hall, 1990), and Benjamin Keen, *A History of Latin America,* 4th ed. (Boston: Houghton Mifflin, 1992).

2. Recent general data about Guatemala and other Indo-American nations may be obtained through any of the many international human rights organizations dedicated to the protection of indigenous peoples in the Americas and elsewhere. Always reliable sources are Amnesty International and Americas Watch.

3. On the link between Western fashion, modernity and capitalism, see Elizabeth Wilson, *Adorned in Dreams: Fashion and Modernity* (London: Virago, 1975).

4. *Popol Vuh: The Sacred Book of the Ancient Quiché Maya,* English version by Delia Goetz and Sylvanus G. Morley, from the translation of Adrián Recinos (Norman: University of Oklahoma Press, 1983).

5. Quoted in Elisabeth Burgos-Debray, ed., *I . . . Rigoberta Menchú: An Indian Woman in Guatemala,* trans. Ann Wright (New York: Verso, 1984), 59.

6. For excellent discussions of the cultural and social significance of Indian dress in Middle America, see Donald and Dorothy Cordy, *Mexican Indian Costumes* (Austin: University of Texas Press, 1978), and Sheldon Annis, *God and Production in a Guatemalan Town* (Austin: University of Texas Press, 1987).

7. In the narrowest sense, *ladino* refers to persons of mixed race or Indians who speak Spanish as their primary language and wear Western garb. In a broader sense, it refers to anyone who represents a system that oppresses the Indian.

8. For outstanding pictorial analyses of Maya dress, see Carmen L. Pettersen, *The Maya of Guatemala: Their Life and Dress* (Seattle: University of Washington

Press, 1976), and Linda Asturias de Barrios, *Comalpa: El Traje y Su Significado* (Guatemala: Ediciones del Museo Ixchel, 1985).

9. These figures come from UNICEF, *State of the World's Children,* 1989, and the Worldwatch Institute.

10. An interesting case in point is that of artist Frida Kahlo, who wore native Indian garb as a means of discovering her own and the collective Mexican identity.

11. See Tim Johnson, "Sweater-knitting Project Giving Guatemalans Hope for Better Life," *The Miami Herald,* June 29, 1992, 8A.

12. Ibid.

13. Burgos–Debray, ed., *I . . . Rigoberta Menchú,* 204.

Andrew Ross

*t*ribalism in Effect

For a while, in 1991, the dopest versions of homeboy and homegirl style included items of clothing featuring their original price tags. This was nothing if not a fiercely logical move in the street style wars, and so its meaning belongs to common sense more than to any individual act of bravado, although we can't help imagining that someone, somewhere, was the first to do it. These days, the purist search for a single style-auteur is always a step in the wrong direction, although it is still one of the most comfortable ways of locating a scene, or giving a narrative to a social motive. Thus we find that a white roadie with The Happy Mondays is credited with favoring the thirty-inch flares that came to decorate the re-cent "Madchester"/Manchester "summers of love"; just as an African-American bus worker from Georgia (and not a pachuco from East L.A.) was once honored by the *New York Times* as the first zoot-suiter, encour-aged to take up the style by the debonair manner of Rhett Butler. There are no iron laws of fashion, but it is equally misleading to perpetuate the theory of individual tastemakers, whether it applies to singularly inspired fashion victims or for haute designers, who have been ransacking street style for over twenty years now.

With youth style going international at breakneck speed, the logic of the marketplace has itself become an object of sartorial terrorism, and so, for outsider sleuths in pursuit of the vox pop, the best tip, more often than not, is to "follow the money." The visibility of the homie's price tags, then, may remind us of how B-boys and B-girls ripped off Gucci paraphernalia a few years back, but it also signals that there's a new game in town—calling the commodity. The faux-fashion Gucci appropriations, among other things, fit very neatly into classic subcultural theory that sanctioned the cocky emulation of a status well beyond the social reach of the style pirate. In the terms that become so familiar, it was confrontational dressing that both resisted and affirmed the subordinate status of the subculture. But the function or meaning of these price tags was less easy to discern. To certify that the goods are freshly purchased or freshly stolen? To mock or to sanctify the accompanying designer (usually sports) label? To supplement the visual address of the clothes or to hijack their fetish appeal? To parade the wearer's buying power or to savagely expose middle-class phobia about the dollar value of taste?

Semioticians might say this uncertainty proves that while everything has its price, the price is never right. But the price tag is no Barthesian floating signifier, liberating the use value of the goods from their exchange-value. On the contrary, it hangs as a kind of challenge to the subcultural premise that street style is created by reference to an alternative market economy—either by withdrawing goods from the orbit of their target taste markets or by elevating the value of neglected goods well beyond the currency of the market. Whatever else it does, the price tag bluntly comments on the ritual omnipresence of the "enterprise culture" that has come into full effect in youth marketing in the last decade, and had engendered at least one anguished debate over the so-called commodification of Malcolm X products. Consequently, today's codes of youth style embrace not only the act of creative consumption but also the very terms of entrepreneurship; design and style as market value. Sometimes this involves more than simply choosing against the corporate consumer grain; the growing preference, for example, for Old School sneakers—the early Adidas, Nike, and Converse classic hightops once available only to college/pro teams—as a reaction against the technologically overdeveloped high-octane sneakers that have fueled the intercorporate sportswear wars in recent years. It can also involve the bootlegging of brand names in back-street screen printers. Ever since the multinational sportswear manufacturers declared their unwillingness to produce clothes for fashion purposes, their logos have become fair game for clothing bootleggers who ply a necromancer's trade at producing not only fakes, but also originals that don't legally exist—a sweatshirt, for example, bearing the logos of Nike, Fila, and Champion.

Street style and fashion marketing are now locked into a frantic polka, a spectacle that MTV has succeeded in programming around the world. But it is often all too hastily assumed that the production of sumptuary style, especially in youth culture, is now global: that the world has become a wardrobe of pure exchange-value to choose from and to cruise with; that it is outfitted according to the just-in-time production schedules pioneered by Benetton; that it markets street style as fast as the street can produce it; that its consumer class marches inexorably to Nike; that its gourmet class robotically conforms to international styles like the sculpted, streamlined Alaïa of the eighties; that the once "resistant" DIY ethic has done itself in (only to be resurrected ironically in the name of grunge by style sluts slumming in thriftshops); and that all that is solid melts into air. Some of this may be true, but just as the new global politics has developed in tandem with the sectarian upsurge of ethnic nationalisms and regionalisms, so too local style tribalism, with a new eye on international trends, has never been more pronounced.

The classic Third World example is the cult of the *sapeurs* and *sapeuses* (devotees of the Société des Ambianceurs et des Personnes Elegantes) in Zaire's Kinshasha, a community of young men who boast their own language, their own religion of the cloth, *kitende,* and who worship at the fashion houses of Gaultier, Kumagai, Matsuda, Versace, Armani, and Miyake in a culture where Western consumerism is officially discouraged in favor of ethnic authenticity. The dandyism of the *sapeurs* and *sapeurses* (who parade their status appearance but who do not enjoy the wealth and power associated with these clothes) clearly has something to with the vestigial patterns of village initiation rites, but its more dynamic function is to allow the socially downscale to employ the designer products of global style in order to challenge the rigid pecking order of cultural capital in Zaire society. There is obviously much more going on here than Western cultural imperialism going through its paces.

In the West itself, the most advanced forms of style tribalism are still to be found in Britain, where the savvy mechanism that churns out teenage subcultures is as well oiled as ever: in recent years, clans of dressy casuals, moody goths, smiley-bearing scallies, ecstatic ravers and travelers, "dirty" crusties, and motormouth ragamuffins have reigned, long since matched in sartorial fervor by the upper-crust dynasties of Sloane Rangers, New Georgians, and Young Fogies. Rave culture has brought with it a whole new vernacular of tribalism (Electribe, Finitribe, and other dance music ensembles complement the rapping significance of A Tribe Called Quest or the Booyah Tribe). The cult of the DJ, in particular, has been attended by all the trappings of technoshamanism and trance-induced primitivism. While much of the tribalist spirit owes its communitarian feel to New Age doctrines of togetherness, Britain's ever changing style map of regional, class, and ethnic divisions seems to have deepened and fragmented further in the face of what Tory stalwarts phobically fear as the "federalist" absorption of British sovereignty into the United European States, another example of transnationalization being saluted with an explosion of subnational diversity.

Britain's youth cultures may boast the highest batting average, but New York City alone has more than its share of territorial divisions and style communities; in Manhattan, Alphabet City's "theory of poverty" bohemians, SoHo hippychicks, gay West Village mannerists / East Village cloneboys, Upper West Side lipstick and nylon girls, homies from Harlem, the new renaissance hipsters from Fort Greene, and, yes, even the Masters of the Universe, still "hemorrhaging money," albeit less loudly, en route from the Upper East Side to Wall Street in their taxicab caravanserai. In Crown Heights, Brooklyn, African-American youth in the Polo Posse have long appropriated the preppy WASP aesthetic by wearing Ralph Lauren togs as part of a subculture known as Lo Life. In the outer boroughs, a host of peer style cultures spell out the differences of musical allegiance, sexual preference, and ethnic loyalty, and further out still, in suburbia, Freud's "narcissism of minor differences" flourishes under the sign of Deadhead, thrash, speed metal, hardcore techno, and so on.

There is no question, however, that style priorities run highest of all in the hip hop nation where the street theater of refashioning black cultural identity is open for performance twenty-four hours a day. Here the symbolic ultraviolence associated with the hard profile of gangsterism—street warrior posses in the old school style of fat gold, kangols, and bomber jackets or in the more sinister hoodies, ski caps and hockey masks of today—faces off against the softer, baggy contours of the beaded, dreadlocked Daisy Ager hybrid in contests over the definition of young black masculinity. Where black male youth is posed alternately as a discomforting threat and as a front of fun-loving innocence, the battle over attitude between Compton "niggaz," neonationalist brothers from the East Coast, and Afrocentric kid 'n' play funsters is more than just bicoastal rivalry with a pan-national third wheel thrown in as the diplomacy option. This aggressive contest over the "realness" quotient of these communities speaks directly to the vanishing solidity of the young black male's existential status in society. What is the authentic style of a group whose official participation in public life is eroded with each fresh round of "genocidal" social and cultural policies? Realness, in this context, is more than just the elusive object of braggadocio, more than just a postmodern game of identities and surface appearances. But if the hard / soft homeboy style divisions seem to fall back upon traditional racist stereotypes of African-American youth as hoodlum and / or as entertainer, the dialogue between the two types is no longer imposed from above or from outside; to some extent, it is selected from within, and is fully debated by the rappers who belong to the most verbally articulate musical culture of the entire modern period. The tenor of this debate wavers when the burning topic of the day happens to be how hard N.W.A.'s dicks really are (black women's disgust has never run higher), but the urgency of even the smallest symbolic outcomes should escape no one.

Style tribalism is fashioned out of moments of merely temporary urgency. Nothing is quite so tribal as fan loyalty to local sports teams, and yet the second, third, and fourth coming of sportswear on the youth style market has proved how easy it is to convert that loyalty into other kinds of cultural values. Unlike the international white "youth class" solidarity of blue jeans, or the later (overseas) status cult of wearing American college sweatshirts, today's passe-partout of the team-identified baseball cap presents a more flexible code of allegiances, seemingly unregulated by class, race, or gender, while offering a cheap alternative to manufacturer brand-name loyalty.

Sometimes, the choice of cap is sports-related—that is, related to how certain teams are playing at any one time; sometimes, it's the aggressive names or reputations of the teams that count most—the Pistons, Raiders, or Pirates; sometime it's their ethnic profile; sometimes it's the game itself—baseball, basketball, hockey, football; more often, it's the color combination, or the appeal of the logo design (caps from the 1950s and 1960s are currently in vogue). For baseball illiterates, especially overseas, the cap is a cheap and stylish source of fantasies of Americanicity. But even in North America, the strong iconography of this belligerently youthful wardrobe item has been radically altered in recent years. The adoption of the cap by urban homeboy and homegirl culture has forever compromised its pastoral Rockwellian associations, not to mention its purity as a symbol of working-class integrity, as worn by the truck driver or the farmer or the assembly line worker. The lily-white legacy of Little League innocence further dissolves when the cap is worn back to front along with the banji realness of full gangsta regalia. This is not the old utopia of a world turned upside down; it is a world where the back is brazenly and disruptively out in front, or else twisted to one side, or pulled down to the eyebrows to act as a "cultural visor." The cap worn askew is no longer a cute tomboy affectation, it is now part of the iconography of social crisis, unmistakably marked by the visual language of the ghetto, where sport and competition often coexist with internecine street warfare. The attitude suggested by the cap now lies in the domain of risky pleasures, at some kind of outlawed remove from the carefully controlled pleasure economy of the baseball leisure industry but still within its orbit.

It may be that the baseball cap has become the first truly global symbol of youth, not unlike the iconic function of the uniform flat cloth cap for the old international proletariat. Just as the flat cloth cap was redolent of labor and productivity, so the baseball cap is tied to leisure and consumerism. Both are fully expressive products of their respective economies; the older economy of scale with a base in standardized mass production, the newer economy of scope with its range of diverse consumer markets. Like the cloth cap, the political meanings carried by the baseball cap are familiar and common, but they now bear the mark of diverse affiliations, choices and loyalties. By contrast, the international denim style of the sixties and seventies exploited workers' clothing in order to distance its white, middle-class devotees from the familiar, everyday cycle of commerce and consumerism. In a similar vein, the ripped jeans of eighties suburban high school fashion displayed a costly contempt for cloth that was not generally shared in other class cultures and in most minority cultures.

Demotic and relevant to the daily life of consumers, the sportswear revolution, spearheaded by the baseball cap, engages young people where they work and play, and puts style where it ought to belong—in everyone's league, with or without a price tag. But there is no minimum level of consumer enfranchisement to guarantee people safe passage to the arena of style. Popular style, at its most socially articulate, appears at the point where commonality ends and communities begin, fractioned off into the geography of difference, even conflict. That is the point at which visual forms of creative consumerism, no matter how tidy or ingenious, are less important than the shared attitudes and social values that come to be associated with the wilfully sundry use of consumer culture. Tribalism is then in effect. Everyone cannot be anyone.

TRIBALISM AFTER L.A.

Despite what Gil Scott-Heron once so erroneously sang, the revolution will be, and has been, televised. But what is it supposed to look like? Eastern Europe 1989, or Los Angeles 1992? In Eastern Europe, the authorities withdrew the tanks, in L.A., M-16 toting marines in full combat gear were called in to patrol the streets. During the disintegration of the old socialist bloc, the media emphasis was everywhere upon the grisly collapse of the old, rather than upon the popular insurgency of the new. In Southern California, participants and sympathizers accorded a variety of romantic names to the events that were unearned, for the most part. Uprising. Rebellion. Insurrection. Intifada. Given the clear association of the events with widespread anger at an appalling case of white justice, it took more than a day for the official designation of "riots" to take hold. By that time, the network spin-control editors and image feeders had come up with a montage of video clips that signified riot, and a narrative that described a scenario "out of control." But live coverage (people forget Scott-Heron's second line—"the revolution will be live"), mostly from the air, of the first eight hours of street activity revealed much more about the practice of urban policing than about any of the causes, conditions, or effects of the rebellion. In the initial absence of the police—immobilized by fear, apparently, and not by a communications breakdown—television cameras performed the work of low-altitude helicopter surveillance that is standard policing procedure in a hypersegregated city like L.A., where control of the citizenry is seldom conducted at ground level alone. In many ways, the streets had already been ceded long before by policing strategies that concentrate on airborne surveillance and on securing whole neighborhoods by controlling the arterial freeway system. The streets of Simi Valley, for example, where the fateful Rodney King verdict was delivered, and where the presence of the Ronald Reagan Presidential Library speaks volumes, are a twelve-mile grid system that the L.A.P.D. (the mother of all police departments, as they are known) can seal off simply by blocking the valley's four highway exits. In a sprawling urban area ringed by the maximum-security suburbs of its self-incorporated satellite cities, the policing of Los Angeles County, as the L.A.P.D. responses showed, is aimed above all at the protection of the predominantly white, middle-class sectors that make up the West Side. When heavily armored police eventually got around to patrolling Hollywood and Beverly Hills on the day after the verdict, Koreatown and South Central were quite conspicuously left to burn to the ground.

Whether or not you saw it as a "rebellion," what was being televised was widely distrusted. No amount of strategic media editing could disguise the fact that the only true riot going on was a riot of consumerism. Guy Debord and his fellow Situationists would have appreciated the invitational spirit—"Let's Go Shopping"—that governed the three-day redistribution of wealth in South Central L.A. From staple foods and material necessities to the notorious theft of all the crotchless panties from Frederick's of Hollywood, the systematic possessing of commercial goods amounted to a utopian version of the daily promises of consumer capitalism, promised but never delivered. Stock footage of fires raging out of control could not conceal the fact that the burning of stores was quite methodical—two thousand incinerated Korean grocery and liquor stores stood in for the Jewish-owned stores that were systematically burned during the Watts riots of 1965. The power of the torch was being wielded against the no less systematic exploitation of poor Black and Latino residents by small business owners, mostly Korean, from outside the community. The most infamous footage from the air, of truck driver Reginald

Denny being hauled from his cab and assaulted, was force-fed into the national media's memory bank of worst white nightmares about black male behavior (a recent study showed that 56 percent of whites believe that "blacks are prone to violence"), but could not cover over the fact that participation in the uprising was truly multiethnic (Latinos alone accounted for a third of those killed, and almost 45 percent (12,500) of those arrested, as compared to 41 percent African-Americans and 11 percent Anglos). South L.A.'s majority Latino population (60 percent) was "discovered" by national media attention at the same time as the undocumented among them were being illegally handed over in droves to the dreaded *migra* (immigration service) under cover of the riots. And lastly, while the spectacle of armed insurrection was confined to the level of low-intensity sniper fire, the gang truce between the Crips and the Bloods that preceded and facilitated the revolt clearly spelled out the message that a unified and well-armed gang population (estimated at 100,000 strong) was quite capable not only of defending underclass neighborhoods and of taking on the police on limited fronts but also of producing from within itself a politically developed vanguard cadre akin to the Black Panther organizations that emerged from gang war zones in the 1960s to make class alliances across the racial lines demarcated by nationalist organizations at the time. The first comprehensive plan for urban renewal—covering education, rebuilding, welfare, law enforcement, and economic redevelopment—was issued by the OGs (original gangsters) themselves in the week following the insurrection, only to be met with deafening silence by city and state authorities.

From a cultural angle, the starting point, for most folks, was that the events in L.A. seemed to have already been scripted and cast a thousand times over in the high-density image and sound environment of hard-core urban hip hop, or in the shock realism of the black film renaissance that has shared the limelight with rappers (in the wake of L.A., Universal Pictures postponed the release of a gangsta film called *Looters*—it would become *Trespass*—starring Ice-T and Ice-Cube). If so, George Bush, touring L.A. the week after, was probably the last to know it. When asked about Ice-Cube and Ice-T, he said: "I never heard of them. But I know that rap is the music where it rhymes." It was only out of political expediency that Bush was later drawn into the public fuss around Ice-T and Body Count's "Cop Killer"—a rock, and not a rap, track, with close to a 99 percent white audience. As if in response, Ice-T had this to say, in a *Rolling Stone* interview:

This country was founded on the things I talk about. I learned it in school. Paul Revere was running around basically saying, "Here come the pigs, and a fuckup is going down." We had a revolution or else we would be under the queen at this moment. That was revolutionary thought, and those were very honorable thoughts in these days, the Boston Tea Party, all that shit. We just celebrated July 4th, which is really just national Fuck the Police Day. And "The Star-Spangled Banner" is a song about a hell of a shootout with the police. You can call them troops, whatever you want, but basically they're police from the other side. I bet back during the Revolutionary War there were songs similar to mine. If you want to look at it, the cop killer is the first soldier in the war who decides, "Hey, it's time to get out there and be aggressive, and I'm moving against them."[1]

Whether or not you accept Ice-T's historical analogy, it's difficult to imagine anyone making sense of the burned-out South Central neighborhoods without being cognizant of the hip hop graffiti references all over the walls, or without being aware of the hip hop fantasies that had shaped daily life in inner city neighborhoods like South Central L.A., made famous by Ice-T and others as the "home of the body bag" and the drive-by. The scenarios imagined in classic recordings like NWA's "Fuck Tha Police," Public Enemy's "Shut 'Em Down," Ice-T's "Copkiller," Kid Frost's "East Side Story" and Ice-Cube's "Black Korea" were very definitely part of the mix, and were acclaimed as prophetic in the weeks thereafter. Even though none of these scenarios came near to being acted out (there was not a single police fatality), the emotional and political landscape that hosted the insurrection was virtually inexplicable without knowing what these raps had to say about the fantasy of killing cops, the fantasy of combating commercial exploitation of the neighborhoods, and the fantasy of reversing racist hate.

One has to be very careful in making claims like this, because they can all too easily feed upon assumptions about the direct effectivity of rap upon events in the social world. Rappers are no stranger to this kind of linkage, having served as demonic targets of blame for almost every conceivable social ill or act of violence that can be found in the urban griot's repertoire of hip hop commentary. My intention is not to prolong for one second this kind of futile debate anymore than it is to argue that rap music was the "key" to the complex social circumstances of the L.A. uprising, serving as a Greek-chorus-type commentary on a tragedy or as a sound-track for a protest film. Some of the same wack reasoning, lest we forget, was applied to the much less militant sounds of soul music twenty-seven years ago, after Watts and other inner-city rebellions (Martha and the Vandellas' "Dancin' in the Streets" was construed as having agitprop overtones). Nor is it enough to acknowledge that rap—Bush's "music that rhymes"—has become the premier mode of cultural expression for youth of all races in the last decade. Hip hop, from the first, has been a social movement, which has come to bear all of the full-blown contradictions of a counterculture in its own right. Having emerged in the Bronx as an explicit alternative to gangland culture, hip hop's subsequent rise to international prominence has been shaped by the tension between its status as socio-political commentary, and its status as a commodity. On the one hand, it has been a medium for recording popular memory, for renovating activist histories and ideas, for renewing nationalist and postnationalist consciousness, and for shaping the attitudes and sensibilities of youth culture as black music and style always have done. On the other hand, the successes of its independent record industry have encouraged the growth of a black entrepreneurial sector that exploits social prejudice—as nasty as they wanna be—as unscrupulously as the lords of narcotraffic exploit social poverty and despair.

In light of these contradictions, consider the ease with which some rappers continue to move from organized neighborhood gangs to the musical subculture, carrying their newfound status as community spokesman into the public arena, and eventually creating their own political affinity groups or seeking membership in larger national organizations like the Nation of Islam. Afrika Bambaataa is the classic example, but many high-profile rappers have made the same moves in recent years (consider that KRS-One, the exemplary politico "humanist" of today, more or less invented the gangsta rap genre in 1987 with his album *Criminal Minded*). These are well-worn paths, and well-defined fantasies (there are, of course, many more wannabe gangstas than the real thing), and the fluidity with which rappers pass from one community to another accounts for their rich cultural clout and influence. Even the most sold performer, like Hammer, who more or less formulated rap as a visual medium, still gets props for videos that are visual anthologies of up-from-the-street dance moves, a tribute that is rarely extended to Michael Jackson, whose dance repertoire seems irrevocably frozen in time in the early eighties. Perhaps the most telling symptom of these street ties occurred during the L.A. insurrection, when the media feeders tried in vain to reach Ice-Cube for comments; he had been too busy, he said, looking for friends and relatives in the rubble of South-Central.

Twenty years earlier, the white counterculture strove in vain to maintain the credibility of its founding premise—that its most respected performers would continue to circulate roughly within the same social orbit as their audience, and that they shared the same alternative value system. But the Woodstock Nation was not socially beseiged in quite the same way as the

Hip Hop Nation; draft-dodging, dropping out, and voluntary poverty led to different forms of outcast status from those occupied by black youth today, especially if you consider the one in four black males aged twenty to twenty-nine who are currently incarcerated under the U.S. criminal justice system. To compare the two as functional countercultures, however, is quite instructive. The white counterculture's coexistence with the organized political movements was uneasy and discordant at best. Hip hop culture enjoys a more intimate relationship with black political and intellectual leaders, and maintains its own highly ritualized tradition of dissing as a framework for dealing with internal factional discords. As for the racial constituency of the music, consider the bottomless irony of "media assassin" Harry Allen's comment that, in twenty years time, a Black Rap Coalition may have to exist to take back rap in the same way as Black Rock Coalition bands today are redefining rock music as black. Allen need hardly worry. The existence of an extensive hip hop counterculture has not in itself put paid to the recurring prospect of white appropriation, but it has played a large role in determining that hard-core rap is the most attractive commodity for white hip hop junkies, for whom no music is "too black, too strong." Consequently, the short shelf life of Vanilla Ice was a weak farce to the sick tragedy of Pat Boone first time around. In the intervening years, moreover, the culture industries have come to depend upon the existence of a mass market of "white negroes": millions of white consumers whose identity depends upon appreciating the real black thing.

Consider, also, the difference in conceptions of nationhood between the two countercultures. The Woodstock Nation may have been generationally bound, but it presented its libertarian agenda as an alternative American national ideal that could be shared by international youth; in this respect, it was a redemptive version of American cultural imperialism, where the nation's founding principles could truly be universally desired. The Hip Hop Nation seeks its nationalist credentials elsewhere, either in the revival of sixties-style militancy, or in the Afrocentric cultural sourcing of Egypt as the wellspring of Western civilization, or in some patchwork appeal to both forms of consciousness that is part of the new gutsy post-nationalist cosmopolitanism. For many, concepts of nation are no less a language of empowerment today than for a civil rights generation that took its cue first from the national liberation movements in postwar Africa and then from the Third Worldism of the postcolonial bloc. But there is no truly secular line to toe, just as separatist rhetoric is no longer circulated with innocence. The spiritual Afrocentric wave rocks the house as powerfully as the rhymes of the militant and the Daisy Ager. No doubt this is a symptom of the larger, global currents that are often termed tribalist;

federalism, secessionism, and demands for regional autonomy and cultural pluralism that are sweeping the spectrum of 5,000 nations that inhabit the world's 190 states. With the tribal-based breakup of one party rule in much of sub-Saharan Africa, the return of ethnocentrism and race-baiting in Europe and North America, and the rise of stateless ethnic nations all over the old socialist bloc, it is not surprising that the emphasis today is more upon the variety of African-American nationalisms.

In North America, the call for brotherhood and sisterhood coexists with the watchword of diversity. Multiculturalism may be the official liberal response to the desire to "live differently," but tribalism is its most potent expressive form in the culture at large. In hip hop dance, for example, which is really a family of dance styles that evolved around breakdancing and resonates with martial arts, fraternity/sorority stepping, and with older dances like the lindy-hop and the Charleston, the most recent move has been the inclusion of African steps, even from traditional warrior dances. While these steps are seamlessly incorporated, they are still a departure from the techno-urban tradition of the early West Coast robotic poppin' and lockin', the faster East Coast "electric boogie" (the imitation of a current passing through the body), the plain multijointed boogie, or the "running man" step that is the grammatical core for today's precision hip hop choreography. The look of the new rap lineups can also display a fully eclectic style spectrum. Arrested Development, the new hotshot ensemble from Georgia, cover everything in their clothing as well as their bluesy rap music that also incorporates dance-hall and acid jazz as smoothly as gospel and African beat: Southern bluejean bib overalls, dorky homeboy baggie wear, kente cloth, beads, and African prints, and the urban shock effect of shaved head/Doc Marten militancy. Meanwhile, Cross Colors ("post hip hop nation academic hardware") became the first commercial hip hop fashion house to explicitly cross all lines.

Given the enduring political significance of hair in African-American culture, the proliferating shaved head is also indicative of the new tilt toward Africa and away from the dreadlocks of the Caribbean. For the new urban bush woman, the ancestral prototype is the bald black priestess of ancient Egypt (including, of course, Cleopatra herself), while the male boxcut fade with hair carving resonates with the traditions of African tribal markings. But the close crop also belongs to the militant-style puritanism of the Nation of Islam, resonating with doctrinal associations with the lost tribe of Shabazz. Outside of the black communities, the advent of this style accumulates other meanings. In the Queer Nation, and in the postpunk hard-core subcultures, the shaved head can be a parody of the institutionalized look—the penitentiary, the armed forces, the concentration camp, the college sports team—or it can signify ascetic religious sectarianism (the Hare Krishnas are having their day again) and monkishness (especially when worn with a hoodie). The full complement of body-piercing and tattooing adds to the current worship of the "body primitive," breaking up the clean-cut muscle lines of the new gym-wrought jock hardness. In the predominantly white style communities, this celebration of tribalism is quite different from the hippy counterculture's adoption of Native American clothes and bead accessories during the 1960s (an articulation of the "Indian" that also, bizarrely, included the styles of the Indian subcontinent). It is more of a conscious, if still romantic, acceptance of the semicriminalized codes of the outcast (gangs, slavery, Auschwitz) than it is an exercise in colonial exoticism that goes way back to the inscription of the tatooed Other on seafarer's bodies.

This is not to say that exploitive white appropriations of black style have let up (today's culture industries depend upon a permanent market of millions of white negroes), but the dialogue is more of a two-way street than it used to be. The early flourishing of the fake-fashion industry in B-boy style (fake Gucci, Armani, Chanel, and so on) was more than matched by the rapid movement of hip hop style up the fashion industry's food chain: Bloomingdale's was soon stocking five-hundred-dollar baseball caps, quilted B-girl jackets laminated in gold, and hooded sweatshirts from the Gaultier collections. Stussy, whose label Stussy Tribe has become a ubiquitous sign of multiracial style rectitude, has raised itself into the high-end casual market by taking up versions of workwear patronized by rappers who have shifted away from the fierce decade-long passion for major league sports merchandise.

In the gay black style community, where the drag ball institution of vogueing achieved international exposure with Jennie Livingston's film *Paris Is Burning,* the impact of black style on the haute houses was much more immediate and complex. Among other things, the film provided the impetus for consolidating the uptown appropriation of downtown style. Here, in a feature from the Sunday fashion pages of the *New York Times* magazine (the fall after the film opened in 1991) (figure 1), the color black is "no longer the exclusive property of rock musicians, bikers and artists with a nihilistic bent." Heralding the upgrading of biker jackets and biker boots, the feature deploys the talents of the new black supermodel Naomi Campbell, while the deathless prose of the copy reads:

> The old black was discreet, it was flattering to every figure, the perfect background shade. The new black is something else. Sleek and aggressive, it says: 'Look at Me!' This season, designers are using black to shape their most provocative silhouettes. They can be sharp or sinuous.[2]

FASHION

BY CARRIE DONOVAN

THROWING

Figure 1. Naomi Campbell "throwing shade." Photograph by Sheila Metzner.

Either way, they spell out their sexy attitude clearly. One way of reading this is simply to transpose people for colors, and to read "African-American" for "black." "The old African-Americans were discreet. . . . The new African-Americans are something else. . . . This season, designers are using African-Americans . . . etc." It may sound crude, but this is more or less what the fashion industry has on its mind when it wants to add a little color, or "throw" a little "shade," as the feature's title puts it. "Throwing shade" is, of course, a term taken from the competitive rituals of ball-vogueing culture, so many of which are themselves parodic versions of haute couture. Here, "throwing shade" is appropriated to describe the style game of oneupwomanship among white, upper-class fashion victims. In drag-ball culture, throwing shade is a highly developed form of "reading" competitors—an art form of personal insult in which a rival's minor flaws are exploited. Vogueing is basically a way of throwing shade on the dance floor, but its originality lies in the syncretic mix, as a dance form that combines poses from *Vogue* fashion and from Egyptian hieroglyphics with hip hop moves from early breakdancing onward. In this respect, its hybrid character recalls semimartial diasporic arts like the limbo dance of the Caribbean, or the capoiera in Brazil. The aggressively competitive nature of these dance forms is more than a vestigial reminder of their evolution as a medium for preserving the arts of martial resistance outlawed throughout the period of slavery. In vogueing, the terms of the contest are still physical agility, but the contest is not fought over physical skill, it is fought over beauty, whose deficiencies in style rather than prowess are exploited by your opponent. Understanding the politics of style here depends upon knowing that beauty conquers precisely because of the exclusion from power and wealth of these dancers—gay, black (or Nuyorican), and poor, and thus subordinated thrice over. For the bourgeois shade-thrower, on the other hand, beauty is quite simply the competitive outcome of power and wealth.

Appearances to the contrary, there is no less of an interplay between the voguer and the hardcore rapper. While the voguers are quite removed from the main target of their desire—white, bourgeois femininity—their art insists on "realness"—a measure of accuracy in imitating roles played by people with a more secure identity in the world: High Fashion, Town & Country, Business Executive, Miss Virginia Slims, even the identity of bhanjy realness. Realness depends upon the knowledge that social power is primarily exercised through the fantasies woven around such roles. This knowledge about fantasy and roles makes the world less dangerous and threatening to those who have most to fear from discrimination. In white performance or appropriation, this knowledge is liable to be reduced to a utopian statement about indifference, where everyone can be anyone, as Madonna demonstrated in "Vogue"; "It makes no difference if you're black or white/If you're a boy or a girl."

For the hard-core rapper, realness in the form of unreconstructed masculinity is the latest form of protection for the black male body, threatened on all sides with social and economic redundancy, if not extinction *tout court*. As gangbanger or militant, the hard-core performance of "real niggaz" has become the new byword in musical authenticity for a huge sector of North American youth culture. The apocalyptic attitude—"we are at war" in Sister's Souljah's male-supportive opinion—that accompanies these roles may well be merely a frustrated prelude to an emergent political culture more defined and polarized by race than at any time since the early civil rights movement. In the wake of L.A., the hard-core attitude is more likely to be linked to self-defense than to self-destruction, and the new tribalism will be put to the test as it responds to the call to Unite or Perish. The most widely circulated images of self-defense in April of 1992 were those of Korean shopkeepers (some even wearing Malcolm X-with-rifle T-shirts) shooting back at looters (but who were the looters? African-Americans? Salvadoreans? Anglos? We never got to see them). In North American iconography, these were legitimate images, with a long historical resonance, of the new (structurally white) settlers protecting their property with weapons. The more challenging images of self-defense were ones that we never saw but that will no doubt populate hard-core hip hop culture in the near future; they are scenarios where the barrels of the gangsta Uzis no longer point inward. Again, it should be emphasized that these are spectacular images of self-defense that do not readily translate into action. And if we have learned anything about the cultural politics of formations like style tribalism, it is that they cannot simply be read off as articulate statements of purpose, let alone as binding agendas for cultural justice. But with so many gangsters in charge of so many of the nation's institutions, one can hardly be surprised that popular street style has come up with its own up-to-date version of the motivated outlaw.

NOTES

1. *Rolling Stone*, August 20, 1992, 12.
2. *New York Times*, September 22, 1992, 65.

Selected Bibliography

Barthes, Roland. *The Fashion System*. Trans. Matthew Ward and Richard Howard. New York: Hill and Wang, 1983.

Baudrillard, Jean. *For a Critique of the Political Economy of the Sign*. Trans. Charles Levin. St. Louis: Telos Press, 1981.

Benstock, Shari. *Textualizing the Feminine: On the Limits of Genre*. Norman: University of Oklahoma Press, 1991.

Berger, John. *Ways of Seeing*. London: Penguin, 1972.

"Cherchez La Femme: Feminist Critique/Feminist Text." *Diacritics* (Summer 1982).

Davis, Fred. *Fashion, Culture and Identity*. Chicago: University of Chicago Press, 1992.

De Lauretis, Teresa. *Alice Doesn't: Feminism, Semiotics, Cinema*. Bloomington: Indiana University Press, 1984.

———. *Technologies of Gender: Essays on Theory, Film, and Fiction*. Bloomington: Indiana University Press, 1987.

Doane, Mary Ann. *The Desire to Desire: The Woman's Film of the 1940s*. Bloomington: Indiana University Press, 1987.

———. "The Economy of Desire: The Commodity Form in/of Cinema." *Review of Film & Video* 11 (1989): 23–33.

———. "Film and the Masquerade: Theorizing the Female Spectator." *Screen* 3–4 (1982): 74–87.

Ewen, Stuart. *All Consuming Images: The Politics of Style in Contemporary Culture*. New York: Basic Books, 1988.

Ewen, Stuart, and Elizabeth Ewen. *Channels of Desire: Mass Images and the Shaping of American Consciousness*. New York: McGraw-Hill, 1982.

Evans, Caroline, and Minna Thornton. *Women and Fashion: A New Look*. London: Quartet Books, 1989.

Finkelstein, Joanne. *The Fashioned Self*. Cambridge, England: Polity Press, 1991.

Flügel, J. C. *The Psychology of Clothes*. London: Hogarth Press, 1930.

Foucault, Michel. *Discipline and Punish: The Birth of the Prison*. Trans. Alan Sheridan. New York: Vintage, 1979.

Gaines, Jane, and Charlotte Herzog, eds. *Fabrications: Costume and the Female Body*. New York: Routledge, 1990.

Garber, Marjorie. *Vested Interests: Cross-Dressing and Cultural Anxiety*. New York: Routledge, 1992.

Grossberg, Lawrence, Cary Nelson, and Paula A. Treichler. *Cultural Studies*. New York: Routledge, 1992.

Hebdige, Dick. *Hiding in the Light: On Images and Things*. New York: Routledge, 1988.

———. *Subculture: The Meaning of Style*. London: Methuen, 1979.

Hollander, Anne. *Seeing Through Clothes*. New York: Viking, 1975.

Jameson, Fredric. *Postmodernism: Or, The Cultural Logic of Late Capitalism*. Durham, N.C.: Duke University Press, 1991.

Kaplan, E. Ann. *Women and Film: Both Sides of the Camera*. New York: Methuen, 1983.

Kellner, Douglas. *Jean Baudrillard: From Marxism to Postmodernism and Beyond*. Stanford: Stanford University Press, 1989.

Kroker, Arthur, and Marilouise Kroker, eds. *Body Invaders: Panic Sex in America*. New York: St. Martin's Press, 1987.

Kroker, Arthur, Marilouise Kroker, and David Cook. *Panic Encyclopedia: The Definitive Guide to the Postmodern Scene*. New York: St. Martin's Press, 1989.

Kuhn, Annette. *The Power of the Image: Essays in Representation and Sexuality*. London: Routledge & Kegan Paul, 1985.

Lacan, Jacques. *The Four Fundamental Concepts*. Ed. Jacques-Alain Miller. Trans. Alan Sheridan. New York: Norton, 1978.

———. *The Seminars of Jacques Lacan, Book II: The Ego in Freud's Theory and in the Technique of Psychoanalysis*. Ed. Jacques-Alain Miller. Trans. John Forrester. New York: Norton, 1988.

Lurie, Alison. *The Language of Clothes*. New York: Random House, 1981.

MacCannell, Dean, and Juliet Flower MacCannell. "The Beauty System." *The Ideology of Conduct*. Ed. Nancy Armstrong and Leonard Tennenhouse. London: Methuen, 1988. 206–239.

McRobbie, Angela, ed., *Zoot Suits and Second-Hand Dresses: An Anthology of Fashion and Music*. Boston: Unwin Hyman, 1988.

Mulvey, Laura. "Visual Pleasure and Narrative Cinema." *Screen* 16 (Autumn 1975): 6–18.

Rose, Jacqueline. *Sexuality in the Field of Vision*. New York: Verso, 1986.

Rykiel, Sonia. *Célébration*. Paris: Éditions des femmes, 1988.

———. *La Collection*. Paris: Grasset, 1989.

———. *Et je la voudrais nue*. Paris: Grasset, 1979.

Steele, Valerie. "The F-word." *Lingua Franca* (April 1991): 17–20.

Wilson, Elizabeth. *Adorned in Dreams: Fashion and Modernity*. London: Virago, 1985.

Wolf, Naomi. *The Beauty Myth: How Images of Beauty Are Used Against Women*. New York: William Morrow and Company, 1991.

Contributors' Notes

SHARI BENSTOCK is Professor of English and Women's Studies at the University of Miami. Editor of several books on modernism, feminism, and autobiography, she is the author of *Women of the Left Bank* (1986), *Textualizing the Feminine* (1991), and a forthcoming biography of Edith Wharton (Scribners, 1994).

BARBARA BRODMAN is Professor and Coordinator of Latin American and Caribbean Studies at Nova University. She has published a variety of texts on indigenous Latin American cultures and literature. As a Fulbright scholar she conducted research on indigenous cultures and art in Brazil and Indonesia. In 1989 she helped organize the Women's Convoy to Central America and continues to travel extensively in Latin America.

MARY ANN CAWS, Distinguished Professor of English, French and Comparative Literature at the Graduate Center at City University of New York, is the Past President of the Modern Language Association and the American Comparative Literature Association, and the author of many books on poetics and art, among them *The Eye in the Text, The Art of Interference, Reading Frames in Modern Fiction* (all Princeton University Press), and *Women of Bloomsbury* (Routledge). She has also translated René Char, André Breton, Stephane Mallarmé, Tristan Tzara and Reverdy.

HÉLÈNE CIXOUS teaches at the University of Paris VIII—Vicennes. Author of many works of feminist theory, her most recent publications include *The Book of Promethea* (1991) and *Coming to Writing & Other Essays* (1991, edited by Deborah Jenson).

LINDA BENN DELIBERO teaches media and cultural criticism at The Johns Hopkins University and is a doctoral fellow in American Studies at the University of Maryland, College Park. Her essays have been published in *The Village Voice, The Voice Literary Supplement, The Boston Review,* and other magazines.

SUZANNE FERRISS is Assistant Professor of Liberal Arts at Nova University. She has published articles on British and European Romanticism and is currently completing a book, *Post-Revolutionary Letters*.

DIANA FUSS is Assistant Professor of English at Princeton University. She is the author of *Essentially Speaking: Feminism, Nature and Difference* (1989) and editor of *Inside/Out: Lesbian Theories, Gay Theories* (1991).

CHERYL HERR teaches modern British and Irish studies at the University of Iowa. She has written *Joyce's Anatomy of Culture* (1986), edited *For the Land They Loved: Irish Political Melodramas, 1890–1925* (1991), and published articles in such journals as *Critical Inquiry, Novel, Theatre Journal, Journal of Modern Literature* and *The James Joyce Quarterly*. In completition are two books, *Outside It's America* and *Regarding Ireland*.

KARLA JAY is Professor of English and Women's Studies at Pace University. She has edited, authored, or translated seven books, the most recent of which is *Lesbian Texts and Contexts: Radical Revisions,* coedited by Joanne Glasgow (New York University Press). She is currently General Editor of a series entitled "The Cutting Edge: Lesbian Life and Literature" (New York University Press).

DEBORAH JENSON is a doctoral candidate in Romance Languages and Literatures at Harvard University. She is currently at work on her thesis, "Romantic Wounds," and is the editor of Hélène Cixous's *"Coming to Writing" and Other Essays*.

DOUGLAS KELLNER is Professor of Philosophy at the University of Texas at Austin and is author of many books and articles on social theory, politics, history, and culture, including *Camera Politica: The Politics and Ideology of Contemporary Hollywood Film; Critical Theory, Marxism, and Modernity* (co-authored with Michael Ryan); *Jean Baudrillard: From Marxism to Postmodernism and Beyond; Television and the Crisis of Democracy; Postmodern Theory: Critical Interrogations* (with Steven Best); and *The Persian Gulf TV War*.

INGEBORG MAJER O'SICKEY is Assistant Professor of German at State University of New York, Binghamton. She has published on "New German Cinema" and is presently working on a book on Marguerite Yourcenar's early fiction.

LESLIE W. RABINE is Professor of French and Director of Women's Studies at the University of California, Irvine. She is author of *Reading the Romantic Heroine: Text, History and Ideology* (1985) and coauthor, with Claire Moses, of *Feminism, Socialism, and French Romanticism*.

ANDREW ROSS teaches English at Princeton University. His books include *Strange Weather: Culture, Science, and Technology in the Age of Limits* and *No Respect: Intellectuals and Popular Culture*. Coeditor of the journal *Social Text,* he is also the editor of *Universal Abandon?* and the coeditor of *Technoculture*.

SONIA RYKIEL, the French fashion designer, has published *Et je la voudrais nue* (1979), *Rykiel* (1985), *Célébration* (1988), and *La Collection* (1989).

CAROL SHLOSS teaches English at West Chester University. She is the author of *In Visible Light: Photography and the American Writer* (1987).

KAJA SILVERMAN is Professor of English and Film at the University of Rochester. She has published *The Subject of Semiotics* (1983), *The Acoustic Mirror: The Female Voice in Psychoanalysis & Cinema* (1988), and *Male Subjectivity at the Margins* (1992).

MAUREEN TURIM teaches English and Film at the University of Florida, Gainesville. She is the author of *Abstraction in Avant-Garde Films* (1985), *Flashbacks in Film: Memory and History* (1989), and many articles on fashion and film history.

IRIS MARION YOUNG has written extensively on gender, politics, and social theory. Her works include *Throwing Like a Girl and Other Essays in Feminist Philosophy and Social Theory* (1990) and *Justice and the Politics of Difference* (1990).

Index

Miyake, Issey, 286
Model, Lisette, 116
Modleski, Tania, 75
Monroe, Marilyn, 56, 166–167, 169, 174
Morrissey, Muriel Earhart, 80, 82, 86, 93
Morton, Melanie, 171, 179
Moschino, 224–225
mothers/maternalism, 13–14, 99, 141, 145, 150, 154, 155, 177, 187, 201–202, 206, 213–218, 220–222, 226–230, 271
Motz, Marilyn Ferris, 34–35, 39
MS, 112
Mugler, Thierry, 5, 23
Mulvey, Laura, 16, 31, 39, 65, 75, 195, 209, 222, 228, 266
Musketeers of Pig Alley, 148
myth/mythologies, 4, 91, 130, 136, 138, 146, 178, 203, 218, 269, 274

Nabokov, Vladimir, 186, 195
Nancy, Jean-Luc, 231
nationality/nationalism, 7, 236–239, 267–283, 286, 291, 294–295
Navratilova, Martina, 91
Nazimova, Alla, 156
Neal, Steve, 210
Nemerov, Gertrude and David, 112
"New Look," 1, 42, 187–190, 192, 194
Newsweek, 46, 57, 168
Newton, Helmut, 229
New Yorker, 45
New York Hat, The, 150
Nietzsche, Friedrich, 178
norms/normative, 9, 13, 24, 34, 39, 141, 142, 152, 159, 175, 191, 246, 254. *See also* cultural norms
Northern Woman, 240–241
Norville, Deborah, 22
Now, Voyager, 189

O'Callaghan, Kathleen, 265
O'Connor, Sinead, 239
Odlum, Floyd, 89
O'Dwyer, Eamonn, 250

Oedipal/preoedipal, 201, 213, 217, 220, 226–229
Oppenheim, Méret, 129
orientalism, *see* exoticism
Orr, Deborah, 57
Osborne, Carol L., 93
O'Sickey, Ingeborg Majer, 8–9, 21–40, 304
Other, 12, 14, 26, 66, 118, 123, 126, 183, 186–187, 189, 191, 200, 214, 217–218, 221, 224, 242, 260, 296
Out of Africa, 26

Paglia, Camille, 176–177, 182
Painted Lady, The, 150
Palmer, Gladys Perint, 265
Pamela, 186
Paris Is Burning, 174, 296
Parker, Suzy, 47
Parks, Bert, 30
Parton, Dolly, 22
patriarchy, 4, 16, 38, 65, 70, 72, 204, 210, 264
Penley, Constance, 75
Penn, Irving, 114
Penn, Sean, 168–170
People, 57, 165, 168, 179
Peppermint Soda, 205
Pettersen, Carmen L., 282
Picabia, Francis, 128
Pickford, Mary, 152
Piercy, Marge, 21
Plissart, Marie-Françoise, 232
Plunkett, Walter, 84
Poiret, Paul, 152, 153
politics, 1, 2, 3, 8, 9, 10, 14, 15, 25, 37, 42, 43, 46, 50, 57, 59, 60, 61, 66, 68, 70, 73, 144, 145, 159, 162, 172, 176, 179, 180, 193–194, 204, 235–266, 278–281, 289, 291–295, 299
Pollock, Griselda, 230
Pontalis, Jean-Bertrand, 64, 74, 231
Popol Vuh, 269, 271, 282
popular culture, 2, 12, 14, 42, 61, 155, 159, 161–163, 165–166, 173, 176, 246
postmodernism, 10, 12, 60, 63, 69,